International
Library of the
Philosophy of
Education

**Educational
judgments**

International
Library of the
Philosophy of
Education

General Editor

R. S. Peters
**Professor of Philosophy of Education
Institute of Education
University of London**

Educational judgments

Papers in the philosophy of education

Edited and with an Introduction by

James F. Doyle

Associate Professor of Philosophy
University of Missouri - St Louis

Routledge & Kegan Paul

London and Boston

First published 1973
by Routledge & Kegan Paul Ltd
Broadway House, 68–74 Carter Lane,
London EC4V 5EL and
9 Park Street,
Boston, Mass. 02108, U.S.A.
Printed in Great Britain by
C. Tinling & Co Ltd, London and Prescot
Copyright Routledge & Kegan Paul 1973
No part of this book may be reproduced in
any form without permission from the
publisher, except for the quotation of brief
passages in criticism

ISBN 0 7100 7458 1

Contents

General editor's note

There is a growing interest in philosophy of education amongst students of philosophy as well as amongst those who are more specifically and practically concerned with educational problems. Philosophers, of course, from the time of Plato onwards, have taken an interest in education and have dealt with education in the context of wider concerns about knowledge and the good life. But it is only quite recently in this country that philosophy of education has come to be conceived of as a specific branch of philosophy like the philosophy of science or political philosophy.

To call philosophy of education a specific branch of philosophy is not, however, to suggest that it is a distinct branch in the sense that it could exist apart from established branches of philosophy such as epistemology, ethics, and philosophy of mind. It would be more appropriate to conceive of it as drawing on established branches of philosophy and bringing them together in ways which are relevant to educational issues. In this respect the analogy with political philosophy would be a good one. Thus use can often be made of work that already exists in philosophy. In tackling, for instance, issues such as the rights of parents and children, punishment in schools, and the authority of the teacher, it is possible to draw on and develop work already done by philosophers on 'rights', 'punishment', and 'authority'. In other cases, however, no systematic work exists in the relevant branches of philosophy—e.g. on concepts such as 'education', 'teaching', 'learning', 'indoctrination'. So philosophers of education have had to break new ground—in these cases in the philosophy of mind. Work on educational issues can also bring to life and throw new light on long-standing problems in philosophy. Concentration, for instance, on the particular predicament of children can throw new light on problems of punishment and responsibility. G. E. Moore's old worries about what sorts of things are good in themselves can be brought to life by urgent questions about the justification of the curriculum in schools.

There is a danger in philosophy of education, as in any other applied field, of polarization to one of two extremes. The work could be practically relevant but philosophically feeble; or it could be philosophically sophisticated but remote from practical problems. The aim of the new International Library of the Philosophy of Education is to build up a body of fundamental work in this area which is both practically relevant and philosophically competent. For unless it achieves both types of objective it will fail to satisfy those for whom it is intended and fall short of the conception of philosophy of education which the International Library is meant to embody.

One of the most persistent demands in recent times has been that subjects such as philosophy, which are studied predominantly in universities, should be made more 'relevant'. The meaning of this demand is not altogether perspicuous, but there is certainly a growing tendency for philosophers to concern themselves, as they have done in previous periods of history (e.g. the seventeenth and nineteenth centuries) with the practical problems of the community. A journal called *Philosophy and Public Affairs*, for instance, has just been started in the USA. Another example of this trend is the growing interest in philosophy of education.

In February 1971 the American Council for Philosophical Studies sponsored a working conference at St Louis on philosophy of education. Topics such as the right to education, freedom in education and indoctrination were discussed by a small group of philosophers of education and moral philosophers. This volume is the result. It represents precisely what the International Library of the Philosophy of Education is attempting to supply—a series of works in philosophy of education that are both practically relevant and philosophically competent.

R.S.P.

Preface

With the exception of the introductory essay, all the papers included in this volume were initially prepared for a small working conference held in the United States in February 1971. This was one of several such conferences which the Council for Philosophical Studies has sponsored to encourage original work and co-operation in philosophy. Well in advance of this particular conference, several of the participants wrote fresh position papers on selected issues in education, and these in turn elicited written responses from the other participants. The purpose of the conference itself was to submit all of these papers to intensive criticism, with the hope that the results would merit wider study by those who are seriously interested in the philosophy of education.

Each of the contributors has had an opportunity to revise his paper in light of the critical discussion it received at the conference. In some cases this revision has been quite extensive. The result is a reasonably coherent collection of arguments and counter-arguments about what is at stake in some of the most important issues in education today. At a more practical level many of the papers also propose how one may best try to resolve these issues. As the title of the volume suggests, the aim of each contributor is to offer as much guidance as his discipline and perspective afford to the making of intelligent educational judgments.

One of the contributors, Arnold Kaufman, was killed in a collision between a commercial airliner and a military aircraft shortly after he submitted his revised paper for this collection. His untimely death was a grievous loss to everyone who knew him, and this loss was deeply felt by those of us who had so recently enjoyed his trenchant but good-humored criticism. We should like to offer this volume as a tribute to his memory.

It should also be explained that Professor Kaufman, through an oversight, had not submitted his footnotes before his death. Unfortunately these have not been found among his papers. I am grateful to Richard Rodewald of the University of California, Los Angeles, for conducting a thorough search for these notes. As editor I have taken the liberty of supplying the missing citations where these could be confirmed.

Preface

Earlier versions of three of these papers have been published elsewhere. The paper by Professor Scheffler is included in *Reason and Teaching*, a collection of his essays published by the Bobbs-Merrill Company and Routledge & Keegan Paul, Professor Price's paper on the issue of relevance has appeared in *Studies in Philosophy and Education*, Southern Illinois University, and Professor Edel's paper was published in *Educational Theory*, University of Illinois. Professor Feinberg has included a substantial part (about eight paragraphs) of his paper in the first chapter of his book, *Social Philosophy*, published by Prentice-Hall.

Finally, I should like to acknowledge the skilful assistance of Janiece Fister in preparing the final typescript.

J.F.D.

Introduction: Philosophy and educational judgments

Education, like art, politics, science, and other activities on which men pinned their highest hopes, has become the object of heated controversy and even disillusionment in many quarters. One reason for this dramatic turn of events, no doubt, is that many new demands are being placed on educational institutions which they in turn have not been able to satisfy. Witness, for example, current demands for relevance, freedom from indoctrination, and the cultivation of greater sensitivity to human suffering and social injustice. At the same time, new demands are being placed on the various kinds of education which people have acquired and which were thought to be adequate for their purposes, but which are now found to be wanting in many important respects. When confronted by such unprecedented demands as those of rapid technological change, the environmental crisis, and world citizenship, many people have concluded that they are not the beneficiaries of an education, but are rather the victims of mis-education.

A further source of controversy and disillusionment is education in yet a third sense—not as a distinctive activity or personal achievement, but as a specialized field of study, including, among other disciplines, the philosophy of education. The field of education in general, and the philosophy of education in particular, have not satisfied the growing demands of students, teachers, administrators, and the general public for more cogent explanations of what is at stake in contemporary educational issues. Specialists in the field of education, whether they be philosophers, historians, or social scientists, have all too frequently been content merely to address the results of their studies to one another, much as specialists in other fields do. As a consequence, the philosophy of education, for example, has tended to become isolated from general philosophy and even from the general intellectual life of society. By the same token, philosophers outside the specialized field of education have practically ignored the kinds of demands I have just alluded to and the searching educational questions which they raise. There are, to be sure, notable exceptions on both sides; but as a rule, philosophers have not been as concerned as they should be with the judgments

I

which all of us must make about particular educational issues or about education in general.

Fortunately, the papers included in this volume provide tangible evidence that this criticism does not apply to all philosophers, either in the philosophy of education or in general philosophy. These papers bear the collective title of *Educational Judgments* because each of them is concerned, in one way or another, with judgments which most people are called upon to make about contemporary educational issues. The contributors to this volume are diverse in their philosophical orientations and fields of specialization. Yet they share the view—in part, perhaps, as a result of their collaboration in this effort—that the primary aim of the philosophy of education is to enhance our understanding of educational judgments and of the demands made upon us in the name of education. They would also agree that education, today as in the past, raises philosophical issues which are too important to be left to philosophers; that, in the final analysis, all of us must make our own educational judgments. All that philosophers can hope to do is first to establish what is relevant to such judgments, and then to explain why it is relevant.

The philosophical import of current demands for greater relevance in education, as Professor Frankena points out in his paper, is that they reveal an underlying conflict among different concepts or definitions of education. These range all the way from traditional concepts of education as 'socialization' or 'enculturation' of the young, at one extreme, to currently fashionable notions of education as 'freedom' or 'ecstasy' at the other. This conflict raises the issue of which (if any) of these different concepts one should reasonably adopt in his thinking about education. Frankena's paper, and the two critical responses to it by Professors Gewirth and Kaufman, present a series of arguments about what is at stake in this most general of all educational issues.

By way of anticipating their arguments I should like to comment on the formula or matrix which Frankena offers as a guide to judgments about this issue. He argues that any general concept or definition of education as a distinctive activity can be understood as a variation on the following formula: Education is an activity in which X is fostering or seeking to foster in Y some disposition D by method M. (By 'dispositions' he means approximately what Professor Peters has described as 'states of mind'; i.e., beliefs, habits, attitudes, skills, forms of thought and knowledge, and the like. He also intends for the other variables in this formula to be interpreted as generously as possible.) Thus, in making critical comparisons among different concepts of education, one would be well advised to begin by identifying what these concepts substitute for each of the variables in this formula. This will serve to make more explicit how alternative concepts differ from one another and in what respects they are logically or practically incompatible. The crucial elements in any concept of education, according to Frankena, are the dispositions which it emphasizes as the distinctive outcome or purpose of educational activity. Considerations of who is to do the educating, who is to be educated, and by what methods, all depend upon judgments about the dispositions to be fostered by education.

What, then, is relevant to judgments about the dispositions to be fostered in any activity which merits the title of education? Here, of course, Frankena's formula offers no help, and it would be a mistake (as Gewirth appears to have done in his paper) to interpret this abstract formula as expressing another substantive concept or definition of education. Rather, as Frankena himself emphasizes, it is nothing more than a formal matrix which is intended to accommodate any concept of education which one might encounter (though perhaps not these concepts exclusively). Once it has served its limited purpose as a way of analyzing and comparing different concepts, one must then proceed to raise other and more difficult questions before one can judge which concept of education it would be most reasonable to adopt. This in fact is what Frankena, Gewirth, and Kaufman do in their respective papers, and their debate with one another is primarily over the adequacy of different accounts of the dispositions to be fostered by education. They are in agreement that the descriptive concept of education as socialization or enculturation of the young is inadequate from any point of view—except, perhaps, that of the detached scientific or historical observer who is completely neutral (if that is possible) toward the particular educational activity he studies. To the extent that one is not neutral toward this activity—and especially toward the dispositions it fosters—one must take seriously the question, 'What dispositions are desirable, and why are they desirable?' As Frankena rightly insists, this is a very different question from one with which it is often confused; namely, 'What dispositions are actually desired—by society, by those doing the educating, or by those being educated?' This is not to deny that answers to the latter question may be relevant to answering the former; but the point still holds, that the two questions call for different kinds of answers.

Many people consider the question, 'What dispositions are desirable, and why are they desirable?' to be the most fundamental and far-reaching in the philosophy of education. Perhaps it is just for this reason that they look for ways to answer this question once and for all, so that it will never again have to be raised. However,

3

fundamental and far-reaching though this question certainly is, it is not the sort of question which yields to final answers. The best that one can hope to do, whether he be a philosopher or anyone else, is to consider rationally and on their merits such answers as have been proposed in the past, together with the answers expressed or implied in current educational demands—meanwhile leaving the way open to adopt better answers in light of further argument and fresh evidence. A careful reading of Frankena's paper will show that this is the way he himself proceeds to answer this question, and the same is true of his two critics. In the end he opts for an answer which, in his judgment, preserves what is most defensible in new as well as older concepts of education. His own concept of education is one which emphasizes the complex dispositions of personal autonomy, responsibility, and mastery of relevant forms of life, thought, and action. Educational relevance, he suggests, is on the one hand a matter of cultivating individual interests and potentialities, and on the other a matter of preparing people to engage in genuinely new forms of life, thought, and action. In the course of justifying this concept he also addresses the related issues of who should be the agents of education, who should be its recipients, and what methods should be used to foster the dispositions which define education as a distinctive activity.

Both Gewirth and Kaufman, in their critical responses to Frankena's arguments and conclusions, raise important questions about the adequacy of his concept of education. In particular, they question the adequacy of this concept as a basis for judgments about contemporary issues in moral, political, and social education. Both seize on the disposition of personal autonomy (discussion of which recurs in several of the papers in this volume) as being a worthy and yet an extremely problematic goal of practical educational activity. For Gewirth, the problem arises from the fact that personal autonomy and moral goodness, which Frankena also espouses, would appear to be antithetical dispositions. Moreover, it is far from clear that the methods most appropriate to the fostering of autonomy are compatible with the methods by which we can achieve moral goodness and responsibility. Gewirth sets for himself the task of demonstrating how this apparent conflict can be resolved—first by examining the concept of the 'self' as the subject of these different dispositions and educational methods, and then by explaining how the 'rational self' can be both autonomous and morally good. He points to the danger of pegging the requirements of the rational self too high— as some philosophers have done in the past—and adopts in his own account a view of rationality which he thinks is relatively uncontroversial and generally attainable. Gewirth concludes that

4

fostering rational dispositions which can be achieved by any ordinary person is an indispensable part of any educational activity which is seriously directed to the joint achievement of personal autonomy and moral goodness.

For Kaufman, the crucial question raised by Frankena's concept of education is whether personal autonomy should be given, in his words, the 'place of pride in our educational scheme of things.' Autonomy, he suggests, is the sort of general educational aim to which it is all too easy to pay lip-service, especially in liberal democratic societies. Yet in practice it is often not clear what is involved in becoming an autonomous person, how this can be achieved educationally, or even whether this is desirable from a moral, political, or social point of view. Nor is it clear that autonomy —even assuming that it is a desirable achievement for everyone— is relevant to judgments about all educational activities or all stages of education. These are all important educational issues about which philosophers need to be more concerned, and Kaufman points the way to their clarification and resolution. Like Gewirth, he finds it necessary to consider the various ideas of the self which are often tacit and unexamined in our beliefs about personal autonomy. He argues that the autonomous person is one who is able to judge, act, and think authentically as well as rationally. Without authenticity, a person either lacks a 'core self' or else fails to express this self in his judgments, actions, and thoughts. However, without the dispositions of the rational person one is, so to speak, at the mercy of his 'core self,' no matter how authentic his judgments, actions, and thoughts may be. Viewed in this light, autonomy is not necessarily incompatible with what Kaufman calls 'the ideals of communal life.' Indeed, the achievement of autonomy in this sense may be a necessary condition for the fulfillment of these emerging ideals. If this is true and these ideals are valid, then autonomy ought to have a central place, especially in moral and political education. However, according to Kaufman, moral and political education is not likely to foster autonomy unless its methods include the presentation of radical alternatives to the dominant norms of society, and, at the same time, the opportunity for those being educated to participate in the making of substantive educational decisions.

Left unresolved in these first three papers is the issue of whether indoctrination is defensible as a method or aim of educational activity. One might, with some justification, infer from Frankena's conclusions that indoctrination, to the extent that it is incompatible with the achievement of autonomy, has no legitimate place in education as he defines it. However, it is not clear that his concept of

5

education would rule out indoctrination at every stage and in every instance of educational activity. The same is true of Gewirth's and Kaufman's conclusions, though both suggest in their papers that indoctrination is incompatible with the methods and aims of moral, political, and social education. Thus, one might view the two papers in the second section of this volume as taking up the preceding arguments and establishing in a more explicit way what is relevant to judgments about indoctrination.

Professor Pincoffs, and Professor Baier in his critical response, are both primarily concerned with the relations between indoctrination and moral education. However, Pincoffs sets the stage for his criticism of moral indoctrination by giving reasons for thinking that indoctrination is sometimes defensible as an educational method or aim. The issue raised by indoctrination, he argues, is not, 'When does education become indoctrination?' as if the two were always incompatible. Rather, it is expressed in the two questions, 'When does education become indefensible indoctrination?' and 'When does education indefensibly become indoctrination?' He cites, as an obvious answer to the first of these questions, the form of indoctrination known as 'brainwashing.' The general answer to the second question is that education indefensibly becomes indoctrination when a person is indoctrinated under the pretence of being educated. He recommends this general interpretation of indoctrination as a basis for judging whether moral indoctrination is ever justified.

Although, on Pincoffs' view, indoctrination is sometimes defensible in education, he denies that this is ever true of moral indoctrination. In this respect he supports the demand, frequently heard these days, that education should be entirely free of moral indoctrination—in its methods, its content, or its aims. This demand raises the issue, however, whether moral education is even possible without resort to indoctrination, especially in the early stages of moral development. Assuming, as most people would, that moral education is desirable for everyone, are we not bound (in practice at least) to accept indoctrination as a necessary part of this kind of activity and achievement? Pincoffs, after criticizing the positions taken by John Wilson and R. M. Hare on these issues, argues that, as an adult, everyone is held answerable, not only for what he does, but for what he is—at least as far as his moral character is concerned. It is this basic moral demand which makes the fostering of personal autonomy, responsibility, and other moral dispositions desirable (indeed obligatory), and which at the same time makes moral indoctrination indefensible. However, Pincoffs insists that moral indoctrination is one thing, and moral training is quite another. As a part of everyone's early moral education he ought to be trained, for example, to

6

regard dishonesty, cruelty, and injustice as morally wrong. Such training need not (and ought not) involve either the methods or the aims of moral indoctrination (imbuing someone with a moral doctrine or belief), but is rather the inculcation of moral excellences of character. According to Pincoffs, these moral excellences of character are not debatable in the way that moral doctrines are, and this difference helps explain why training is consistent with the methods and aims of moral education, whereas indoctrination is not. In other words, moral indoctrination, no matter how humane and well-meaning it may be, would always involve indoctrinating someone under the pretence of educating him.

Baier's criticisms of this position are subtle and complex. What he finds most problematic in Pincoffs' arguments is the claim that certain moral precepts, such as 'dishonesty is wrong,' are undebatable from the moral point of view. He agrees that such precepts may be undebatable from the moral point of view adopted by a society or by a particular reference group. This, however, is not good enough, as Baier sees it; for there are other points of view which have a claim to being the moral point of view, and this means that the moral precepts and point of view cited in Pincoffs' paper are after all rationally debatable. If they are debatable, then moral training which treats them as if they were immune to debate would be, even on Pincoffs' own terms, merely another form of moral indoctrination. Does this mean, then, that indoctrination is an unavoidable feature of moral education? Baier, like Pincoffs, concludes that moral education can be, and ought to be, free of the methods and aims of indoctrination. He defends this conclusion by a series of arguments designed to establish, as he says, what is 'necessarily involved in being a moral agent,' and why. Among these necessary conditions of being moral is participation in what he calls 'the practice of justification' (thus the title of his paper). In his recommendations for moral education, Baier invites comparison with the views expressed by Frankena and Gewirth.

What place should be given in education to fostering dispositions we associate most closely with the arts—dispositions such as appreciation, sensitivity, imagination, the ability to make or cherish something unique, the skills of artistic performance, creativity, originality, and the like? The papers considered above have responded to this question only indirectly, largely because they were not primarily concerned with judgments about the issues it raises. Yet these issues are clearly involved in a number of current educational demands. Criticisms that our educational institutions neglect the cultivation of affective and creative dispositions are, of course, not new. However, in recent years these criticisms have become much more specific and cogent, as more and more people have discovered that their education has prepared them for little more, aesthetically speaking, than willing complicity in the banalities of mass culture. This discovery has often provoked a reaction against the traditional emphasis, especially in formal education, on cultivation of verbal and rational skills and mastery of cognitive disciplines. At the very least, it has prompted demands for what one might call 'aesthetic education' as a necessary complement of intellectual and practical education.

In the two papers in the third section of this volume Professors Broudy and Price take up the challenge of these new demands for aesthetic education. Broudy in particular examines the motives and reasons underlying these demands, many of which he finds justifiable in light of a general concept of education. For example, like Frankena, he emphasizes the desirability of autonomy and of being prepared to engage in genuinely new as well as traditional forms of life. There are conceptual as well as practical connections, Broudy suggests, between these general goals of education and the cultivation of people's capacities to enjoy, create (or re-create), and cherish aesthetic objects. He explicates these various connections in terms of a theory of the arts and of aesthetic experience. However, the main thrust of his paper is practical rather than theoretical. After considering the various constraints (one being a concern about indoctrination) under which aesthetic education would have to be instituted, he defends as the most practicable (though perhaps not ideal), an approach which would stress the cultivation of imaginative perception rather than artistic performance or appreciation of art. Price, in his reply to Broudy's paper, raises doubts about the adequacy of aesthetic education which is limited to the cultivation of imaginative perception. He argues that the activity of aesthetic education, if it is to achieve the educational aims to which both he and Broudy subscribe, must also involve the cultivation of abilities to engage in aesthetic creation and performance. As Price interprets them, the dispositions of imaginative perception, though clearly desirable, are essentially passive and do not include the skills and abilities of the aesthetically educated person.

The argument that aesthetic education is relevant, and perhaps essential, to the achievement of personal autonomy raises several questions of a more general nature. First, what kinds of learning are involved in becoming what has been called an autonomous person? Secondly, what is the connection between each of these kinds of learning and the eventual achievement of autonomy? And finally, what are the conditions in which the kinds of learning that eventuate in autonomy can flourish? (Of course, one could raise similar questions about other distinctive aims of education.) Several of the papers already considered suggest ways in which the first two of these questions might be resolved—at least as far as they can be resolved philosophically. However, almost no attention has been given to the third question, perhaps because it is viewed as the kind of question which can only be resolved by scientific study and educational experimentation. That it is also a philosophical question becomes more clear when one asks, What are the conditions which must be satisfied in order for people to learn to be autonomous and to lead autonomous lives? This is the question raised by Professor Peters and Professor Feinberg in the fourth section of this volume—though they choose to raise it, initially at least, about the more familiar ideals of 'freedom' and the 'free man.' As it happens, their responses to this question are complementary. Peters is primarily concerned in his paper with the connections between freedom as a characteristic of institutions and the educational development of free men. In effect he asks, 'Is freedom in the schools, the family, and other institutions a necessary condition for learning to be a free man?' His answer involves an analysis of the conceptual and instrumental connections between 'freedom' and 'learning to be a free man.' Feinberg, on the other hand, seeks to clarify the complex and often puzzling relations among the different things we may mean by 'freedom' and being a 'free man.' Among these things, of course, are 'autonomy' and 'authenticity,' and he devotes a substantial portion of his paper to an analysis of how these current educational ideals are conceptually related to more familiar meanings of 'freedom' and being 'free.'

Peters makes use of the notion of 'man as a chooser' as the mediating link between 'freedom' as a social principle and the educational ideal of the 'free man.' He analyzes both the 'objective' or social conditions and the 'subjective' or psychological conditions which must be satisfied in order for anyone to be 'free' in the sense of being a chooser. He recognizes, of course, that we usually think of a free man as being more than merely a chooser. For this reason we sometimes characterize the man who is 'free' in the ideal sense as being 'autonomous' or self-regulating. Like Kaufman, Peters considers autonomy in this context to be the result, on the one hand, of having adopted an authentic code or way of life of one's own, and on the other of possessing the abilities required for rational reflection and criticism. In addition to having the traits associated with authenticity and rationality, the autonomous man may also exhibit what we call 'strength of will' or 'self-control.' However, Peters argues that this is only a contingent condition of autonomy, whereas the other two appear to be necessary conditions.

This analysis of the conceptual connections among 'freedom' as a characteristic of institutions, 'being a chooser,' and being a 'free man' serves as the basis for a detailed examination of the educational and social conditions which must be satisfied in the activity of learning to be a free man. In making judgments about these conditions, Peters draws upon the theories of learning of Jean Piaget and Lawrence Kohlberg—at the same time acknowledging that their accounts of the invariant and necessary stages of learning have not been conclusively established. He shows, however, that if these accounts are correct, then learning to be a free man is more a matter of appropriate 'cognitive stimulation' from the whole institutional environment than it is of overt instruction. This would be especially true in the early stages of learning; for unless one first learns to be a chooser within a general system of social regulation provided by institutions, he cannot learn to be a free man in the sense of becoming autonomous. Peters also suggests that these theories of learning would seem to dictate a policy of 'cautious conservatism' rather than of permissiveness in the early stages of education directed to the ideal of the free man. It is worth pointing out that his arguments and conclusions have an important bearing on judgments about the role of indoctrination in moral, political, social, and aesthetic education.

Peters remarks in his paper that the educational ideal of the free man as 'autonomous' is more clear in what it denies than it is in what it asserts. Interpreted in one way, this is not a serious criticism —for autonomy, like many other aims or ideals, may be such that we can state its necessary conditions more easily than we can state its sufficient conditions. However, the point of Peters's remark appears to be that even the necessary conditions of the special kind of freedom we call 'autonomy' are not clear enough to make it very useful as an aim of education. He suggests that this relative obscurity tends to invest the idea of autonomy with magical powers which it may not deserve, at least as a basis for educational judgments. Feinberg's paper is in large part a response to just this sort of challenge. He seeks to dispel some of the magic often associated with talk about 'freedom' and 'being free' by elucidating what is involved in the various senses of 'being free' and how each of these senses functions in our personal and social ideals of freedom. In much the same spirit as Frankena does in his paper (for judgments about the concept of education) Feinberg offers a formal schema as a guide for analyzing and comparing what is meant in the statements we make about freedom. He argues that singular judgments about 'being free,' in the sense of enjoying absence of constraint, necessarily involve three variables: first, *who* is free; second, what he is free *from*; and third, what he is free *to do* (or omit, or be, or have). This schema has the merit of drawing attention to the different kinds of factors which may count as constraints, depending upon the substitutions which are made for the other variables. On the basis of his detailed analysis and classification of these kinds of constraints, Feinberg shows how comparative judgments of more or less 'freedom on balance' can be interpreted and justified. He points out, however, that judgments about someone being 'free on balance,' or 'a free man all-told,' depend for their justification upon independent standards of the worth and importance of what he is free *from* and free *to* do.

As Feinberg reminds us, 'being free' originally meant 'having the legal status and rights of a freeman.' By extension, this expression has acquired the further meaning of 'possessing the traits of character and personal qualities appropriate to the status of a freeman.' Now that the legal status of 'being free' no longer conveys an important distinction, the traits of character and personal qualities associated with this status have become part of other meanings of 'being free,' such as 'being autonomous.' Regarding autonomy, Feinberg shows in his analysis that there are several different ways of not being free in this distinctive and complex sense. Rather than being self-governing, as the political metaphor of autonomy would seem to require, we may be ruled by another (heteronomy), or we may fail to rule ourselves (be 'anomic' or 'out of control'). A third and fairly common way of not being autonomous is to exhibit one or another form of passive adjustment or conformity to one's social group and its culture. On its positive side and as an ideal way of 'being free,' autonomy is related to the desire to decide for oneself what one will do and be—at least as far as important issues are concerned. Feinberg agrees with those who assert that constraints of this desire are ones which are most worth being without. However, as he makes clear, fulfillment of this desire presupposes that there is already an authentic or core self which is sufficiently developed in its character, critical abilities, knowledge, imagination, etc., to make such decisions. He concludes that it would be a mistake in education to adopt unrealistic standards of autonomy or to foster autonomy prematurely. Moreover, he recommends the adoption of a more comprehensive ideal of individual freedom—'a free man all-told'—which includes autonomy as one of several inter-related components.

The authors of the papers in the first four sections of this volume have deferred judgment, so to speak, about the issue of whether education as they describe it should be available to everyone as a matter of right. They do, of course, present a number of arguments which are directly relevant to judgments about rights and duties in education. For example, if the positions defended by Pincoffs and Baier are correct, then they provide relevant (though not conclusive) grounds for judging that freedom from moral indoctrination is a right of those being educated, and at the same time a duty of those doing the educating. There remains the larger issue, however, of whether everyone has a right to education as a matter of moral if not legal entitlement. Many people today believe that everyone does have this right, and their conviction is reinforced by legal and quasi-legal declarations of a universal (or human) right to education. This growing consensus would appear to have a shaky foundation, however; for there is less agreement than one might suppose about how this right should be interpreted and justified. Moreover, the belief in a universal right to education, despite its evident importance, has not received the critical attention that one might have expected from philosophers—especially those concerned with issues in education. In the fifth section Professor Olafson, and Professor Melden in his responding paper, seek to overcome this neglect by showing in detail how one might reasonably proceed in explicating and defending a universal right to education.

Both Olafson and Melden recognize that, quite apart from a *right* to education, there may be good reasons for making education of various kinds available to everyone. For example, considerations of public policy may dictate that this be done, as presumably they have in societies which provide free and compulsory education to all children. This, of course, does not include 'everyone,' but only every member of a given society who is of a certain age and capable of benefiting from education. Moreover, moral considerations of fairness may justify extending education to everyone (literally), on the ground that it would be unfair to provide education only to some people when it is needed and deserved more or less equally by all. Neither of these kinds of reasons for making education available to everyone depends upon an appeal to a right to education. Why, then, is it important to assert and defend a universal right to education? The short answer to this question, as Melden makes clear, is that a right invests the holder of it with special moral or legal authority over the conduct of others; and granting such authority to everyone (at least every child) is a way of insuring that others will provide for their education. This only explains the *purpose* of granting everyone a right to education, however. It does not explain why this *ought* to be done as a matter of obligation and entitlement. Can this kind of justification be given for recognizing and implementing a universal right to education? Both Olafson and Melden give reasons for answering this question in the affirmative. They disagree, however, about the merits of different strategies one may adopt in defending this right.

The strategy adopted by Olafson is one which avoids the difficulties of attempting to derive a universal right to education from wider human rights. He argues that if we view 'the various contexts of human co-operation as so many concentric circles,' then the outermost circle of mankind is 'more ideal than real,' whereas the innermost circle of the family is 'unquestionably operative' in most parts of the world. Moreover, he insists that a right to education must be correlated with positive duties of others to provide the requisite means of education. Duties not to interfere with anyone's access to these means, though important, would not be sufficient by themselves to sustain a right to education as something more than a formal freedom to acquire an education. These two considerations suggest to Olafson that we would be well advised to interpret rights and duties in education as the outcome of relationships between generations, the paradigm of which is the relationship between parents and their children. He argues that a universal right to education derives its rationale from the moral responsibility incurred by parents to care for their children. They incur this moral responsibility, and the duties associated with it, by knowingly performing the procreative act by which their children come into being. The duties of parents to care for their children include the special duty to provide for their education, which Olafson interprets as the development of at least the various kinds of competence without which an individual cannot exist as an independent person. He shows how this duty to provide for education can be construed, not only as one belonging distributively to all parents, but as a collective duty of a whole generation with respect to the generation which succeeds it. One can view this collective generational duty as based on one's obligations as a member of an ongoing political community and, more generally, on one's moral obligation to make restitution for the collective cost to others of one's own education. Olafson concludes that a universal right to education attributed to the members of each new generation rests on these moral, political, and legal obligations which are shared collectively by the members of the preceding generation.

In his critical response Melden contends that this argument from the reciprocity of educational rights and duties between different generations does not fully justify the conclusion that everyone has a right to education. He agrees with Olafson that the appeal to human rights as the justification for a right to education is idle talk if nothing is done to relate these rights to the concrete conditions and possibilities of the world in which we live. Under those circumstances, one would be justified in describing a right to education derived from human rights as a 'soft' rather than a 'hard' right. However, Melden offers reasons for thinking that a growing recognition of basic human rights is in fact an important influence today on legislative measures, judicial rulings, and public policies designed to protect and enforce a universal right to education. This is particularly true, he claims, of a right to moral education, which is the most fundamental of all educational rights.

Clearly the questions raised by contemporary educational demands are myriad and complex, and they are not the kind of questions which will yield to isolated or unreflective answers. In practice as well as in theory, questions about the general features which distinguish education as an activity cannot be detached from related questions about the goals, the methods, and the social environment of teaching and learning. Nor can any of these questions be pursued in isolation from other queries about who should be educated and in what ways, who in turn should be responsible for their education, and the rights and duties of each with respect to one another. These are the kind of educational questions which stand very much in need of systematic study by philosophers and others of a philosophical bent. In this sense at least, the relevance of philosophy to the making of intelligent educational judgments can hardly be doubted. Nor can it be doubted that philosophy as a discipline would be a more significant force in human affairs if these educational questions were given a higher ranking on its agenda. What may not be so clear, at least on the basis of reading the papers already considered, is the relevance of philosophy to the practical judgments of educators and to education as a field of study. Those who are particularly concerned about this issue in contemporary philosophy of education will find that it has not been neglected in this volume, but is in fact the common theme of the three independent papers in the concluding section.

In the first of these papers Professor Scheffler responds to current doubts about the relevance of philosophy to the professional preparation and activity of teachers. As he points out, these doubts have become more acute as the philosophy of education has developed in ways which threaten to sever its past connection with educational practice. He argues that it is essential to maintain this connection, not only for the sake of enlightened practice but also to insure that the philosophy of education will not lose its significance as a branch of practical philosophy. In the course of his argument he recommends a number of different roles which philosophy might reasonably play in programs of study for prospective teachers. The one to which he gives most attention, however, would involve serious study of the philosophy of a subject as an integral part of the preparation for teaching it. Scheffler explains in detail how study of the philosophy of a subject—such as mathematics, or science, or art—would enhance a teacher's ability, first to initiate others into this subject, and then to foster a progressive mastery of it. These, of course, are the objectives of the kind of curriculum adopted by most schools. If these objectives have merit, then it is important that teachers have a philosophical understanding of their subject as a 'form of thought' with its distinctive aims, methods, and standards. Moreover, they need a critical perspective—which the philosophy of their subject provides—from which to evaluate this form of thought and relate it to other forms. Even their ability to judge which materials will best exemplify this form of thought, and which ones will make it most accessible to the novice, would be enhanced by a philosophical understanding of their subject, according to Scheffler. He recognizes, however, that teachers have broader responsibilities as well, such as fostering personal autonomy and responsibility in their students. For this reason he recommends that they also study the more general philosophical disciplines, of which the theory of knowledge, philosophy of language, and moral philosophy are relevant examples.

As his title suggests, the aim of Professor Price's paper is to elucidate what is involved when educators or others judge something to be educationally relevant or irrelevant. Thus one might interpret his paper as a demonstration of the use of philosophical analysis to clarify familiar but often perplexing terms in educational discourse. This particular analysis serves to make explicit what is presupposed and implied in uses of 'relevant' and 'irrelevant' to express educational judgments. Such judgments, Price shows, are always about an educational practice of some kind, and they are always incomplete unless they identify what it is to which the practice in question is alleged to be relevant or irrelevant. This relational character of such judgments makes it necessary for at least two conditions to be met before an educational practice can be truthfully said to be relevant. First, the practice in question must in fact be conducive to an identifiable state of affairs; and secondly, this state of affairs must be one that ought to exist. However, this same relational character makes it possible for educational practices *not* to be relevant in a number of different ways, only two of which can be plausibly described as ways of being irrelevant. According to this analysis, an educational practice can only be irrelevant if it is *not* conducive to what ought to exist, or if it *is* conducive to what ought not to exist. Price also employs this analysis to establish what is involved in judging degrees of educational relevance or irrelevance. Two questions which emerge in bold relief from his analysis are these: First, how does one judge whether an educational practice is conducive to a state of affairs that ought to exist? Secondly, how does one judge whether a state of affairs ought to exist as an appropriate goal of education? It will be recalled that the first of these questions figures prominently in the paper by Peters, as does the second in Frankena's paper.

Professor Edel's paper also invites comparison with the discussions which precede it in this volume. As is fitting in a general concluding paper, it is both a critique of recent analytic responses to contemporary issues in education, and a challenge to philosophers to employ all the resources they can muster to respond to these issues in more constructive ways. Edel points to the growing dissatisfaction of students and even philosophers of education with the kind of analysis of educational discourse which purports to be independent of any empirical or normative considerations. The result of this kind of detachment, he argues, is that the most important theoretical and practical questions in education escape the net of philosophical analysis. Edel cites, as a case in point, the recent analytic literature on the uses of 'knowing' and 'learning' in ordinary language. He claims that progress in clarifying educationally relevant distinctions among different kinds of knowing and learning has been due, not to the identification of uses in ordinary language, but to a tacit appeal to the experience of teaching and learning. Because this appeal is tacit (and illicit), the underlying empirical and normative assumptions are left unquestioned. Much the same is true, he contends, of recent analytic studies of the concept of education; and in this connection he cites Peters' successive and influential analyses of the uses of 'education.' Edel himself describes a number of suggestive ways in which philosophical analysis could be enriched and made more relevant to educational theory and practice. His general recommendation is that philosophers should integrate their analytic studies with socio-historical, psychological, and normative studies of education. Fortunately, there is much evidence in this collection that the philosophy of education has already advanced well beyond the crossroads which Edel describes.

Part 1

The concept of education today

William K. Frankena

There has been much talk recently about relevance and irrelevance in education. It is sometimes suggested, on the one hand, that education is relevant by definition—that, if what the schools are doing is not relevant, it is not education. On the other hand, many of our young people seem almost to think that education is by definition irrelevant—that what is called education is what the elders in the establishment want passed on to them, not what they themselves want or need. The fact is that both of these ways of thinking about the relevance of education have a certain justification. For there are (at least) two rather different concepts or definitions of education that obtain both in common usage and in educational circles (a third will be introduced later).

In the *first* place, education is often thought of as a process of 'enculturation' or 'socialization' of the younger generation by the older. I could give any number of examples of such definitions of education from writers of various sorts, but will quote only two, just to convey the idea involved. One, by four educationists, reads: 'In the very broadest sense, education is the process by which the individual acquires the many physical and social capacities demanded of him by the group into which he is born and within which he must function. Sociologists have called this process socialization.'[1] The other is by a distinguished historian of ancient education: 'Education is a collective technique which a society employs to instruct its youth in the values and accomplishments of the civilization within which it exists.'[2] Let us call this the social science concept of education, though it appears also in common discourse and even in philosophy. As our four educationists say, it is a 'purely descriptive-analytical' definition of education. But, as they also indicate, there is *another* concept of education that appears in educational thinking, which they describe by saying, 'Most educators use it [the word 'education'] to mean something more than the process of socialization . . . their discussion of what they are doing tends to presuppose some idea of what they ought to be doing.'[3] That is, 'most educators' think of education 'in a way that [contains] value-judgments about what ought to go on in education' or about the sort of result education should produce. Such a concept of education is implied if one says of so-called Nazi education, 'I don't call that education. Look what it does to people.' This kind of a concept of education is a *normative* one and has been emphasized by the British philosopher, R. S. Peters, in several of his writings.[4]

> 'Education' relates to some sorts of processes in which a desirable state of mind develops . . . 'education' implies the intentional bringing about of a desirable state of mind . . . to call something 'educational' is to intimate that the processes and activities . . . contribute to or involve something that is worthwhile . . . being worthwhile is part of what is meant by calling it 'education.'

These two concepts of education, both involved in our contemporary thinking, are clearly very different. Roughly, one defines education as the transmission to the young of the dispositions or states of mind (beliefs, knowledges, skills, habits, traits, 'values,' etc.) that are *regarded* as desirable by their elders, while the other defines it as the fostering in the young of the dispositions or states of mind that *are* desirable. Different as they are, however, both definitions may be generated from the same basic matrix, as I shall now try to show.

We must remember that the word 'education' is today used sometimes for the activity, process, or enterprise of educating or being educated, and sometimes for the discipline or field of study that concerns itself with this activity, process, or enterprise. In the latter sense, education is the discipline (or would-be discipline) that studies or reflects on education in the former sense—its aims, methods, effects, forms, history, costs, value, relations to society, etc.—and the results of its studies and reflections constitute the content of courses in departments and schools of education and of books and articles in the history, psychology, philosophy, etc., of education, the content, for example, of papers like this one. But, while this essay is an example of education in the latter sense, it is concerned about education in the former sense. And education in *this* sense—as an enterprise or process—always consists in cultivating, fostering, or acquiring what I call dispositions and Peters calls 'states of mind' (beliefs, knowledges, skills, habits, traits, 'values,' etc.) by certain sorts of methods. Thus, Bertrand Russell says, 'Education, in the sense in which I mean it, may be defined as the *formation, by means of instruction, of certain mental habits and a certain outlook on life and the world.*'[5] To put the matter abstractly and generally with the help of variables, every activity of education can be represented by the following formula: in it X is fostering or seeking to foster in Y some disposition D by method M. This is the basic matrix of every conception of education as a process or enterprise. Different views of what education is or should be differ simply in what they substitute for the variables in this formula, i.e., in what dispositions they say are or should be cultivated, by whom, in whom, and by what methods. This formula makes it clear that the first and central question for every theory, philosophy, or program of education is the question, 'What dispositions are to be fostered?' It should also be noted that X and Y, the agent doing the educating and the patient being educated, may be the same person; this is true in every activity of self-education. It may even be said—and often has been said—that all education involves self-education. Indeed, it may even be said—and seems to be said by some extremists today—that all education should be done entirely by oneself or that only self-education is really education. Both things may be said, but while the first is true, the second is incredible.

It is easy now to see how the two concepts of education mentioned earlier can be generated from this matrix. The *social science* concept of education as socialization is generated simply by making the following substitutions:

X = society or its representatives
Y = its younger members
D = the dispositions regarded as desirable by society
M = the methods regarded as satisfactory by society.

Then education is the fostering by the older members of society of the dispositions they *regard* as desirable in its younger members by methods they (the older members) regard as satisfactory. On the other hand, the *normative* concept of education is generated by making these rather different substitutions:

X = those doing the educating, whoever they are
Y = those being educated
D = the dispositions it *is* desirable Y should have
M = the methods that are satisfactory.

Then education is the enterprise, or any enterprise, in which anyone fosters desirable dispositions in anyone by satisfactory methods. Notice here that by 'satisfactory methods' is not meant simply 'any methods whatsoever that succeed in fostering the dispositions in question'; it may be that a good habit can be inculcated effectively by a method that is questionable on other grounds, e.g., by using drugs or threats of corporal punishment that are unsatisfactory from a moral point of view.

It is also easy to see now how some can feel that education is by definition relevant and others that it is by definition irrelevant. Anyone who thinks consciously or unconsciously in terms of the normative definition is bound to feel that education is relevant just because it is the fostering or acquiring of desirable dispositions. As Peters says, being worthwhile is part of what is meant, on this conception, by calling something education. However, anyone who thinks consciously or unconsciously in terms of the social science concept of education, if he himself regards the dispositions society is fostering in him as undesirable, will naturally think that education is by its very nature irrelevant at least for him. In fact, I believe that this is just what is happening in the minds of many of the student critics of our system of education who raise the cry of irrelevance. They hear on all sides, especially from the social sciences, so dominant in our scheme of education, the equation of education with socialization, i.e. with enculturation in the beliefs, 'values,' etc., of their society. Even Riesman and Jencks, who otherwise write so perceptively about our academic scene in *The Academic Revolution*, sometimes simply equate education with socialization. I know there is also the conception of 'education as ecstasy,' which represents the other extreme and is often adopted by the same readers. But, still, it does seem to me that much of the cry of irrelevance in education stems from an implicit or explicit adoption of the social science concept of education. If one adopts it and then takes it as an accurate description of our actual program of education, then one is likely to draw the conclusion that our actual education is simply socialization by society and personally irrelevant—at least if one does not accept the values implicit in such socialization.

There are, as we shall see, other concepts of education that can be generated from our matrix. Let us, however, look further at the two before us. The social science definition of education may serve the purposes of the history or sociology of education. As Peters says, '. . . in the context of a theory of social cohesion education may be harmlessly described as a socializing process,' when one is taking 'the point of view of a spectator pointing to the "function" or effects of education in a social . . . system.' But this definition will not do 'from the point of view of someone engaged in the [educational] enterprise.'[6] It has, indeed, a number of defects from the point of view of those participating in education, those educating and those being educated. (1) It takes too passive a view of the role of those who are being educated. (2) It gives too little place to experiment and science in determining what methods education is to use. (3) Most important, as Peters points out, it encourages 'a conformist or instrumental way of looking at education.' In fact, it defines education as essentially conservative or traditional, since it limits education by definition to the cultivation of dispositions *already* regarded as desirable by society by methods *already* regarded as satisfactory. Then the fostering by anyone of other dispositions by other methods simply is not education, no matter how desirable the dispositions may be or how scientific the methods. This makes the social science definition of education too narrow for the purposes of the philosophy of education. Even in ordinary discourse we use the term 'education' in a much broader and less intrinsically conservative way; we speak, for instance, of educating society itself. Today's younger generation even thinks of itself as educating its elders; it may be mistaken in this, but it is not misusing the word 'education,' as it would be if the social science definition were correct.

It appears, then, that the first of our two definitions of education is neither true to our actual use of the term 'education' nor satisfactory from the point of view of the practical educator or of the educational philosopher who seeks to guide the enterprise of education, possibly along new paths. The normative definition obviously comes much closer to filling both bills. I propose that we adopt it, except, perhaps, when we are doing social science, i.e., that we adopt it when we are engaged in educational activity or in thinking about what it should do. If we do this, then we will have to say that education *is* by definition relevant, for then it will by definition foster desirable dispositions, but, of course, it does not follow that what is taught in our schools is relevant, for it does not follow that our schools are fostering desirable dispositions. It may be that our so-called educational enterprise is not really educational, as so many now think is in fact the case, e.g., those who see it as 'mis-education.' Notice, that in calling our putative education 'mis-education' such people are implicitly adopting the normative concept of education. They are not denying that our program cultivates dispositions, nor that it promotes those regarded as desirable by elder society, but that it fosters desirable dispositions, and they are implying that if or since it does not issue in desirable states of mind, it is not education but mis-education.

In effect, I am suggesting that, at least when we are not just doing social science, descriptive or explanatory, we all of us—parents, teachers, students, legislators, society as a whole—should think in terms of the normative concept of education rather than in terms of the social science concept that so many of us have picked up in recent years. Only then will we have a concept of education that can guide us as a pillar of cloud by day and a pillar of fire by night, rather than the other way around. Then, for example, we can get the question whether the 'education' offered our young is relevant or not in proper perspective. As I have already implied,

C

the social science concept of education is partly responsible for the feeling so many have that our 'educational' program is irrelevant, conformist, traditionalistic, authoritarian, etc. If we define education as socialization *and* identify socialization with the internalization of the prevailing culture, and *also* call our school program education, we simply invite our children, if they have any logic in them, to conclude that that program is committed to the *status quo* and should be reconstructed from the ground up.

Actually, we and they are both unfair to our program in doing this, quite unnecessarily unfair. No program that teaches science, history, art, literature, or philosophy as well as these are in fact taught in our schools, that promotes autonomy and critical thinking as much as ours does, or that produces so many critics of its own results, can be fairly described as wholly bent on the mere internalization of the prevailing culture or judged to be mis-education from beginning to end, no matter how deficient it may be in some of its parts or aspects—and I do not deny that it is deficient in many ways. I only suggest that we unfairly make it look more deficient than it is to our children, if we represent it to them as simply what the social scientists call socialization.

On the other hand, if we use the normative concept of education as the fostering and acquiring of desirable dispositions by satisfactory methods, then we can address ourselves directly to the questions, 'Which dispositions are desirable?' and 'Which methods are satisfactory?' leaving open as possible answers both the extreme conservative alternative that we already know what these are and the extreme liberal alternative that we still have to find out—and, of course, all of the less extreme alternatives in between.

Here I should like to digress a bit for a moment. I have just been indicating that our actual 'education' is neither relevant by definition (though education as normatively conceived is) nor irrelevant by definition (though education as conceived in the social sciences may be thought so). But why are people saying that it is 'irrelevant,' rather than just that it is unsuccessful or seeks to promote the wrong dispositions—which is the sort of thing educational critics have been saying for centuries? Perhaps the answer has the following parts, at least so far as college and university education goes: (1) we have an unprecedentedly large proportion of our population going or seeking to go to college, including many for whom there is no very *clear* reason for thinking they should be there at all; (2) it is not *clear* (perhaps even not true) that the dispositions our colleges and universities foster or seek to foster are or will be necessary or useful to them *all*, more necessary or useful than others they do not foster; (3) when these two conditions *both* obtain, the feeling that something is wrong with higher education increases in volume, requires a new vocabulary, and generates a greater sense of urgency.

If this is so, it must also be pointed out that there are at least two ways in which our society and its colleges might react to the charge that their 'education' is irrelevant (or not really education). They might take the line that they should promote other dispositions in students than they do—this is the line their critics themselves tend to take. But they might also take the line that it is a mistake to think that everyone or nearly everyone should go or needs to go to college —this would be a hard and unpopular line, but it is in principle as open as the other (and, indeed, former Chief Justice Earl Warren has suggested that what this country needs is a new type of institution, besides the state, the church, and the school). Either way there would have to be a revolution in our educational thinking, of course, but perhaps it is to this *dilemma* between revolutions that our current academic unrest points, rather than to either answer to it.

Suppose, then, that we agree not to define education as the transmission of the prevailing culture, or even as whatever we do to shape our minds and characters or those of others, but as what we should do in shaping them. Then the next question is, 'What dispositions and methods are desirable or satisfactory?' And here all sorts of problems, ethical and meta-ethical, arise that we cannot possibly deal with now. We must, however, say at least a word about desirability or satisfactoriness before we can proceed. Many people equate what is desirable with what is desired or regarded as desirable by society, by oneself, or by some class or group to which one belongs. This is a mistake, made again, I fear, at least partly under the influence of the social sciences. If one says that something is desirable or satisfactory one is not just saying that it is desired or regarded as desirable by someone or some group. One is making a normative or value-judgment, not a descriptive or factual one, though it may be based on descriptive or factual judgments. Neither is one merely expressing one's own favorable feelings toward the thing in question. One *is* taking a favorable attitude toward the thing (not just stating a fact about it), but one is also claiming, at least implicitly, that one's favorable attitude is justified or rational in some objective sense. If one is not doing this—if he only means to state a fact about his or other people's feelings, or to vent his own desires or feelings and evoke similar feelings in others, or if he disowns making any claim to objective validity— then he really has no business using the words 'desir*able*' or 'satis*factory*,' as Dewey among others pointed out.

One may say, as students (and teachers) sometimes do, that the dispositions fostered by a program of 'education' are not desirable unless they are desirable *for* or *to* the ones in whom they are being fostered. This thought appears to underlie some of our current complaints of irrelevance. There is some truth in this. But we must distinguish here between two things: (1) saying that, to be desirable, a disposition must be desirable for the child to have; (2) saying that, to be desirable, a disposition must be desired or regarded as desirable by the child. The first statement is true, the second false. A disposition may be desirable for a child to have even if he does not desire it or regards it as undesirable. It may, in that case, be pointless or mistaken to try to develop it in or teach it to him, but that is another question, one of practical pedagogy.

This is why I think that even in the interest of our children themselves, forgetting that of their elders or of society, we cannot buy a certain concept of education that seems to be finding favor these days, viz. that education is simply the process of fostering in those being educated the dispositions they themselves want, regard as desirable, or judge to be relevant. This third contemporary concept of education can be generated from the matrix formulated earlier by making the following substitutions:

X = anyone, preferably oneself
Y = anyone, again preferably oneself
D = the dispositions Y desires, regards as desirable, or judges relevant
M = the methods Y regards as satisfactory.

It is, as I understand it, the idea behind some of what is called 'free' education, and it is at once 'new', as it is called, and old. Actually, it was nicely formulated by Bianca in *The Taming of the Shrew*:

> Why, gentlemen, you do me double wrong;
> To strive for that which resteth in *my* choice:
> *I* am no breeching scholar in the schools;
> I'll *not* be tied to hours nor 'pointed times,
> But learn *my* lessons *as I please myself.* (My italics.)

But, new or old, this definition of education is not defensible, since it rests on the confusion just pointed out between what is desirable and what is desired or regarded as desirable.

Another, related, reason why I think we cannot buy this 'new' or 'free' conception of education is this. It says that what we are to do in education—else it is not really education—depends wholly on the recipient's sense of what is desirable or relevant. But it seems obvious that one of the things that most needs educating, most needs development by education, is precisely this sense of what is desirable or relevant. People's sense of desirability and relevance needs stretching by education at least as much as education needs to be tailor-made to fit their sense of desirability or relevance. It still may be, of course, that our present 'education' does not do enough to make students *see* the desirability or relevance of what it puts before them. But it is also fair to ask if its relevance or desirability must always be laid out on a platter, or whether students may be expected to try to stretch their own intellectual and emotional visions so as to see it for themselves.

If I am right in this, then the question, 'What dispositions are desirable and what methods of fostering them are satisfactory?' cannot be answered simply by asking what dispositions and methods are regarded as desirable or satisfactory by our society or by those being educated. There is nothing for it but to make a straight-out normative inquiry. How then is it to be answered? I do not mean here, '*What* is the answer, i.e., what dispositions and what methods are desirable or satisfactory?'; I mean, '*How* is the answer to be arrived at by anyone seeking it?' About this I can only be brief and general. My conception of the 'logic' of such an inquiry is this. First, one must look for basic normative premises about what is good, right, etc., with which to begin in trying to see what dispositions education should foster. But one cannot tell this by using such premises alone. One must also look for basic factual premises about man and the world. Then, from these two kinds of premises, one can conclude what dispositions we should acquire or foster. For example, Aristotle argued as follows: (1) the Good=happiness =excellent activity=doing geometry, doing just acts, etc.; (2) man has reason as well as desire and emotion and is capable of doing geometry, just acts, etc. (or at least some men are); (3) therefore all men (or those who are capable of them) should acquire a knowledge of geometry and a disposition to be just. Then, as a second stage in one's reasoning, one must look for further factual premises about the psychology of learning, methods of fostering the dispositions in question, etc., and draw further conclusions about the methods that education should use. Thus, Aristotle reasoned: (4) a knowledge of geometry can be acquired by instruction and a disposition to be just by practice in doing just acts; (5) therefore the young should be given instruction in geometry and practice in doing what is just.

There are also questions, of course, about who is to be taught what and who is to do the teaching—questions about X and Y as well as about D and M—but in general they are to be answered in a similar manner.

27

It may be asked how we are to find the various premises on which we are to rest our conclusions about dispositions to form and methods to use. The only answer, so far as I can see, is 'By doing science, including especially psychology and social science, and philosophy, especially ethics and social philosophy—or, perhaps, theology. Not just by looking to see what the basic premises of our prevailing culture are.' There are problems about this, of course, but there is no other rational alternative.

It may also be asked, '*Who* is to determine what dispositions are desirable and what methods satisfactory?' I find this question particularly baffling. In a way, the answer is, 'Whoever asks the question what education should be like must find his own answer.' Everyman must in a sense be his own educational philosopher— that is the spirit of what Socrates called the examined life as well as of our contemporary culture. In practice, however, every bit of educational enterprise that is not purely personal or wholly experimental must be based on some kind of working compromise between differing views, and I have no formula for effecting such compromises—except to insist that everyone must always be participating in the search for what it is rational to think education should be like, what it is rational to think true education is. This is itself one of the goals education should promote—reflection and dialogue about itself.

In another way, the answer to our question must always be that our best minds must address themselves to the problem of discovering what dispositions we should acquire or cultivate—by the methods I have tried to outline. I do not mean to advocate some kind of dictatorship of the intellectuals, not even of philosophers— I believe that these best minds must still try to sell us their conclusions in an open and free market (or rather that they must 'educate' the rest of us). I only mean that, even in a democratic society, such minds must work on this problem and be listened to, else we are all the losers. Socrates' complaint about democracy had a point—one should not go to just anyone to see what *arete* is, be taught it, or find out how to teach it.

I can, however, at least give some indication here of what *my* conception of the content of education is. I have rejected both the notion that education is the formation of the dispositions that are valued by adult society and the notion that education is the formation of the dispositions valued by the young. It seems clear that the former notion of education cannot be accepted by any self-respecting member of a younger generation, and that the latter cannot be accepted by society as a whole. Is it just a matter of generation-gap or of society versus the individual? I do not think so. It seems to me (a) that a society should not itself accept the first or social concept of education and (b) that an individual, even a youngish one, should not himself accept the third or individualistic concept of education. Let me try, briefly, to say why.

On the first point—I have, of course, read about 'the poverty of liberalism,' but I still think that the point of society is to make it possible for its individual members, including its younger members, to have the best lives they are capable of, granting, even insisting, that this implies that each member must be moral in his relations to others. Besides, no society can safely or rationally assume that it already knows just what dispositions its members need in order to live the best lives of which they are capable, or even what dispositions are required for their being moral in their relations with one another—or that it already knows just what means are best for cultivating the dispositions needed. The second point is somewhat harder to make briefly. Perhaps I can best make it by suggesting that Hegel was right in arguing that the 'subjective spirit' of a human individual must remain empty and unrealized if it does not participate in the achievements of the social 'objective spirit' represented by language, art, science, history, mathematics, morality, etc., not to mention philosophy. John Dewey, who certainly emphasized the child-centered approach in education but was also something of a follower of Hegel, expressed this by saying that even such child-centered education must proceed 'by the participation of the individual in the social consciousness of the race. . . . If we eliminate the social factor from the child we are left only with an abstraction. . . .'[7] He might better have said that we are left only with a wild man, such as Kipling's Mowgli would have been had his animal friends Baloo, Bagheera, and Kaa not been able to talk and hence to teach.

For the rest I should like to follow Peters once more.[8] After saying in effect what I have just said, he goes on to point out that there are a number of 'living' or 'public traditions' or 'forms of life' and activity that have been developed in the course of human history, 'such as science, history, mathematics, religious and aesthetic appreciation, and . . . the practical types of knowledge involved in moral, prudential, and technical forms of thought and action.' Each of these involves 'canons' or 'standards' proper to itself that are independent of the individual, each has its methods, its previous achievements, and its openness to further development. Following Michael Oakeshott, he refers to the methods of such an 'inherited tradition' as its 'language' and the previous achievements as its 'literature.' And he argues, much as Hegel did, that one cannot even 'have a mind' unless one has been 'initiated' into such 'lan-

29

guages' and 'literatures.' In fact, he maintains that the dispositions that are desirable for individuals to have are first of all those that are involved in and fostered by such public traditions or forms of thought and action, and that education is 'the processes by means of which the individual is initiated into them.'

> It consists in initiating others into activities, modes of conduct and thought which have standards written into them by reference to which it is possible to act, think, and feel with varying degrees of skill, relevance and taste.

Its *aim*, however, is not just to indoctrinate or pass on these traditions, as the social science concept of education seems to say; it is to make of each individual, so far as possible, an autonomous speaker of the languages involved, i.e., to make him capable of judging, acting, and thinking on his own in art, history, science, morality, etc. 'The pupil has gradually to get the grammar of the activity into his guts so that he can eventually win through to the stage of autonomy.' But while such autonomy is part of its aim, the *means* of education must include introducing the pupil to the already existing 'literatures' of art, history, dancing, basketball, etc.

> The pupil . . . cannot [win through to autonomy] unless he has mastered the moves made by his predecessors which are enshrined in living traditions. *How* he can come best to do this is an empirical question; but talk of encouraging 'creativeness' is mischievous unless children are also equipped with competence; talk of 'problem-solving' is cant unless children are knowledgeable enough to recognize a real problem when they see one. The only way into mastering what Oakeshott calls the 'language' of any form of thought or activity is by first being initiated into its 'literature.' This is an arduous business.

It 'takes time and determination,' yet, if it is to achieve its end, it must, Peters insists as much as Dewey or anyone, be carried on in such a way that the pupil finds it all enjoyable and worthwhile, perhaps even 'relevant,' for as much of the time as possible. Education must at least be education, but it should, if possible, also be 'ecstasy.'

This is the view about education with which I should like to associate myself. It keeps what is true in Dewey's view of education as growth, but it makes clearer what growth consists in than he ever did. It also keeps what is true in the more recent view of education as ecstasy, without forgetting that education is the *formation* of dispositions, not their *exercise* in experience and life. More generally, it retains what is valid in the social science concept of education, without its built-in conservatism; it does this by insisting that education involves initiation in traditions of thought and action while aiming at creating individuals who can and will make new advances within those traditions, i.e. do new work (or at least make independent judgments) in art, science, basketball, or what have you. At the same time it also retains what is valid in what I have called the 'new' or 'free' concept of education, since it too aims at making individuals as autonomous as possible.

What I am suggesting is that education be conceived of as the fostering and acquiring, by appropriate methods, of desirable dispositions, and that the dispositions that are desirable (and not just naturally possessed or acquired) consist of a mastery of forms of thought and action with their respective standards, together with responsibility and autonomy. If you ask me whether education can take this form, I can only answer that it has done so in the lives of countless individuals in the past. The main question is whether it can take this form successfully in the lives of all of us and our children. It seems to me that it can, *if* we can properly match forms of life and action to individual interests and potentialities. This seems to me, as it did to Dewey, to be the main task of our practical educators—parents, teachers, and students themselves (I do think students have and should be given a large responsibility here; but I mean responsibility and not just freedom).

There is, however, a further point that Peters neglects, one suggested by the 'new' or 'free' (third) concept of education. This is the possibility of our discovering new forms of life, thought, and action, new traditions, if you will, besides those we already have and include in our curricula. It is not clear to me that this is possible, but, if the world lasts, life in it bids fair to be very different from what it is now, and it may be that we will discover or evolve new ways of living, new kinds of activities, with different standards from those with which we are now familiar—and I do not mean those, if any, that are discovered by drug trippers and psychedelic explorers. If such new things may be, then education must keep this possibility in mind, hold it before us, and somehow prepare us to realize it. How it can do this, I cannot say, but I would suppose that it cannot do even this if it does not initiate us into some of the forms of life and thinking we are already aware of. Perhaps here is where talk of 'creativity' is not mischievous.

If, finally, you ask me just what dispositions each individual should acquire or form, which forms of thought and action he should be initiated into, or whether everyone should acquire all kinds of dispositions, be initiated into all forms of thought and action, then my reply is that he should acquire the dispositions, be initiated into the 'traditions,' that are needed for him to lead a morally good life in relation to others and to have himself the best life he is capable of in the world in which he will be living, insofar as this can be envisaged in advance (something educators are now trying to do much more than ever before). Which dispositions or 'traditions' they are may vary considerably from individual to individual. In any case, however, these are the dispositions and traditions that *are* desirable and relevant, whether the individual *thinks* they are or not. At present, for most of us, they must include preparation for a vocation, but the vocations of the future will differ in greater or lesser degree from those of today, and there are even those who tell us that the day is coming when we shall not work any more. Underneath this vocational question, of course, lie the questions of the natures of the good life and of the moral life—but these lie outside the area on which I can try to throw light here.

Notes

1 R. N. Anderson, R. L. Lawson, R. L. Schnell and D. F. Swift, *Foundation Disciplines and the Study of Education*, Toronto, Macmillan, 1968, pp. 12–13.
2 H. I. Marron, *A History of Education in Antiquity*, Mentor Books, 1964, p. xiii.
3 *Op. cit.*, p. 13.
4 *Education as Initiation*, University of London Institute of Education, 1964, p. 15.
5 *Mysticism and Logic*, Allen & Unwin, 1917, p. 37.
6 *Op. cit.*, p. 12.
7 M. S. Dworkin (ed.), *Dewey on Education*, Teacher's College, Columbia University, 1959, pp. 19–22.
8 For the following quotations see *op. cit.*, pp. 33–46.

Morality and autonomy in education

2

Alan Gewirth

Professor Frankena has given us a useful, wide-ranging analysis. While his discussion deserves praise on many points, my comments will be confined for the most part to a series of criticisms in order to bring into sharper focus some central issues.

1. Frankena writes that 'every activity of education can be represented by the following formula: in it X is fostering or seeking to foster in Y some disposition D by method M. This is the basic matrix of every conception of education as a process or enterprise' (pp. 20–1). Depending partly on what is meant by 'fostering,' if this formula is intended to be coextensive with 'every activity of education,' then it is either too broad or too narrow. If 'fostering' is taken to have a general causal meaning, so that it is akin to 'producing' or 'generating,' then the formula is too broad. Suppose X is a gangster who intentionally uses methods of terror to generate dispositions of fear and cowardice in his victims Y. This situation fits Frankena's formula; but it is difficult to see how it could be called an activity of education.

If, on the other hand, 'fostering' is used to mean the employment of formal instructional methods aimed at giving the learners (Y) certain dispositions, then Frankena's formula is too narrow. For it would then fail to describe what may be called 'informal education,' where various life-experiences have a teaching impact on the persons who undergo them. For example, when Henry Adams entitled his autobiography *The Education of Henry Adams*, he meant something much more extensive than the formal education he received in his academic career. He meant also, and far more profoundly, the various physical, emotional, and social experiences from which he learned throughout his life, such as his early severe childhood illness from which he learned that he would never have the robustness and ebullience of most of his peers and that he would have to amend his expectations accordingly. In such a situation, unlike my above example of the gangster, there was no explicit 'X' who was 'fostering or seeking to foster' in Adams some disposition 'D,' nor was there any explicit method 'M' used therein, but only an unorganized process. Yet it would be a mistake to overlook the important respects in which such informal processes may be highly educational in their impact; and indeed much moral, social, and political education is of this informal sort.

These kinds of cases cannot be accommodated to the 'social science' concept of education which Frankena correctly distinguishes from the 'normative' concept. It might be suggested that the dispositions 'D' which figure in the social science concept as 'the dispositions regarded as desirable by society' are at least analogous to the dispositions in my gangster example, for the fear and cowardice which the gangster aims to instill in his victims are 'regarded as desirable' by him as characteristics of his victims. But this indicates, rather, that certain restrictions must be imposed on the concept of 'dispositions regarded as desirable' if even the social science concept as Frankena describes it is to be a concept of education. The question here is: Is it the case that *any* dispositions which *anyone* regards it as desirable that persons have may figure as the 'D' in Frankena's formula? If the answer is affirmative, then not only the gangster but also the school bully who methodically cultivates in his young victims the disposition to surrender their pennies to him on demand would be engaged in educational activity, since surely the bully regards it as desirable that his victims have this disposition.

I suggest, then, that in any positive concept of education (of which the social science concept is a species), the dispositions which are regarded as desirable must be so regarded out of a conviction that they are to some extent for the good of the recipients or learners (Y) themselves, and not only for the good of the agent (X). In other words, every concept of education, positive as well as normative, must contain a moral component, in that sense of 'moral' in which it means a concern for the interests or welfare of persons other than the agent. Those persons might include more than the recipients or learners, but it must be thought that their own welfare is in some way included in the interests or welfare for which the dispositions fostered are regarded as desirable.

Frankena's general formula for education must, then, be amended in at least two respects. First, not every interpersonal activity in which X fosters dispositions D in Y by methods M is an educational activity; the dispositions fostered ('D') must include the moral component just referred to, and the methods ('M') must be correspondingly fashioned insofar as *formal* education is concerned. Second, the educative agent 'X' and the methods 'M' must both be expanded to include cases of informal education, where there is no explicit or formal educative agent at all and where the processes used are far more diffuse, experiential, unorganized, and informal than anything that can be suitably called a 'method.'

2. Frankena rightly urges the adoption of the normative concept of education from the standpoint of practical engagement in educational activity, and he also rightly urges the central importance of the question: 'What dispositions and methods are desirable or satisfactory?' But in giving his own answer to this question, he seems to contradict himself. On the one hand, discussing the concept of so-called 'free' education, according to which 'education is simply the process of fostering in those being educated the dispositions they themselves want, regard as desirable, or judge to be relevant' (p. 26), Frankena rejects this concept on the ground, among others, that 'It says that what we are to do in education—else it isn't really education—depends wholly on the recipient's sense of what is desirable or relevant. But it seems obvious that one of the things that most needs educating, most needs development by education, is precisely this sense of what is desirable or relevant' (pp. 26–7). On the other hand, one page later Frankena writes as follows: 'It may also be asked, "*Who* is to determine what dispositions are desirable and what methods satisfactory?" I find this question particularly baffling. In a way, the answer is, "Whoever asks the question what education should be like must find his own answer." Everyman must in a sense be his own educational philosopher . . .' (p. 28). There is a contradiction here, since Frankena is both denying and affirming that the persons who are being educated (and who are surely included in 'everyman') should determine for themselves what dispositions are desirable.

This contradiction is similar to the one into which moral philosophers sometimes fall when they try to uphold both objective and subjective concepts of obligation, saying on the one hand that what is morally obligatory must be determined by objective criteria bearing on the nature or consequences of actions, and on the other hand that it must be determined by the agent's own convictions as to what is morally required of him.

The contradiction I have attributed to Frankena may be removed or at least mitigated if distinctions are drawn as to persons and methods. He may be interpreted as denying that the unreflective, precritical standards of persons who are to be educated should be decisive in determining what dispositions are desirable, while affirming that this determination should be made by persons who are to be educated insofar as they are willing to embark on a critical quest for enlightenment. This is perhaps what Frankena means when he goes on to say, 'everyone must always be participating in the search for what it is rational to think education should be like, what it is rational to think true education is' (p. 28). There still remains, however, the question whether 'everyone' is here meant to include both the educators and the persons being educated, and if so, whether they should all participate to the same extent and with the same degree of authority in determining the outcome.

3. Frankena says that to deal with the question of which dispositions and methods are desirable we must ask *'How* is the answer to be arrived at by anyone seeking it?' His reply is: 'First, one must look for basic normative premises about what is good, right, etc., with which to begin in trying to see what dispositions education should foster. But one cannot tell this by using such premises alone. One must also look for basic factual premises about man and the world. Then, from these two kinds of premises, one can conclude what dispositions we should acquire or foster' (p. 27). There is little doubt that Frankena views this inquiry as a philosophic one. First he cites Aristotle's way of going about it; next he says that to find the answer 'Everyman must be . . . his own educational philosopher' (p. 28); then he writes that 'our best minds must address themselves to the problem of discovering what dispositions we should acquire or cultivate—by the methods I have tried to outline' (p. 28).

While this conception is praiseworthy on many counts, I wonder about its practical bearings. Let us consider a concrete example. As we all know, there is widespread questioning nowadays among college students and other young people as to the value of constitutional democracy. Many have expressed despair as to the ability of the 'electoral process' to solve the pressing problems of poverty, racism, war, environmental pollution, and so forth. At the same time, there seems to be widespread ignorance among young people—not necessarily the same ones as those just referred to—concerning the very nature of constitutional democracy. What I am thinking of here, for example, is a Gallup Poll published a few years ago in which a broad sample of high-school students, asked various questions about applications of the Bill of Rights, indicated that they did not know what rights were constitutionally protected and indeed evinced a strong preference that many of the protected rights be denied to various unpopular groups.

It seems clear that such phenomena pose important problems for education. The general problem may be put as follows: What should be the role of education in teaching young persons about the rights and responsibilities of citizenship in a constitutional democracy? I shall refer to this as the general problem of *political education*. This problem may be regarded as a specification of a still more general problem about moral education as a whole; but I shall here focus on the former slightly more delimited case.

Now when we consider Frankena's philosophic questions and 'basic premises' in relation to the concrete problems of political education, a certain sense of impracticality may emerge. Let me emphasize that, as a philosopher, I definitely share Frankena's apparent conviction that satisfactory answers to the concrete questions of moral and political education must ultimately appeal, in one form or another, to 'basic premises' of the sorts he outlines, although we would perhaps differ on at least some features of the normative premises. But there still remains the question whether school-children should undertake such philosophic inquiries in anything like the sense in which philosophers do so. If we consider the developmental hypotheses of thinkers like Piaget and Kohlberg, we find that while they indeed view each child as going through various stages of moral awareness to a stage where moral rules themselves are critically questioned, this still involves a far more *specific* subject-matter than the maximally general philosophic inquiry set forth by Frankena.

I suggest, then, that with respect to the problems of political education we must be careful not to confuse the roles of the elementary school-child, the adolescent, the teacher and administrator, and the philosopher. While all of these should indeed engage in rational, critical inquiry to the limits of their ability, and while each would benefit from informed awareness of and communication with the thinking and experiences of the others, the problems of political education for school-children should be approached in far more specific and circumstantial terms than is the case with a philosopher coping with a whole system of moral and political theory. Or, to put it more generally, we must also be careful, in this respect, not to confuse the criteria of the theoretical and the practical. A person may have sufficient practical political virtue or excellence—he may, for example, be a staunch, enlightened exponent of democratic freedoms—without having performed the technical, deeply probing analyses of the philosopher, just as a man may be a staunch, enlightened practitioner of the virtues of temperance in respect of food, drink, drugs, and so forth without having acquired the technical knowledge of a biochemist or pharmacologist.

A question may also be raised here about the relation of the whole program of formal political education to what I have called informal education. With respect to political education as to the Bill of Rights, for example, to what extent is formal education likely to be successful without an antecedent basis in informal education? Aristotle said that moral virtue is acquired by habituation rather than by explicit instruction, and even if this is a bit conservative in some respects, it still seems plausible that perhaps the most effective

37

way for young people to become familiar with, accepting of, and even critically aware of the Bill of Rights and similar moral–political values is through their experience of living in a country where these rights are firmly respected. I am not saying that such informal education is a sufficient condition of an informed respect for these rights, nor even that it is a necessary condition. But I do suggest that where the possibilities of such informal education exist, it is important to take them into account in one's conception of political education. Indeed, there should be a two-way movement between formal and informal political education, with the resources of the informal education being used to support the more explicit and critical methods of formal education.

4. The above difficulties about the methods of determining what should be the ends of education, i.e., what dispositions education should aim to foster, are sharpened when we consider Frankena's substantive statements about these ends themselves. While I have already suggested what I take to be some of the problems in this area, I wish to discuss them more directly and explicitly. Frankena writes that education should aim 'to make of each individual, so far as possible, an autonomous speaker of the language involved, i.e., to make him capable of judging, acting, and thinking on his own in art, history, science, morality, etc.' (p. 30); 'the dispositions that are desirable . . . consist in a mastery of forms of thought and action with their respective standards, together with responsibility and autonomy' (p. 31); the person being educated 'should acquire the dispositions, be initiated into the "traditions," that are needed for him to lead a morally good life in relation to others and to have himself the best life he is capable of in the world in which he will be living' (p. 32).

In obvious respects these statements are unexceptionable. Especially valuable is their recognition that the ends of education should be complex, aiming at more than the fostering of a single, simply specifiable kind of disposition. But this very complexity raises problems about how to interpret the components of these multiple aims and how to relate them to one another.

Crucial to these problems is the difficult question of the relation of autonomy to the other aims of education, especially moral goodness. The difficulty arises from the fact that autonomy seems to mean deciding on or choosing one's own standards for oneself, while moral goodness (like the other 'forms of thought and action' mentioned above) requires that one conform to objective standards whose contents are independent of one's own decisions or choices. To be autonomous is, in a basic sense, to be free of external constraints, while to be morally good is to be subject to certain external constraints. How, then, can one espouse both autonomy and moral goodness as aims of education?

The most direct way of answering this question would seem to be that education should aim at making persons *autonomously* morally good, in that they themselves recognize and choose (or 'internalize') those standards of conduct which are morally right. This answer is, I think, largely correct. But as it stands it does not meet the difficulty. For not only are the two components thus joined together separable from one another, but they seem to be antithetical to one another. That they are separable seems clear: it is possible to be autonomous without being morally good, and it is possible to be morally good without being autonomous. If, as Frankena puts it, an autonomous person is one who is 'capable of judging, acting, and thinking on his own,' the acting which such a person does 'on his own' may vary from the conduct of a Machiavellian prince or a Nietzschean superman to that of a religious mystic or a Gandhi or Schweitzer; and surely not all of these types of conduct are morally good or right. On the other hand, if being morally good consists, in large part at least, in acting in the ways required by justice and the common good, a person may act in these ways not because he has judged 'on his own' that these ways are morally good or right but rather because he has been brought up to act in these ways, or because the law threatens him with punishment if he acts otherwise, or from similar causes that have little or nothing to do with autonomy.

It might be urged that even if a person may be autonomous without being morally good, he cannot be morally good without being autonomous. For moral goodness consists not merely in doing what is morally right, but in doing it *because* it is morally right, i.e., from one's own independent or autonomous recognition and acceptance of the standards of moral rightness. Such a conception of moral goodness or virtue is set forth by philosophers as otherwise different as Aristotle and Kant, and I think there is much that is sound in it. But as it stands, this conception does not take account of the basic antithesis that may be found between being autonomous and being morally good. For if autonomy consists in choosing one's own standards *because* they are one's own, then this rules out accepting certain standards *because* they are morally right or good. To be autonomous, on this view, is to be independent of any standards outside oneself, while to be morally good is rather to accept certain objective standards from outside oneself—'outside' in the sense that, so far as concerns morality, not anything that one thinks, wants, or chooses is right; rather, the relevant criteria are independent of what one may happen to think, want, or choose. Hence, it would seem to be logically impossible to achieve both autonomy and moral goodness, so that to espouse both of them as aims of education is to involve oneself in a contradiction.

To approach a solution of these difficulties we must look more closely at each of their components. Viewed etymologically, 'autonomy' means being a law (*nomos*) unto oneself (*auto*), or setting one's law for oneself. This etymological root already indicates the difficulties just canvassed, for the law one sets for oneself need not coincide even in part with the moral law, and setting one's law for oneself seems to preclude accepting the law, including the moral law, from any source or criterion other than oneself.

The obvious questions here concern the natures of the 'self' which sets the law and of the 'law' which is set thereby. Many discussions of autonomy, however, pay no explicit attention to these questions. In a recent sociological classic, for example, where the 'autonomous man' figures as an ideal type (in both senses of 'ideal'), the author writes: 'The "autonomous" are those who on the whole are capable of conforming to the behavioral norms of their society—a capacity the anomics usually lack—but are free to choose whether to conform or not.'[1] But what if the 'behavioral norms' of the society include equal civil rights for all persons regardless of race or religion? Is the autonomous man then 'free to choose' not to conform to these norms, for example by threatening with a pickax black persons who want to dine in his restaurant in accordance with the society's 'behavioral norms'? More generally, may an autonomous man espouse racist and tyrannical norms as well as egalitarian and democratic ones? If so, then it becomes very difficult and perhaps impossible to effect that connection between autonomy and moral goodness which one wants to include among the central aims of education. For in such a case autonomy is defined simply as 'self-reliance' or 'self-determination' without regard to the content of what one relies on or what one determines oneself to do or be.

When the concept of autonomy is used without explicit concern for this question of content, its obvious correlate is anarchy. For just as autonomy means setting one's law for oneself, so anarchy etymologically means being without any law or government (*arché*) which is set by anyone other than oneself. Hence the conclusion is sometimes drawn that autonomy is logically incompatible with obedience to political or legal authority. But if such authority prescribes even the minimum of just dealings with one's fellows, then it would again follow that an autonomous man may flout the minimum requirements of justice. Hence, once again, it becomes difficult or impossible to effect a positive connection between autonomy and moral goodness.

Modern political philosophers beginning with Hobbes tried to reconcile autonomy with political authority through the device of the social contract. The crucial point of this device was that the obligation to obey political authority, so far from being externally imposed, was rather self-imposed, 'there being no obligation on any man, which ariseth not from some act of his own' (*Leviathan*, ch. 21). The trouble with this solution was that if 'act of his own' was meant literally, it was impossible to point to any such act, any contract whereby men had agreed to take on political or moral obligations. The solution also involved a fictional conception that men are factually equal in power or ability; for otherwise, the stronger would dominate the weaker without having themselves to be subject to the constraints of political authority or moral obligation.

I now want to suggest that the way out of these difficulties requires that autonomy be viewed in a more specific and restrictive way than is done in the doctrines so far mentioned. If no limits are put either on the 'self' which sets laws or standards or on the 'law' which is thus set, then the connection between autonomy and moral goodness becomes either coincidental or self-contradictory. If, on the other hand, the self in question is regarded as having to meet certain rational requirements, then autonomy can be positively and indeed necessarily related to moral goodness because these requirements are also the criteria of morality. To put it succinctly, only if the self of autonomy is the rational self, and its law the rational law, can the above difficulties be overcome.

The basic point is that insofar as autonomy is regarded as affirmatively connected with moral, intellectual, and other norms, it must itself be given a normative definition. According to this definition, autonomy means that the rational self sets or accepts for itself the rational law. To put it less elliptically, to be autonomous in this normative sense means that one acts as a rational person, in accordance with rationally justifiable norms whose rational justifiability one recognizes and accepts for oneself precisely because and insofar as one is rational. Such autonomy does not involve that criteria are imposed on the person from without, because insofar as the person and the criteria are both rational, the criteria are his own. To be sure, to learn to apply these criteria in sufficient detail requires much learning experience; but what one learns is, in one of the classic definitions of education, a leading out of what is implicitly in oneself.

For the understanding of this argument, it is obviously of great importance how rationality is defined. The argument will make its point only if the rationality to which it appeals fulfills two requirements. On the one hand, with a view to autonomy, the rationality in question must be a part of the normal equipment of human persons, so that its setting laws or criteria for persons can realistically be regarded as something done by the person himself. On the other hand, with a view to moral goodness, the law or criteria set by the rationality in question must be able to ground or justify what is morally right.

What sort of rationality, if any, can fulfill this latter requirement has long been one of the most controversial questions of moral philosophy. I cannot here present the detailed arguments required to defend my own answer to this question. But with regard to the conception of rationality which I hold fulfills these two requirements, I can at least assert that its being entitled to the name 'rationality' is quite uncontroversial. For by 'rationality' I here mean the ability and disposition to take due account both of relevant empirical facts and of logically necessary connections. Philosophers have always been concerned with the analysis of each of these dispositions, and anthropologists and others have questioned whether they are the only kinds of rationality. But it would be difficult to question that they are at least among the most basic types of rationality.

This conception of rationality clearly fulfills the first requirement stated above. For all normal human persons have, at least in an elementary way, the empirical and logical abilities in question. That the conception also fulfills the second requirement is, as I just suggested, far more controversial. I have argued elsewhere,[2] however, that these empirical and logical bases are sufficient to justify a supreme principle of morality, which can in turn elucidate and justify all the specific moral rules and judgments constitutive of moral rightness. In so far, then, as a person uses his rationality in the sense just indicated, he will set for himself laws, rules, or judgments which are morally right; hence his normative autonomy will necessarily be one with his moral goodness, so that the conflicts indicated above between autonomy and moral goodness are resolved.

The concept of the rational self, to which I appealed in my normative definition of autonomy, lends itself to easy caricature. It has been satirized both as a Cartesian 'ghost in the machine' and as a sinister buttress for totalitarianism, the latter deriving from the contention that if the rational self is the 'real' self, then men's ordinary empirical desires may be overridden on the ground that it is not what they 'really' want. Neither of these reductions, however, is loglcally necessitated by the idea that the positive linkage of autonomy with moral goodness requires that the self which gives laws to oneself be rational in the sense indicated above. As I have already suggested, the phrase 'rational self' is metaphorical; it refers to that aspect of the total personality whereby one can ascertain and act according to what is logically and empirically justifiable. This aspect of oneself, including the criteria it observes, can be specified without postulating an unobservable guiding entity within the psyche, and appeal to a rational self need not involve denying that the total self is a complex combination of various instinctual, emotional, and conative elements. The use of reason in the sense indicated above does not involve suppressing these elements but rather, in important respects, guiding them and coordinating them both with one another and with the corresponding elements in other persons.

Let us look somewhat more closely at the general point of my above argument. I have suggested that the potential conflicts between autonomy and moral goodness as aims of education can be resolved by regarding both of these as involving rational criteria. The general point, then, seems to be when there is a conflict between two aims or values, the conflict can be resolved by finding a criterion common to both, such that each can be either defined or justified by reference to that common criterion. The following question may hence be raised: even if this general point is sound, why must the criterion in question be reason or rationality? Isn't it possible, for example, to appeal to emotion or feeling as the common criterion?

This was in fact what David Hume tried to do. He held that moral distinctions derive not from reason but from a 'moral sentiment,' and although he did not address the problem of autonomy explicitly, he could be interpreted as arguing that this basis in moral sentiment preserves autonomy as well as moral goodness because the sentiments in question are the agent's own. (I here ignore problems arising from Hume's distinction between moral agents and moral spectators.) After all, persons are emotional as well as rational, so that autonomy might just as well mean that the emotional self sets for itself an emotional law or standard; and since this emotional law can be the basis of morality, autonomy is thus reconciled with moral goodness.

While I would not want to foreclose all the possibilities of such a solution, I think there is strong ground for doubting that it will meet the second of the two requirements presented above. For emotion, in so far as it is to serve as the basis of morality, does not have the same kind of relative fixity and universality as is found in rational criteria. Hume himself, of course, held that moral sentiments *qua* moral are invariant and universal, in that the features of actions or qualities which give to a spectator 'the pleasing sentiment of approbation' are the same for all spectators, these features consisting in what is either useful or immediately agreeable either to the agent himself or to other persons. But, even taking into account Hume's requirement that the point of view from which moral spectators judge is or must be general rather than self-interested, it is difficult not to see in his assertions about what universally and invariably pleases them the optimistic innocence of the Enlightenment. Hume himself had to admit that some moral judges or spectators approved of the 'monkish virtues' which are quite different from the virtues he himself had denominated moral, and that many nations, in esteeming the martial virtues, have also departed from what gives his moral spectator a pleasing feeling of approval.[3]

More generally, to derive criteria of moral goodness from emotions or feelings commits one to relativism because judgments based on feelings may vary from one person or group to another. In so far as judgments of moral goodness and rightness are to be characterized by such features as universality, impartiality, and consistency, the justificatory criteria on which they are based must be rational ones.

In conclusion, I want to bring the above considerations about rationality together with my earlier caution about not confusing the criteria of the theoretical and the practical. Any realistic conception of moral and political education must recognize that the intellectual requirements of philosophical analysis are far more rigorous than the standards of adequacy found in ordinary thought and action. Hence, if the rational self which figures in the normative conception of autonomy as I have presented it is conceived at so philosophic a level that its standards cannot be met by ordinary persons, then one will indeed have succeeded in rescuing the concept of autonomy from the difficulties mentioned earlier, but at the cost of depriving it of practical relevance by confining it to a select group of intellectuals.

This is not, however, the only possibility. For as I have already suggested, the rationality I briefly described above is available to the ordinary person. He can take sufficient account of relevant empirical facts (even though he may not be able to discover all or most of them for himself), and he can grasp (at an elementary level) the kind of logically necessary connection which is involved in a rational moral principle. He can note, for example, that it is inconsistent of him to apply to others a rule he is unwilling to have applied to himself, in so far as he is relevantly similar to those others. The Golden Rule is the most famous but not the only example of such an appeal to logical consistency. Moral and political education may well begin from the Golden Rule; by exposing its difficulties in the face of the complexities encountered in moral and political experience, the teacher can bring his students to recognize a principle which is more adequate to those complexities. The development of the appropriate rational dispositions in the student can thus lead concomitantly to the development both of autonomy and of moral goodness.

I do not wish to be understood as holding that the points I have tried to make above are necessarily in disagreement with Frankena's position. On the contrary, I think they correspond to at least part of what he intends when he says that 'everyone must always be participating in the search for what it is rational to think education should be like, what it is rational to think true education is' (p. 28). My concern here has been not at all to confute this, but rather to consider how the appeal to rationality can be used to resolve the problems raised for education when its central aims are held to include both autonomy and moral goodness.

Notes

1 David Riesman, *The Lonely Crowd*, Garden City, L. I., Doubleday-Anchor, 1954, p. 278.
2 See A. Gewirth, 'Categorial Consistency in Ethics', *The Philosophical Quarterly*, vol. 17, 1967, pp. 289–99; 'Obligation: Political, Legal, Moral', *Nomos*, vol. 12, pp. 55–88; 'The Justification of Egalitarian Justice', *American Philosophical Quarterly*, vol. 8, 1971. In a forthcoming book, *Reason and Morality*, I present a detailed development of the argument.
3 Hume, *Enquiry Concerning the Principles of Morals*, secs VII, IX, Selby-Bigge (ed.), 1902, pp. 254–5, 270.

Comments on Frankena's 'The concept of education today' 3

Arnold S. Kaufman

I agree with Professor Frankena that autonomy is education's central aim. Though he proposes certain educational methods as means of promoting autonomous lives, Frankena understandably gives us only a glimpse of what he means by 'autonomy,' even less of why he values it. But unless we have a clearer idea of the first his proposals can not be assessed for their effectiveness as means. And unless we have grounds for confidence that the purported ideal is morally defensible his proposals can not be morally evaluated.

Except for a concluding discussion in which I critically examine Frankena's proposed methods, my aim is to develop those central moral aspects of Frankena's position with which I basically agree.

I Autonomy

Frankena says that an autonomous person is 'capable of judging, acting, and thinking on his own.' We must clarify the idea of *ownership* that is at work here as well as in most other discussions of autonomy. For, in a trivial sense, any action someone performs is his own just in virtue of the fact that it is *his* action. And so with judgments and thoughts. Clearly something special is intended when *ownership* is attributed in order to convey the idea that the action, judgment, or thought is autonomous. What is that special something?

One might claim that ownership is attributed to a special part of the whole person; to what he really is; to some core self. It is this core self that exercises control over other, less central parts of a person's total self. This is right as far as it goes. However, the expression of one's core self makes that thought, act, or judgment authentic. And authenticity is not the whole of autonomy. For an individual might, with perfect authenticity, always and unreflectively obey laws or customs merely because they are socially accepted. At the core he is quite authentically, but also quite unreflectively, law-abiding and imitative. His being so authentic in these respects *adds* a measure to his lack of autonomy.

46

Autonomy requires that we act, judge, or think as we do because our core self is controlling *in a certain way*—in general, the way of the rational person.

An autonomous person is then one who possesses two inter-dependent and overlapping virtues: authenticity and rationality. I shall first *very briefly* sketch the lines along which I think these ideas ought more fully to be elucidated. Then, in the same tentative spirit I shall sketch a moral rationale which justifies autonomy's place of pride in our educational scheme of things.

(i) An authentic thought, judgment, or action is an *expression* of one's core self. (For purposes of simplicity I shall hereafter restrict myself to discussion of actions unless it is important to draw distinctions.) An inauthentic action *conflicts* with that core. An action may not be authentic, yet not be inauthentic. That I brush my teeth with a certain brand of toothpaste is irrelevant to what I am at the core: neither its expression, nor in conflict with it.

What then is a person's core self? Consider the following illustration. John, Mary's boss, snaps at her for coming to work two minutes late. He is grumpy and grouchy through the day, giving Mary a very hard time. Peter, watching all this, says, 'John is not himself today.' What is Peter trying to convey?

Let us suppose that Peter thinks John is very kindly: that he has evidence for this judgment, garnered over a long span of years. That is to say, Peter thinks John has deeply rooted, important dispositions that provide a basis for expecting him to be kind to those he encounters and which help explain why he is kindly when he is. But, on this day, John is acting in ways that conflict with these basic dispositions. Peter supposes that whatever it is that causes John to be so unmannerly, it is nothing as rooted and important as his kindly-making dispositions. It does not matter whether Peter is right about this. I am trying to say what he means, not whether what he says about John is true.

More generally, a person's core self is that constellation of relatively deeply rooted, important dispositions, knowledge of which helps us to anticipate and explain his actions over a relatively extended stretch of his total behavior. And when he acts in conflict with those dispositions they enable us to expect and to explain his discomfort or worse:[1]

> ... Oh, the *guilts*. It's a very easy dodge to say, look, I'm gifted, I'm talented, so you have to put up with my foibles. ... And the minute you try to make people accept the ugliness of you because of *this*, you've done an ... unfair thing. And something indecent, actually. ... And every time I did it I

47

knew that I was going to do it before I did it and was ashamed of doing it all along and was ashamed after I'd done it.

Obviously, for someone else accurately to judge that my anxiety, guilt, shame, or whatever is a symptom of an inauthentic nature he must have some idea of how I normally act in similar circumstances. And even then he might be mistaken. For some reason, I might until this moment have deliberately tried to mislead him whenever we were together. For someone to judge that another has acted authentically he must rely on normal behavior. But actually acting authentically (or inauthentically) is quite another matter.

A given person may not have a core self. He may not be capable of getting himself 'all together.' For he may have basic dispositions that do not cohere. Who was inauthentic, Jekyll or Hyde? He may have an anomic self.

Of special importance is the inauthenticity of self-deception. Not all self-deception is inauthentic. A gambler deceives himself about the influence a rabbit's foot has on his fortunes. Hardly a case of inauthenticity. Indeed, in some cases such foolishness might testify to the fact that he has a gambling-nature. But if a person deceives himself about some aspect of his core self he is likely to be inauthentic. In Kafka's novel, *The Trial*, K at first inauthentically protests that he is innocent. (This example brings out another important feature of authenticity. Even if actually innocent, if someone is strongly disposed to feel and think himself guilty, then *that* is part of his core self.)

Self-deception that is inauthentic is specially important for two reasons. First, it involves failure to acknowledge truths about oneself so basic that education must especially aim to correct the situation. Second, whatever may be a correct account of self-deception (and I do not try to offer an explication here), it certainly involves breakdown of one's capacity for rationally assessing evidence which plainly warrants, and would normally be taken by the individual himself to warrant, beliefs contrary to those he sincerely expresses. In this respect, self-deception that is inauthentic overlaps the second essential component of autonomy, rationality.

One final comment about authenticity. Many of the authors for whom ideas similar to that of the core self (real will, real wants, real belief, etc.) have played a central theoretical role have intended something very different than the idea sketched here. They have had in mind an *ideal* of the core self—ideas about what someone's core self should be. Or perhaps they have meant to claim that, given the core self a person actually does have, were he to act rationally he would express it in certain ways and not others. But if he fails to act rationally, if indeed he is not even disposed to act rationally, then he can not be said to be inauthentic in the sense specified here. In either case, the important thing to note is that authenticity is only one virtue, not the only one. And authentic action is not, on balance, always either morally right or prudentially sound.

(ii) It is important to indicate what is *not* involved in the rationality attributed to the autonomous person. The temptation is persistent in philosophy and in more practical affairs to invest the idea of rationality with significance that defeats the very ideal of autonomy. Thus Benn and Peters, trading on a defective analogy with objectivity, insist that a moral agent must be impartial on pain of being irrational.[2] John Rawls says that envy is irrational.[3] And a noted columnist observes that 'Pouring animal blood on government records is an act that is no less *inherently irrational* than planning to kidnap Henry Kissinger or to destroy the underground heating system for government buildings.'[4] One does not have to condone lack of impartiality, envy, or militant tactics like the ones mentioned to recognize that building the requirement that they be absent into the very concept of rationality is usually intended to protect such ideas from scrutiny by autonomous minds. Such conceptual maneuvers are typically devices for ideological insinuation, not efforts to achieve conceptual clarity. Even when it is not part of the intent of the individual who invests the word, 'rationality,' with 'surplus' content so as to exempt certain ideas from criticism, such definitions are functionally likely to promote this outcome. Hence, from the point of view of an autonomous life, it is better to avoid this kind of definitional maneuver when explicating 'rationality.'

More generally, the concept of rationality that develops within a given culture is bound to incorporate customary beliefs and practices, and thereby, in a functional sense, to protect them from criticism. But, as should be obvious, at the heart of the justification of the ideal of autonomy is precisely the effort to avoid accepting customary things in this way. As John Stuart Mill insistently and passionately held, it is desirable to give 'the freest scope possible to uncustomary things, in order that it may in time appear which of these are fit to be converted into customs.'[5]

II Justification

Having all too briefly discussed autonomy I turn now to an equally cursory sketch of a justification of the ideal of autonomy. And here

49

I do no more than indicate the general lines of John Stuart Mill's defense of autonomy as well as my reasons for accepting them.

In what is certainly the most passionate chapter of his essay, *On Liberty*, ('Of Individuality, As One of the Elements of Well-Being') John Stuart Mill defends the ideal of autonomy (he calls it, 'individuality') on two broadly different kinds of grounds. He thinks that individuality is intrinsically good; it is a proper object of value just in virtue of what it is. But he also develops many consequential arguments; partly to persuade others to accept the ideal, partly, I think, to justify his own commitment to it. Thus he argues, not only that without autonomous individuals social progress is impossible, but that autonomy is an essential condition of that kind of individual development without which one can never come to live the best life of which he is capable. This, of course, includes acquiring one's 'fair share of happiness.' With this general defense of autonomy I agree.

It is worth passing mention that the ideal of autonomy, as constructed here, is not only different from the Kantian theory of moral autonomy, it is incompatible with it. For Kant, the morally autonomous person is probably inauthentic, and certainly non-authentic. Believing that human beings are depraved, Kant saw the central problem of the moral life as curbing one's appetitive nature through self-legislation—which is what he meant by 'autonomy.' The central aim of a morally autonomous, rational individual is to counteract his all too deeply rooted dispositions.

Autonomy in all its senses has recently encountered heavy criticism from an unexpected quarter. In one defense of the counter-culture Philip Slater writes:[6]

> The belief that everyone should pursue autonomously his own destiny has forced us to maintain an emotional detachment (for which no amount of superficial gregariousness can compensate) from our social and physical environment, and aroused a vague guilt about our competitiveness and indifference to others; for, after all, our earliest training in childhood does not stress competitiveness, but cooperation, sharing, and thoughtfulness—it is only later that we learn to reverse these priorities . . . [So] Individualism finds its roots in the attempt to deny the reality and importance of human interdependence. . . . Unfortunately, the more we have succeeded in doing this the more we have felt disconnected, bored, lonely, unprotected, unnecessary, and unsafe.

And in a different way, as Frankena indicates in his passing remark about the alleged poverty of liberalism, Robert Paul Wolff is making a similar point.[7]

Though Slater and Wolff seem to me in part to confuse a kind of laissez-faire, 'materialistic' individualism with autonomy as I have sketchily defined it, it does seem to me that a residual and serious criticism remains. While I am inclined to think that the ideals of communal life and of autonomy are not in such fundamental conflict as Slater, and possibly Wolff, suppose, there is something in what they claim. But the issue needs to be dealt with more clearly than they or anyone else has yet done.

III Autonomy and methods of education

Given the ideal of autonomy that I have sketched, what can we say about the adequacy of Frankena's discussion?

First, though I agree that autonomy is a central ideal of education, it is not as important in *all* educational respects as Frankena seems to suppose. Training in basketball would not be significantly impaired if autonomy were neglected. More importantly, if Thomas Kuhn's views about the nature of normal science are correct, then there are long stretches of time during which it is desirable to discourage the overwhelming majority of budding scientists from cultivating a taste for autonomous inquiry. For, according to Kuhn, achievement in doing normal science depends, not primarily on creative departure, but on assimilation and application of what he calls 'the textbook tradition.'[8] I do not claim that Kuhn is right: only that his arguments are sufficiently cogent that we cannot foreclose the possibility that a special zeal among scientists for probing first principles and presuppositions may, on the whole, be undesirable during specific periods of time.

Yet in many spheres, surely all those that pertain to moral topics, the ideal of autonomy has basic value. Would the methods Frankena proposes promote autonomy in these appropriate areas? I will, with misgivings, express some doubts. For his methodological views are not sufficiently elaborated to warrant confidence that he actually accepts the positions I will attribute to him. If I am mistaken, then my remarks may be considered both as requests for further clarification and suggestions about how the topic of the correct educational methods should be further developed.

Frankena holds, and it should be clear that I agree, that rationality lies at the heart of what it is for thought, judgment, and action to be autonomous. But what are the appropriate standards of rationality? Or, what comes to the same thing, what conception of rationality ought to be educationally fostered?

They are, Frankena tells us, the standards of 'skill, relevance, and taste' that are valid for any practice. And, following Oakeshott, he supposes that these are standards embedded in a subject's traditional language and literature. One is tempted to add that these are also standards customarily accepted by those who engage in the practice. Oakeshott is clear on this point. He writes that 'the view I am recommending is that the conduct of a scientist may properly be called "rational" in respect of its faithfulness to the traditions of scientific inquiry,'[9] making it clear that those traditions are embedded in customary practice. As it is with scientific conduct, so it is with all other forms of activity.

Oakeshott does not deny that standards of 'rationality' may usefully change. But this will not usually, if ever, result from autonomous scrutiny of an activity. Rather, salutary change will normally be the indirect result of such things as 'an earthquake, a plague, a war, or a mechanical invention.'[10] There is, in other words, no evidence that Oakeshott shares Frankena's robust faith in autonomy's efficacy. Like Burke, Oakeshott seems to be more appreciative of those[11]

> men of speculation [who], instead of exploding general prejudices, employ their sagacity to discover the latent wisdom which prevails in them. If they find what they seek, and they seldom fail, they think it more wise to continue the prejudice, with the reason involved, than to cast away the coat of prejudice, and to leave nothing but the naked reason; because prejudice, with its reason, has a motive to give action to that reason, and an affection which will give it permanence. Prejudice is of ready application in the emergency; it previously engages the mind in a steady course of wisdom and virtue, and does not leave the man hesitating in the moment of decision, sceptical, puzzled, and unresolved. Prejudice renders a man's virtue his habit; and not a series of unconnected acts. Through just prejudice, his duty becomes a part of his nature.

Education's main function must be, not to examine the world in order to change it, but to rationalize what exists in order better to preserve what has, after all, stood history's tests.

This general posture should put Frankena on guard against the likelihood that Oakeshott's proposed educational method is the best way to promote autonomy. And, indeed, there is good reason to think that immersing students in the traditional language and literature of a given discipline is more likely to fulfill Oakeshott's goal than Frankena's contrary one. (Surely Frankena does not mean by 'reason' anything that would conform to Oakeshott's criterion of fidelity to customary practice. For Frankena to accept that criterion would, in effect, be to abandon commitment to autonomy.)

From the point of view of an autonomous person, prevailing standards and practices, even if they happen to go by the name of 'reason,' are themselves the very sorts of things that should be detached and, in some culturally non-profound sense, examined. Training in the traditional language and literature of any discipline tends, on the whole, to reinforce nerve-deep habits of thought, judgment, and action that form long before an individual acquires the skills of autonomous inquiry. This is even more true in those very areas most in need of the play of autonomous minds; moral topics generally, political topics in particular. Socialization in prevailing 'prejudices' invariably occurs long before education for autonomy.

That is, early processes of socialization tend, in the overwhelming majority of cases, to promote unreflective identification with the prevailing culture. Pervasive, deep, and tenacious, this process of acculturation tends to be reinforced by traditional ways of practicing a discipline. For these traditions are not immune from the shaping power of the prevailing culture. As the central task of education for autonomy is to break the hold that this network of mutually reinforcing habits of thought, feeling, and judgment exerts upon us, our method must systematically encourage challenge to traditional forms of activity.

The likelihood that traditional language and literature are so shaped is supported by another consideration. In general, something like the Marxian theory of ideology is a warranted hypothesis. Historically any culture is mainly shaped by predominant interests acting through influential elites. Over the stretch of ages we should expect that surviving ideas reflect, not the outcome of disinterested trial and error, but instead the inherent biases of dominant elites. More important, even when the traditional language and literature do contain outstanding examples of autonomous inquiry, the very processes of educational selection are likely to be influenced by gut-level cultural biases unless deliberate effort is made to avoid their impact.

The best way to educate for autonomy lies, then, not in rejecting traditional works but, at least in part, by carefully selecting from among them those works most likely to help a student win through to autonomy; that is, selecting those that pose the most thoughtfully radical challenge to prevailing modes of thought, feeling, and judgment.

This is not to imply that an autonomous person cannot be

conservative. My point is rather this. Taking students in large numbers, pre-reflective conservatism about most matters is the almost inevitable byproduct of early socialization. To help those students to win through to autonomy it is necessary that this inherent social bias of any social order be corrected. To make this correction requires that radical alternatives to customary thought, feeling, and action be persuasively presented. So doing does not inculcate radicalism as much as it frees individuals from a deeply ingrained, unreflective conservatism. If the student is *autonomously* reconfirmed in his originally conservative viewpoint, so be it. His conservatism now has a basis in reasoning it previously lacked. Even a Burkean can gain his outlook autonomously. But that very fact should move him to reject the Burke-Oakeshott views in at least one respect. He ought to repudiate an educational theory that discourages others from achieving what he has achieved. If he has confidence in his point of view he will not try to shield them from the play of autonomous minds.

To illustrate how the alternative method I am proposing would work, suppose one is devising an introductory course in political philosophy. Then two things seem desirable. Rely heavily on the best radical thinkers, past or present. Buttress those texts with Socratic dialogue that aims at promoting rational scepticism about even the standards of reason discovered in those texts. Hence, for example, if Hobbes is used, Macpherson's interpretation of Hobbes' theories would provide an appropriate counterpoint.

Perhaps the misgivings I have voiced are precisely what Frankena himself has in mind when, in his brief, almost casual concluding remarks, he suggests the possibility of a ' "new" or "free" (third) concept of education,' a concept he claims that Peters neglects. This approach focuses on discovery of 'new forms of life, thought, and action, new traditions, if you will, besides those we already have and include in our curricula.' My contention is that it is precisely that sort of educational method that Oakeshott's views tend to preclude. If, as I suspect, Frankena in fact agrees with the line of argument I have taken, then my remarks should be regarded as an invitation to him to pursue the possibilities in his concluding paragraph more straightforwardly and systematically than he has done. For the possibilities he describes as 'not clear' are real; and, I have argued, require substantial modification of his main methodological proposal.

IV Autonomy and educational elitism

One final point: in one respect Frankena's views exhibit surface paradox. His supreme educational goal is autonomy. Yet throughout his essay he expresses the conviction that a student may properly be subjected to authoritative discipline by his elders. The elders generally know, better than a student himself, what best serves his interests in respect of autonomy.

My observation is not intended as a criticism. I happen generally to agree with Frankena in this regard, though I am perhaps much less sanguine than he about the typical educator's genuine commitment to education for autonomy. However, it is useful to indicate the extent of Frankena's agreement on this point, not only with John Stuart Mill, but with Herbert Marcuse. Both consider it permissible coercively to interfere with individual development for the sake of promoting autonomy—Mill, for example, in his defense of compulsory education, Marcuse in his attack on what he regards as a spurious, counter-productive tolerance.[12] Whether either is justified in the particular case cited is another matter. My point is that there is a broad area of theoretical agreement here that, for obvious ideological reasons, tends to be ignored or denied.

One explanation might be that coercive interference on behalf of autonomy ought to be restricted to youths who have not yet completed their formal educational programs and only in relation to their educational activities. But I can see no plausible justification for this restriction. For adult citizens in this, or any other society, may, as Marcuse insists, be so deficient in the skills of the autonomous person that one may be justified in proposing coercive interference for the sake of autonomy. That is, even forty-year-old businessmen, astronauts, army officers, or, heaven help us, professors may lack autonomy and require a coercive discipline. I do not say this is so. And I know there are many arguments that weigh against the judgment that this is so. I only point out that the educational elitism implicit in Frankena's views about the teacher–student relationship has a more general theoretical basis and *may* have wider practical application.

At the same time, the case for an enlarged student 'power' does not depend principally on any right of participation in educational decisions that affect their lives. Rather it is that such participation, like democracy generally, is one very important means of educating youngsters for the autonomy their elders claim to cherish.

Notes

1 I was unable to ascertain the source of this quotation (Editor).
2 S. I. Benn and R. S. Peters, *Social Principles and the Democratic State*, Allen & Unwin, 1959, p. 56.

3 John Rawls, 'Distributive Justice', in *Philosophy, Politics and Society* (third series), Laslett and Runciman, (eds), Blackwell, 1967.
4 I was unable to ascertain the source of this quotation (Editor).
5 J. S. Mill, *On Liberty* (Everyman's Library), Dent, 1910, p. 125.
6 Philip E. Slater, *The Pursuit of Loneliness*, Boston, Beacon Press, 1970, pp. 25–26.
7 See Robert P. Wolff, *The Poverty of Liberalism*, Boston, Beacon Press, 1968.
8 See Thomas S. Kuhn, *The Structure of Scientific Revolutions*, 2nd ed., University of Chicago Press, 1970.
9 Michael Oakeshott, 'Rational Conduct', in *Rationalism in Politics*, New York, Basic Books, 1962, p. 103.
10 *Ibid.*, p. 107.
11 I was unable to locate the page reference of this quotation (Editor)
12 See Herbert Marcuse, 'Repressive Tolerance', in *A Critique of Pure Tolerance*, Boston, Beacon Press, 1969.

Part 2

On avoiding moral indoctrination

4

Edmund L. Pincoffs

Morality in his sleep! Place the Mortutor (copyright) under your child's pillow, tuck him in, and set him on the road to rectitude. Operates at a cost of less than 2¢ per day.
Designed by noted psychologists and engineers; approved by leading public figures; widely used in public institutions. Just clip the form below. . . .

Philosophers and ordinary men, or some of them anyway, shudder at the notion of moral indoctrination. It is not clear what is the object of this reaction, nor why shuddering is more appropriate than cheering. In a recent debate, three suggestions have been made for what indoctrination consists in: method, content, and aim. In this paper, I want to examine these suggestions and to offer some distinctions which I hope may advance the discussion.

I

I will begin with remarks made by John Wilson and R. M. Hare.[1] Wilson starts out by rejecting the suggestion that to indoctrinate is to employ any particular method of instruction. That it cannot be defined in this way is, he thinks, apparent from the fact that whereas the employment of certain methods, such as hypnotism, would be regarded as indoctrinating if they were used to inculcate religious, political, or moral beliefs; the same methods, employed for the teaching of Latin grammar or the multiplication tables would not count as indoctrination. According to Wilson's way of looking at the matter, a Mathtutor would not be an indoctrinating device, whereas a Mortutor would, even if the devices were electronically identical.

If, however, indoctrination does not consist in the employment of any particular method, it must have to do, Wilson holds, with the content of instruction. Indoctrination consists in teaching what is uncertain as if it were certain. Beliefs are uncertain if '. . . it is not true that any sane and sensible person, when presented with the relevant facts and arguments, would necessarily hold the beliefs.

We might put this by saying that there was no *publicly-acceptable* evidence for them, evidence which any rational person would regard as sufficient . . .' (pp. 27–8). Education, on the other hand, consists in instructing in such a way that the certainty with which a doctrine is taught is directly related to the publicly-acceptable evidence available for its support. Moral beliefs are uncertain, not merely in the sense that there is not enough such evidence for their support, but in that we are not sure what kind of evidence it takes to support them. 'We cannot even be sure that any question of truth, falsehood, or evidence arises at all with metaphysical and moral issues . . . we do not know exactly how they are important. We do not know how to tackle them . . .' (p. 30). Yet moral beliefs, even if not completely certain, may be taught in such a way that only that degree of certainty is claimed for them which is warranted by the public evidence available for their support. There will, then, be beliefs and behavior which every sane and sensible person believes should be taught because enough evidence is available to warrant our teaching them. How Wilson can qualify, as sane and sensible, people who (1) do not know whether there can be evidence for moral beliefs, and (2) hold that there is sufficient evidence for a moral belief to teach it to our children, I do not understand. At any rate, he holds that it is not so much a matter of how morality is taught, by what devices or methods, as of the uncertain nature of the subject-matter taught as certain which warrants our labeling the teaching as indoctrination.

Hare thinks that Wilson's way of analyzing indoctrination will not do, since it would allow indoctrinators to pose as educators. 'For who are to count as sane and sensible people? Most people think that they themselves and the majority of their friends are sane and sensible people. So if that is what Mr Wilson says, he will not succeed in barring the way to a great many educational practices that I am sure he would want to call indoctrination' (p. 48). Once we admit Catholics, Communists, Anglicans and other potential indoctrinators into the fold as sane and sensible, then we have no ground on which to reject their claim that the beliefs they teach are certain, since the criterion of certainty in a belief is that sane and sensible people when presented with the relevant facts and arguments necessarily hold it. Hence, we have no ground for rejecting the inculcation of religious or moral catechisms, by whatever means, as indoctrination.

In place of method or content, Hare would put aim. Aim is what enables us to distinguish the indoctrinator from the educator. '. . . indoctrination only begins when we are trying to stop the growth in our children of the capacity to think for themselves about moral questions. If all the time that we are influencing them, we are saying to ourselves, "perhaps in the end they will decide that the best way to live is quite different from what I am teaching them; and they will have a perfect right to decide that," then we are not to be be accused of indoctrinating' (p. 52). The aim, on Hare's view, will influence the method of moral education, and this in turn will influence the content. Given the aim of keeping the child's mind open on moral matters, we will not use methods which will shut off teacher and pupil from 'the fresh winds of argument.' The aim of the educator is to get the pupil to think for himself, so his method is to discuss moral questions with him 'with no holds barred and no questions banned, and is himself prepared to ask the questions again—really ask them—and is prepared to answer them in a different way from the way he has up till now, if that is the way the argument goes' (p. 53).

The form of moral education which flows from its aim has to do, as readers of Hare's moral philosophy might suspect, with pre-scriptivity and universalizability. 'What we have to teach people, if we are educating them morally, is to ask themselves the question "What kind of behavior am I ready to prescribe for myself, given that in prescribing it for myself, I am prescribing it also for anybody in a like situation?" ' (p. 61). Pupils must be educated in such a way that they will be free in later life to adopt different principles than we have taught them, provided the new principles are prescriptive and universalizable too. 'At the end of it all, the educator will insensibly stop being an educator, and find that he is talking to an equal, to an educated man like himself—a man who may disagree with everything he has ever said; and, unlike the indoctrinator, he will be pleased' (p. 70).

II

Indoctrination need not be a bad thing. To say that a person has been indoctrinated is, according to the *OED*, to say that he has been 'imbued with a doctrine, idea, or opinion.' Indoctrination, if this definition be accepted, need not be a bad thing; because it is sometimes morally justifiable to become imbued with a doctrine. Peace Corps volunteers, new teachers in an experimental school, or workers for a political party may expect to undergo indoctrination. That is, they may not only learn the full implications of the commitment they have made, but they may try to absorb the doctrine, to make it a part of themselves, so that they do not have to wonder or worry about what to say or do in situations likely to arise. To this end, they may with clear consciences attend classes, feign debates, and memorize passages of the relevant literature. They may even, when they feel that they are getting rusty on matters of doctrine, attend reindoctrination classes so that they will get a fresh grasp on doctrinal matters which bear on the problems that arise in the lives that they have set for themselves. The question, then, is not, When does education become indoctrination? as if indoctrination were necessarily a bad thing; but When does education become indefensible indoctrination? or When does education indefensibly become indoctrination?

To say that education becomes indefensible indoctrination is to say that it becomes a form of brainwashing. 'Brainwashing' may be used as the generic term for indoctrinating techniques (involving torture, electronic devices, or what have you) which make it psychologically impossible for a person to deliberate to any purpose about certain matters. In the present context, the deliberation in question would be about what one ought, morally speaking, to do. The brainwashed person would typically be imbued with the belief that there is some authority (the Pope, the King, the Univac) which will infallibly tell him what is right, and that there is nothing to do but obey. Or he might be brainwashed into accepting some more abstract principle as the universal determinant of right action, as for example that whatever promotes eternal salvation, or is in accordance with natural law, or forwards the cause of Communism is right.

To say that education indefensibly becomes indoctrination is to say that the pupil is indoctrinated under the pretence that he is being educated. He has not deliberated about and then chosen certain doctrines in which he then wishes to become indoctrinated, but he is indoctrinated willy nilly. He is indoctrinated unawares by means which would be permissible had he freely and justifiably chosen to be indoctrinated. Sometimes the term 'orientation' is used to refer to this normally inoffensive form of indoctrination. 'Orientation' presupposes the will of the student to entrust to the indoctrinator the task of helping him to find his bearings. But the trust is revocable, and is understood as such by student and teacher. The indefensibility of indoctrination arises here from the lack of any such tacit or explicit understanding, from the student's being indoctrinated by means which insensibly confirm him in beliefs he has not freely chosen, from his being led toward an irrevocable trust in the landmarks with which the indoctrination supplies him. An example of education indefensibly becoming indoctrination might be the kind of instruction in military techniques which takes the volunteer all unawares into a kind of political indoctrination in which he is imbued with the belief that there are no legitimate grounds upon which the command of a military superior may be questioned. Whether it is brainwashing or orientation in, and thus confirmation in, a belief not freely chosen, the consequence is that the right to think for oneself has been surrendered or taken away.

III

What is it about *moral* beliefs that gives the child the right (eventually) to make up his own mind about them? I do not find a very satisfactory answer either in Wilson's or in Hare's account. Wilson's notion, as we have seen, is that these beliefs tend to be uncertain, and that if we don't honor the child's right to question them, we are treating what is uncertain as if it were certain. Therefore we may drum in the multiplication tables in a way in which we have no right to drum in moral beliefs. But even if it is certain that five times five is twenty-five, why should we try to prevent a child's questioning it? It is not clear that we should drum in anything in this mindless way; hence it is not clear that different methods are appropriate to certain and uncertain subject matter. And, as Hare argues, the criterion of certainty becomes crucial on such an account. If it is that a certain class of people, self-nominated as sane and sensible, believe the doctrine for reasons they regard as true and relevant, then Wilson's definition has failed to catch indoctrinators in its net. Therefore, we need not, fortunately, in criticizing Wilson's account, take up the question whether there are any moral beliefs that are certain, or what, exactly, Wilson means when he says that there are none.[2]

Against Hare's insistence that indoctrination consists in teaching a child in such a way that he is not free to think for himself, I would insist that all indoctrination is not of this sort, but only bad indoctrination. I would agree, however, that all moral indoctrination is bad. The question then is what grounds we have for presuming that children have a right, when they become adults, to be able to make up their own minds on matters of moral belief. It is to this subject that we now turn.

Hare's answer can be put roughly by saying that children have a right to make up their own minds concerning moral beliefs because they will need to be able to do so in the circumstances in which they will live.[3] These circumstances are likely to be sufficiently different from those in which their parents and teachers live that the beliefs (principles) which the adults live by will not suffice when the child becomes an adult. The child must therefore be free to adapt himself to the world in which he must live. Moral indoctrination would be bad on this account because it would interfere with the child's right to adjust his moral views to the changing world in which he must live. In *The Language of Morals*, Hare makes use of the analogy of teaching a person to drive. Since you can't always be telling him exactly what to do next, you must try to give him some general principles to follow which he will learn to make use of only gradually, by applying them to very many different kinds of situations. In the moral life, we must not only flesh out the principles we are taught, but even on occasion abandon them altogether, or adopt new ones.

The right not to be indoctrinated may be said, then, on Hare's account, to rest on the right to adapt oneself to change: call it the right of adaptation. In a way this is a perfectly satisfactory account. Indeed, as a parent I cannot possibly claim to foresee every situation my child will have to face in his life. Truth is stranger than prediction. It would be a sin against him if I teach him in such a way that he cannot figure out for himself what to do, but feels bound by beliefs I have given him, or immobilized by my ghostly and inappropriate admonitions. I will, then, give him something procedural. I will not teach him in such a way that he will have to use my principles forever, but I will tell him how, when the time comes, he can find principles of his own. This he will be able to do if I teach him the place that logic, facts, imagination, and inclination should have in his thinking.[4] But when I think about Hare's account a second time, I find that I am not so clear.

The right of adaptation rests upon a supposed need, the need to adapt. But what kind of need is this? In Hare's analogy, we can see the point. Hare does not, I think, have so much in mind that cars or traffic rules will change, as that new situations will arise which will require a change in driving tactics. (Hare might have distinguished these possibilities, since the choice of one interpretation over the others bears on the account one might naturally give of Hare's key term, 'principle.') The need of the student, in any case, is to *cope with new problems*. These problems are such, because if he does not cope successfully, he will have collisions. But what, in moral education, corresponds to collisions? The student needs to adapt to new situations, meaning that he must learn to solve new problems, because if he does not do so, he will . . . what? What is the danger or unhappy consequence which the student must avoid? I do not wish to deny that there is a need to adapt to changing circumstances, to shrug off the dead hand of the past; but how does this apply to the moral life? The only thing to say that sounds plausible is that the student must avoid immorality, he must be moral. He must cope with new problems in such a way that he will not jeopardize his claim to be a moral person. And a moral person is . . . ? How am I to avoid a circle? If I say that he is a person who lives by certain principles, then I am begging the question. For the question is why a person may need to change his principles, any of his principles. But if I say that he is a person who adapts his principles to the situation in which he lives, then I am saying that a student must not be indoctrinated, because he has a right of adaptation. Why? Because he must be the kind of person who can adapt. We must begin again.

IV

When Hare says that the aim of education, lest it become indoctrination, must not be to stop the growth of the capacity of a child to think for himself about moral questions, what does he have in mind as a moral question? The examples he gives (pp. 52–3) are of widely different sorts. He mentions the questions of the 'best way to live', i.e., as a Catholic, a Communist, or a bearer of the American way of life. He mentions the question whether one should lie, and the problems of sex and pacificism. These curt references must be considered against the background of *The Language of Morals* and *Freedom and Reason* where, for example, he distinguishes[5] between decisions of principle which presuppose a way of life, and decisions regarding which way of life to follow.

Communism, Catholicism, and the American way of life are large and amorphous sets of beliefs which it is not at all difficult to imagine the pupil's coming to reject, for reasons which he would gladly give his tutor. It is easy also to imagine his having a debate with his tutor, and rejecting his tutor's views, when the question is whether trial marriages are morally defensible, or whether there can ever be a war in which a man can participate with a clear conscience. He might also come to a more liberal interpretation of lying, so that the tutor's rigorism is tempered by qualifications the tutor would not have admitted. But how far can this ultimate disagreement, this thinking for oneself on moral matters, go? What does and does not count as a moral belief, when Hare asserts that the pupil must be free to think for himself? Is it a belief, which the pupil may return in adulthood to debate with his tutor, that he should be honest (straightforward, non-devious), humane (sympathetic, not cruel), or just (fair, equitable, even-handed)?

When we speak of beliefs, and even more when we speak of principles, the picture we have is likely to be that of people taking positions in a debate. If it is a belief, then it must be open to challenge. A principle must be a place where we can begin in an argument. When Hare says that the pupil must come to be a 'man who may disagree with everything [his teacher] says,' we want to ask

65

whether he can by the same token reject everything the teacher is: not just his beliefs and principles, but the traits of character that are evident in his life.

If the teacher teaches that what is dishonest is wrong, he must do so out of his life: he must, if he is to succeed as a teacher of morality, show himself (not exhibit himself) to be an honest man. It is not something he says, not a principle he adopts, not a doctrine that is promulgated. When he exhibits his repulsion at a cruel act, or punishes his pupil for torturing a cat, he is not *ipso facto* taking a position.

I suspect that Hare and Wilson presuppose a certain background of moral education which 'everyone' has: an education in which qualities of character like honesty and courage are inculcated early. It is only against this background that the appearance of extreme relativism can arise, that disputes between teacher and erstwhile pupil are even possible. How can we suppose that the old pupil will come to his teacher's house to argue the 'belief' that one should be honest? Not honest in this or that situation, but honest in general. Is he trying to persuade his teacher to be dishonest? If *he* is dishonest, there can be no assurance that he will debate fairly, that he will not misrepresent his own views and his teacher's views, that he will not distort the evidence, and will not make *ad hominem* sallies which he should not make. Dishonesty, if a subject for debate, which I deny, is at least not so in the way that Catholicism or Communism or trial marriages are.

We might say that it is only people who have a certain character who are free to disagree upon, to debate, matters of doctrine. For debate, there must be a certain degree of respect and trust. There must also be some agreement on what would count for or against a position. If Wilson is right that we do not know how to 'do' morals, then we do not know how to carry on a moral discussion. It might be said, on the other hand, that the agreement presupposed in carrying on a moral debate need not be moral agreement, since without that we can agree to reject positions which can be shown to be inconsistent. But this is not much of an advance. A 'position' which is inconsistent, is not a position at all. It cannot be stated; it is unintelligible. Indeed, anyone who is able to recognize and point out an inconsistency is able to show that a 'position' is not a position.

But not everyone is eligible to discuss moral issues. As Hare may recognize, but does not emphasize, only the person who can be affected by moral reasons, is amenable to moral reasons, is eligible. Among other things, this means that he must be able to entertain counter-examples. He must be the sort of person who can recognize that if a doctrine entails that he must do a certain thing, then it must be wrong, since he could never do such a thing; because to do so would be dishonest, or cruel, say. If it were open—a matter for discussion—whether to be dishonest or cruel, then a whole range of counter-examples could have no effect on him, and consequently he would not be qualified to debate matters of doctrine from the moral point of view.

What would a debate be like over the question whether cruelty is a bad thing? What sorts of considerations would count for or against the thesis? Would it be said, for example, that cruelty aids self-expression, and that whatever aids self-expression is right? But, then, how are we to know what counter-examples would be acceptable against the self-expression theory of moral rightness, if examples of the cruelty that it could entail would not count? Would it be said that the 'policy' that one should be as cruel as possible could not become a universal prescription? How are we to know, if everything is up for grabs, that this will count either? Why should the debater, if there are no requirements regarding what qualities of character he should have, not argue that we live in a cruel world and that we should be realists, giving and taking our lumps as the occasion makes possible or demands.

It is hard to imagine what a debate would be like of the 'doctrine' that cruelty is a bad thing. It would amount, I suppose, to a discussion of the question whether and why one should be moral. And it is certainly the case that intellectually curious men will want to raise and discuss that question. It is a peculiar issue, in that it can't be kept at arm's length, but inevitably takes an *ad hominem* turn. I suspect this is because it is not clear who is supposed to be discussing the matter. If he is a person for whom 'that would be cruel' counts as a reason against doing an action, then he is in that respect moral, and the argument is pleonastic. If he is not, then how is it to be settled? By appeal to his self-interest? But how is it going to make a man amenable to moral counter-example to show him that it is in his self-interest to be so? This is a matter of character, not of beliefs or principles; of what he is, not of what he holds.

It might even be said that it is precisely in his being amenable to counter-examples showing the cruelty or dishonesty of a course of action, that a man is free to debate the issue whether a principle or belief which would require that course of action should be accepted. If he does not know what would count *pro* or *con* in such a discussion, whether he is ahead or behind, has won or lost, then he can only be free to enter the discussion in a Pickwickian kind of way. He is free to engage in it in the way that a child is free to play chess, by shoving the pieces around on the board.

V

So far, I have agreed with Hare that to say that *A* is a moral indoctrinator is to say that he has a certain aim: to prevent the child from thinking for himself. I have raised the question of what kind of thing the pupil may think for himself about, and I have expressed reservations about the kind of rationale Hare might give for the thesis that the child must not be prevented from thinking for himself. That thesis, which I hope I have not unfairly attributed to Hare, but which is interesting in its own right anyway, is that because the child must adjust to the unpredictable world, he has the right not to be educated in such a way as to make this adjustment impossible. I want to return to this matter now, with another kind of account, which Hare might accept too, of the wrongness of moral indoctrination.

The demand that each person should be free to think for himself is the consequence of his responsibility for the moral beliefs that he holds. When he becomes an adult, he will be held answerable for his wrongdoing. He cannot avoid this responsibility by saying that he did what he did because his parents or his teacher told him to do it; nor can he appeal to the command of a dictator, the canons of his church, or the laws of the state. If parent, teacher, dictator, church, or state provides him with general principles which he must follow in making decisions, then if he invokes these principles in justification of his action, they become his principles; and he is responsible for them, too. By accepting them, he signals acceptance of himself as the kind of person who is governed by those principles. If they are attacked, he must defend them. He could have chosen other principles, but he has not done so.

It is as if, in preparing for battle, he has a choice of the weapons he will carry into the fray. He will then not be able to blame the outcome on his weapons. He cannot excuse himself by saying 'If only I had chosen a sword instead of a dagger, I would surely have won,' since it was open to him to have chosen a sword. The excuse is even less successful if he is free to exchange weapons as the nature of the battle changes; and here the analogy with moral education can be made closer, if we imagine that the first distribution is made by a tutor who tries to foresee what the exigencies of the battle will require, but who realizes his limitations as a prophet, and therefore makes it possible for the pupil to exchange weapons as the battle progresses. The point is not just that the pupil must adjust, but that he is responsible for what he makes of himself. It is he, not his teacher, who will be approved or disapproved, punished or rewarded, sainted or anathemized. It is this ultimate responsibility, not just for his actions, but for being the kind of person that he is as revealed by the kind of reasons (principles) he cites in justification of his actions, which makes it morally mandatory that the pupil should be educated in such a way that he can think for himself. He wants to become an adult for the very good reason that he will be treated as an adult; to shove him into the world an eternal child is morally unjustifiable.

A principle can, on Hare's view, be something which can be discovered by observing a man's behavior,[6] or it is something that is offered in justification of his behavior:[7] but the distinction is too important to risk losing under a common term. (It might be helpful to refer to a principle in the first sense as a character trait, and to use the generic term 'moral belief' for [non-factual] reasons why an action is held to be right.) The important point, for moral education, is that even if we worry with and about our moral characters all of our lives, they tend to be formed early. The teacher, then, must be actively interested in the way they are formed. He must encourage the development of some character traits, and discourage the development of others. To raise the question whether, in pursuit of these objectives, he is engaged in moral indoctrination is confusing. If he is not inculcating moral beliefs, then he is not doing so in an indefensible way. The individual who has had a good moral education will not only give and be guided by the right reasons, he will have the right instincts, the right reactions. This is not a result of indoctrination but of training. There can be bad training as well as bad indoctrination. Fagin's training of Oliver Twist was bad, not because he aimed to make it impossible for Oliver to think for himself, but because he made him into a thief and an artful dodger. That Oliver would not be likely, as a result of his training, to bother his head about moral matters was incidental. Fagin was not notorious for the doctrines he taught, but for forming his boys' characters in the way that he did. To have been subjected to bad training is to have the wrong reactions; to have been the victim of bad indoctrination is to have a closed mind where minds should be open.

To return to the reason why moral indoctrination is bad: it is so because it makes the pupil liable to be held answerable for what should be, but is not, his own thinking. He is not held answerable in the external way in which the criminal law holds a man answerable for the violation of a law he had no way of knowing existed, but for a blameworthy fault: the failure to live by morally defensible beliefs. If he was brainwashed he has an acceptable excuse, but if indoctrination merely inhibits his capacity to think for himself, he has not. The point is, that he cites his moral beliefs as reasons why he acts as he does, but if the belief really requires the action and the action is morally wrong, then something is morally amiss with the person who lives by that belief, and it will not suffice as an excuse that he was raised to believe as he does.

VI

Aristotle remarked that 'by choosing what is good or bad we are men of certain character, which we are not by holding certain opinions.'[8] This is true or false, depending on how we interpret 'opinions.' If 'opinions' are the beliefs we hold on doctrines over which moral men can disagree, such as the question whether participation in a war can ever be justified, or trial marriages be a permissible practice, then what Aristotle says is true. Moral men must be free to debate such issues. No position can be ruled out in advance as a position not open to a moral man. Indoctrination is a way of closing off debatable issues from debate, by making a person believe that to take the 'wrong' position is *ipso facto* to be immoral. We cannot, however, rightly accuse a man of dishonesty, cruelty, injustice, or lack of integrity *merely* in virtue of his holding that trial marriages are morally justifiable. What we can do is attempt to show him that his position *pro* or *con* would entail his making choices which would require him to be cruel, dishonest, etc. He may or may not admit this. But if he does freely choose to do a cruel thing, on the basis of any doctrine or belief whatever, then he is, in that respect, a 'man of a certain character': he is cruel. More, if his beliefs are his justification for being cruel, then he is blamable for holding a belief which, as he believes, justifies his being cruel. For no belief can do this; and he cannot avoid blame by appeal to one. He is in this sense responsible for his beliefs, that if he 'chooses what is bad' as a consequence of them, he must either reject them or admit that they truly represent him, characterize him.

If, on the other hand (Aristotle surely did not mean this) 'opinions' are to the effect that what is cruel, unjust, or dishonest should not be done, then Aristotle's remark would be false, or rather it would be unintelligible. For an 'opinion' is something which, in the context, can be put forward for moral debate; something on which we can take a moral position. But there can be no moral debate of the question whether cruelty is a bad thing.

This is not to say that it is a 'matter of definition' that cruelty is bad, but that it is a matter of eligibility for moral discussion, or for discussion from the moral point of view. I do not deny that someone can claim that cruelty is a good thing, that life has more savor with a dash of cruelty, that cruelty helps self-expression, etc. and that therefore it should not be discouraged. I hold that if a person takes what he says seriously enough not to recognize that 'that is cruel' is a count against his action, he is ineligible to discuss moral beliefs.

No one is a moral indoctrinator, then, because he inculcates in his pupil a distaste for dishonesty, a revulsion against cruelty, or a sense of outrage at injustice. In teaching his pupil in such a way as to encourage these *qualities of character*, he is not closing his pupil's mind, stunting his growth, or making it impossible for him to think for himself. He is, rather, giving him the *kind of character* without which he would be unable to carry on a moral discussion. To help a child to develop the qualities of character I have mentioned is, in fact, to open up new possibilities for him of thinking for himself. For he cannot be said to have the traits in question unless he has learned to think in a certain way. To become a person who is repelled by cruelty, he must learn to recognize cruelty when it occurs in others or in himself. This means that mindless training will not do. He cannot be trained, if he is to recognize cruelty, simply to be repelled by the presence of suffering. This clearly will be insufficient if he is to have it as a trait of character that he is a humane man. It is not enough, even, that he be trained so as to be revolted by the infliction of suffering. Sometimes dentists and head-masters make others suffer for good reason, and not because they are cruel. He must be so trained (here 'educated' may be more appropriate) that he will be repelled by the taking of pleasure in the suffering of another. But this is not a simple response to a stimulus; understanding is required as an intermediary. Far from closing the mind, moral training provides it with the fundamental considerations against which moral beliefs may be tested. It makes it possible for the child to think for himself. With moral training and, consequently, with a developing moral character, he is able to evaluate the doctrines and principles, the beliefs, that are proposed to him. Without moral training, he cannot.

That the position I have outlined smacks of intuitionism I am uncomfortably aware. It is true that if to be an intuitionist is, at least, to claim that there is a particular kind of knowledge, my position is not intuitionist. For on my view the person who rejects a course of action as dishonest is not making a knowledge-claim. He is saying what he cannot do, and, by implication, what he cannot be. But even if my position is not intuitionistic in the ordinary, epistemological sense, it does say, in common with other intuitionistic positions, that there is an area not open to serious discussion: an area off bounds for a moral man.

As philosophers, we do not take kindly to the suggestion that there are matters which we may not seriously question; but we should

F

understand the price we pay in claiming the right to question. Seriously to maintain that it is an open question whether it is a count against an action that it would be cruel is to maintain that it is an open question whether moral beliefs which require such actions can be evaluated on the ground that they would require cruelty of us. Skepticism with respect to the relevance of charges of injustice and dishonesty remove more criteria of evaluation. But if all of the criteria by which we evaluate beliefs are themselves open to doubt, it is open to doubt whether evaluation is possible. We cannot, however, lapse at this point into a comfortable skeptical acquiescence. For if there were no way of evaluating moral beliefs, then it would make no sense to try to discuss them, to debate which of them we should choose. And if it makes no sense to debate, we cannot object to indoctrination on the ground that it unjustifiably teaches what is debatable as if it were what all right-minded people necessarily believe.

Postscript

The dispute between Baier and me may be put in this way. I say that moral debate must be between people who are qualified to engage in it; Baier says that we cannot settle moral issues in advance by ruling out of court persons who would take a certain position ('cruelty is permissible,' e.g.) on them. I say that 'moral issues' must be more carefully defined: they have to do with doctrines or practices on which moral men may disagree but that 'honesty is a desirable quality of character' is not a *doctrine* of this kind. Baier holds that if the question why we should be moral can be debated, then the question why we should have a given character trait may be debated. I hold that the question why we should be moral is not a moral but a meta-moral issue: an issue which is not a proper subject of moral deliberation, but of whether moral deliberation is worth while.

I am sensitive to Baier's criticism that I am attempting a move which would close off discussion in which men can legitimately engage. On the other hand, I do want to note that one must be *qualified* to enter into moral discussion, and that there are some topics which, if a person is qualified, *do not arise for him.* In closing, I should concede to Baier that, even if they do not arise for him, this can hardly prevent what I would call a meta-moral or philosophical discussion of them. But I would want to insist nevertheless that moral training which forms character in early childhood in such a way that certain questions do not arise, is not necessarily moral indoctrination, but is in fact a necessary step in moral education.

Notes

1 Wilson's 'Education and Indoctrination' and Hare's 'Adolescents into Adults' will be found in T. H. B. Hollins (ed.), *Aims in Education*, Manchester University Press, 1964, pp. 24–46 and 47–70.

2 The situation is, for Wilson, somewhere beyond dire. 'We know how to do science,' he tells us, 'but we do not know how to do metaphysics or morals . . . this is sufficiently obvious to an intelligent child, though he might not be able to state it clearly' (p. 30).

3 *Language of Morals (LM)*, O.U.P., 1952, ch. 4; *Freedom and Reason (FR)* O.U.P., 1963, chs 3, 6.

4 *FR*, ch. 6.

5 *LM*, ch. 4.

6 *Ibid.*, ch. 1, sec. 4. 3.

7 *Ibid.*, ch. 1, secs 3. 6, 4.1.

8 *Ethica Nicomachea*, 1112a.

Indoctrination and justification 5

Kurt Baier

I

There is at least one field of education, namely, moral education, in which analytic philosophy can still make a substantive contribution. For moral philosophers cannot be content to play merely the role of the philosopher of . . . , a role which Professor Scheffler rightly commended to philosophers of education. There is simply no flourishing non-philosophical first-level discipline, ethics, to which moral philosophy is related as philosophy of mathematics is related to mathematics, or philosophy of mind to psychology. All that is available, apart from simple conformity to the rules followed by members of one's peer group, are the more or less inspired 'teachings' of charismatic leaders whose life styles supplemented by their general pronouncements serve many people as guides to conduct. Philosophical theories in ethics, such as utilitarianism, do not purport to be *philosophies of* (or about) the morality of their authors' group or the morality of such leaders, but are offered as practical, first-level alternatives, by which anyone who believed in them, might attempt to solve the practical problems which confront him daily. However, the trouble with such philosophical theories is that they are too vague to give one clear directives, and that there are a great many different competing ones with little indication of how to choose between them.

At the same time there is, I believe, a deep conviction among people including the young, that effective universal moral education is desirable, since it is desirable that every individual should develop into a moral adult. Why do people think this desirable? Not, it would seem, because they regard a person's being moral as beneficial or profitable to himself, but rather because they regard it as beneficial or profitable to others. People think virtue is *meritorious*, that is, constitutive of a claim to reward, because virtue requires that for the sake of others, we deny ourselves things we want. Admittedly, some claim that virtue is its own reward, but obviously this must mean mainly that it is not something which, like exercise or fasting, is to be recommended solely or mainly because of its pay-offs.

Similarly crime and immorality are not judged bad because self-harming but, on the contrary often only too attractive and rewarding, and therefore calling for punishment. For these reasons, it used to be thought wrong to produce films which showed that crime pays. For the same reasons it is thought that moral education cannot safely be left to the individual's initiative but must be seen to by society.

Prior to the Reformation, that task was adequately discharged by the Church and the family. Even after the Reformation, it could be attended to by the various churches and church-going families, because all or most people were church-goers. But the steady increase in the number of churches and in religious toleration has naturally given rise to a parallel demand for moral toleration. Morality came to be thought of as that sphere of practical matters which did not concern the state; matters such as supernatural beliefs, swearing, dancing, drinking, gambling, and fornication. In these matters, the individual was thought to be autonomous. If he changed his mind on any of them, he could always switch his church affiliation or set up a new church. The prevalence of religious and moral toleration guaranteed that, although the individual grew up in a specific religious and affiliated moral tradition, he could always later change his mind and his way of life when he encountered, and found preferable, other beliefs and ways of life.

Of course, this still left a core of serious practical matters, such as the sanctity of property and of contract, etc., on which all or most of the churches agreed, and which the state forced on those churches which did not agree (e.g., the Mormons). Given the steady growth of tolerance towards differing moral views, the question was soon bound to arise why there should not be moral tolerance also in those matters on which all or most churches and the state had hitherto agreed to be intolerant; why it should not be a matter for the mother to say whether she wanted the child or an abortion; or for consenting adults to say exactly what sexual practices they wanted to engage in; or for the citizen to say whether he wanted to fight for his country or would prefer not to.

This is the background against which the problem of what to teach in a program of moral education looks both acute and insoluble. For when viewed in this light, all moral education seems to be moral indoctrination and so objectionable. The decline of religious and parental authority have created a near-vacuum in moral conviction. This offers a quite novel opportunity for organized moral education, and so for moral philosophers to provide something which can be taught if such teaching can be cleared of the suspicion of indoctrination.

Pincoffs's paper is an attempt to remove this suspicion. He tries to identify some moral subject-matter which is necessarily free of this suspicion. He argues that there are some substantive moral convictions, such as that cruelty or dishonesty is a bad thing, which no one can query. Whereas some substantive moral convictions are arguable or debatable and so cannot be taught as if they were indubitable, others are the very cornerstones of moral argument, the premisses by reference to which the debatable moral judgments have to be debated. A person who does not accept these convictions is not even in a position to engage in moral argument and debate. His doubt about these basic propositions disqualifies him from doubting and debating the really debatable ones. Pincoffs agrees with Hare that moral education would amount to moral indoctrination if (and only if) it produced in the pupil an inability to disagree with the teacher on moral matters, because that would violate the pupil's right to think for himself in moral matters (p. 63). But he modifies Hare's claim by a distinction between moral matters which are and those which are not debatable. A pupil is not indoctrinated by his tutor even if he is taught certain moral matters, namely, the undebatable ones, in such a way that he cannot disagree because he cannot debate with his tutor about them.

If Pincoffs is right, then presumably the task of moral philosophers would be to identify these undebatable moral matters. Educationists could then incorporate such precepts in a program of moral education and the state could, perhaps should, insist that they be taught in all schools in such a way that pupils end up unable to disagree about them with their tutors or with anyone else holding these views.

I have serious doubts about this thesis and shall raise some questions about it: Do Pincoffs's arguments show that there are undebatable moral issues? Are there such issues? Are they the ones Pincoffs mentions? Does undebatability imply that there can be no legitimate disagreement on the issue or that people should or may be trained so that they become incapable of disagreeing on it with one another? Conversely, does the fact that a person is unable to disagree with another on a certain issue show that it is undebatable? How are these questions related to the question of the capacity to think for oneself on a certain issue and through that with indoctrination?

II

Let us begin with the question of what is involved in a teacher's violating the pupil's right to think for himself in moral matters.

Pincoffs says (p. 63) that children have a right, when they become adults, to be able to make up their own minds on matters of moral belief. In other words, they have a right to be taught the skill of thinking for themselves in moral matters. He then asks (p. 65) how this ability to think for oneself in moral matters is related to 'ultimate moral disagreement.' Does ability to think for oneself in these matters involve actual disagreement between teacher and pupil, or else at least actual questioning, argument, debate, between them on all moral problems, including very fundamental ones? He answers that it does not entail this; that the very possibility of disagreement, questioning, argument, and debate involves the acceptance of certain principles, for otherwise the disagreement, argument, debate, cannot begin (p. 66); and it involves the possession of certain traits or qualities of character, such as honesty and courage, for otherwise the pupil lacks the qualification for any kind of debate or at least for moral debate (p. 66).

Pincoffs's main claim therefore is that a pupil's inability to disagree with his teacher on certain moral issues does not show that he has been indoctrinated since these issues may be undebatable ones, hence it may be impossible for anyone to argue, debate, and so disagree on them. Pincoffs supports this main claim by four contentions: (i) That in order for a person to be able to disagree with another, the matter must be debatable, open to disagreement and argument, an open matter (p. 67). (ii) That the person must be qualified to debate the issue from the moral point of view (p. 67). (iii) But that neither he nor anyone else would be thus qualified to debate unless there were some things, which count for him, which weigh with him, as reasons against doing it, and others as reasons for doing it (p. 67). (iv) That things such as 'that would be cruel' or 'that would be dishonest' must be among the things that count for him as *moral* reasons against doing it; as reasons from the moral point of view, against doing it (p. 67).

Now these reasons cut fairly deep and seem to me of the first importance, both in themselves and for the issue at hand. Yet they do not seem to me conclusive.

Ad (i). Are any moral matters, such as whether something, say, cruelty is wrong, or is a bad thing, open to question, to debate, to doubt? Pincoffs finds it 'hard to imagine what a debate would be like of the "doctrine" that cruelty is a bad thing. (p. 67). He supposes that it would amount to a discussion of 'the question whether and why one should be moral' (p. 67). He does not say why he thinks it would amount to that but I imagine it is because he thinks that anyone familiar with the English language would acknowledge the implication from 'N acknowledges that "it would be cruel" is a reason against it' to 'N acknowledges a moral reason' and that this gives rise to the question why one should acknowledge moral reasons and follow them, i.e., why one should be moral. However, he regards 'why be moral?' as a peculiar issue, in that it 'inevitably takes an *ad hominem* turn' (p. 67), that is, an issue which can be settled only by those who know the psychological make-up of the person with whom they are arguing. One cannot begin to argue on that issue with a person, he seems to think, unless one knows whether 'that would be cruel' counts with him or whether only 'that would be against my best interests' does. But once one knows that, Pincoffs appears to hold, the question loses its grip. For in the first case, if 'this would be cruel' weighs with the man, then a moral reason weighs with him, and so he is moral, 'and the argument is pleonastic' (p. 67)—which I suppose means unnecessary, pointless —since he already is moral. And if the reason does not weigh with him, if only 'that would be against my best interest' weighs with him, then how could that be used to make him accept the moral reason in question? If being cruel were on that occasion against his best interest and he refrained from cruelty for that reason, this would not demonstrate to him the *validity* of the moral reason, but only the coincidence of this moral reason which he does not accept, with another reason which he already accepts. Even if being cruel could be shown always to be against his best interests, the man would still not be looking at the matter morally. He would still not be a moral man. He would still not be engaging in a moral debate. And so such a demonstration would not demonstrate why he should be moral, since being persuaded by it would not make him moral.

Now, there are many things to be said against this argument. I shall confine myself to three points.

(a) Let it be granted that when the issue is thus turned into an *ad hominem* argument, it has no clear point: If the man in question accepts the moral reason, there is no need to go on; if he does not, he shows that he is not willing to argue from a certain point of view. But whatever that shows, it does not show that the issue is not debatable. All it shows is that it is not debatable from a point of view which entails that one accept 'that would be cruel' as a reason against doing something. And that need not be the only point of view from which to discuss it. It does not even show that the point of view from which it is not debatable really is the moral point of view. Hence even if one accepts everything Pincoffs says, one can still maintain that such an issue is debatable, and even that it is debatable from the moral point of view. Hence one could still maintain that a person has been indoctrinated if he has been taught this 'doctrine' in such a way that he is incapable of entering into argument about it.

(b) Suppose someone argues that acceptance of certain propositions (e.g., 'that would be cruel') as reasons against doing something is by definition looking at something *morally*—is in other words *necessarily* and obviously acceptance of a *moral* reason. In that case, one really cannot consistently maintain that the issue whether cruelty is a bad thing is *debatable* from the moral point of view. One can, however, consistently doubt and debate something else, namely, whether one ought to be moral, whether one ought to adopt that point of view. One can doubt whether a person who accepts such a reason and correctly calls it a moral reason, and so 'is moral,' ought to accept it and act in accordance with it, and so 'be moral.' And one can ask this question about a whole society and its usage. For what holds in our society for 'that would be cruel' might hold in some other society for, e.g., 'that would be helping a slave to escape from his rightful owner' or 'that would be dishonorable' or 'that would be unmanly'; and so on. And once this is said, it should be clear that even a linguistic connection with 'being moral' need be no more than a reflection in a language of the substantive— and possibly objectionable—moral convictions of that community.

Thus, if, as may seem plausible, we cannot legitimately raise the question whether one ought to be moral, this cannot be so for the reasons given by Pincoffs. It seems moreover clear that Pincoffs's reasons appear to explain why we cannot legitimately raise this question only because of a confusion, namely, the confusion between two closely related uses of the expression 'being moral.' In the first use, 'being moral' means 'accepting and following what are *regarded by some reference group* as moral reasons.' In the second use, 'being moral' means 'accepting and following what are *sound reasons* of a strength superior to and overriding all other types of reason with which they may come into conflict.' Clearly, in the second use the question of *whether* one ought to be moral does not arise, since it means much the same as whether one ought to follow the reasons one ought to follow. But the question does arise when it is asked in the first use, since what are *regarded* by some people as moral reasons need not *be* sound reasons superior to and overriding reasons of all other kinds with which they can come into conflict.

Hence Pincoffs may well be quite right (I think he is), in claiming that 'doing that would be cruel' is regarded in our society as a moral reason against doing that, but this does not show that the question whether cruelty is a bad thing cannot be debated. Nor does it show the undebatability of the question whether one ought to be moral, in the first use, i.e., whether one really ought to accept and follow those reasons which in our society are recognized as moral reasons.

Lastly, it must be emphasized that although the second use of 'being moral' precludes us from raising the question of *whether* one ought to be moral, it does not preclude us from asking *why* one ought to be. For the fact that someone has defined 'moral reason' in such a way that having a sound moral reason implies that one ought to follow it rather than any other reason one might have, especially a reason of self-interest, does not *ipso facto* explain *how* anything *can* be such a reason. On the contrary, such a definition would seem to call for an explanation of how the class of moral reasons *so defined* is possible.

(c) It should by now be clear that the question of whether someone ought to be moral or why he ought to be, is not naturally or legitimately interpreted as the *ad hominem* question Pincoffs has in mind. 'Why be moral?' is not a request to someone to show that moral reasons reduce to other kinds of reason which one already accepts, and to show by such a reduction that there is no real conflict between moral reasons and those others one already accepts and is moved by, and that one would therefore be inconsistent if one did not also accept and follow moral reasons, and thus to show that or why one ought to be moral. 'Why be moral?' is on the contrary a question about the objective (relative) merit of certain types of consideration. It is a request to someone to show that, although moral reasons conflict with others which one already accepts, one should regard and treat moral reasons as superior to and overriding these other conflicting reasons. Of course, such a demonstration cannot then consist in showing that moral reasons after all reduce to reasons of this other type.

It would lead us too far afield to answer 'Why be moral?' But since it may be thought that, so construed, this question is necessarily unanswerable and therefore pointless, I shall say a few words about one possible way of answering it, without of course contending that it is a sound answer. Suppose that 'morality is a system of principles such that everyone may expect to benefit if everyone accepts and acts on it, yet acting on the system of principles requires that someone perform disadvantageous acts' (cf. David Gauthier, 'Morality and Advantage', *Philosophical Review*, Oct., 1967, p. 462). This theory asserts the existence of a conceptual connection between two types of practical reasons, self-related and moral. Self-related reasons are those facts about the consequences of someone's actions which relate these actions to what is the optimal life for *him*. Whatever shows that an action would move his life closer to the optimal life, is a 'self-related pro'; that it would move it away from the optimal life, a 'self-related con.' The theory just outlined stipulates two connections between self-related and moral reasons. Moral reasons must be such as to be capable of coming into conflict with self-related reasons, and they must be such that if everyone always follows them, everyone can expect to do better for himself than if everyone always follows self-regarding reasons.

Such a moral theory enables us to take the first step towards an answer to 'Why be moral?' For it spells out a *generating principle* or criterion of moral reasons, and so provides an answer to the question what moral reasons are, i.e., what makes reasons moral reasons. It enables us to eliminate some kinds of reason which are regarded as moral but do not satisfy the theory's criterion of being moral reasons.

This theory also enables us to take the second step towards an answer to 'Why be moral?' for it elucidates just how it is that moral reasons are superior to self-related ones. The proof is childishly simple. If moral reasons are what this moral theory requires them to be, then everyone whose behavior is guided by the system of reasons in question can expect to be better off if moral reasons are universally regarded and treated as superior to and overriding self-related reasons when the two types of reason come into conflict than if they are not so regarded and treated.

I conclude that if Pincoffs is right in saying that debate over the 'doctrine' that cruelty is a bad thing amounts to the debate whether and why one should be moral, then that 'doctrine' is eminently debatable, and he is wrong in saying that it is not debatable.

In the light of this discussion it is now easy to see the inadequacy of Pincoffs's second point (ii), (that the debatability of an issue is its debatability for persons properly qualified to debate it) as a premiss on which to base his conclusion about moral indoctrination. The conclusion, it will be remembered, is that a tutor is not necessarily morally indoctrinating a pupil even if he teaches him in such a way that (a) the pupil accepts or agrees with, certain propositions held by the tutor, (b) the pupil cannot debate, discuss, argue about these propositions.

If I am right about 'Why be moral?' then we can distinguish three quite different questions: (1) What do we mean by 'the moral point of view?' (2) Is X (e.g. cruelty, dishonesty) a good or a bad thing, from that point of view? (3) Ought we to accept the currently dominant definition of 'the moral point of view'? But if this is right, then there is all the difference between a pupil in fact accepting, or agreeing with, certain propositions held by the tutor, say, that cruelty is a bad thing, and being unable to debate, discuss, or argue about these propositions. For the pupil may agree with the tutor that cruelty is, from what we now call the moral point of view, a bad thing, and that we ought to call 'the moral point of view,' in the current meaning of that expression, the very point of view we now call 'the moral point of view' and that we ought to treat this point of view in the way we now do, and yet be perfectly capable of debating this with someone who disagrees with one or other of these propositions. Again, he may agree with the tutor on (2), that cruelty is a bad thing, but disagree with him on the other two propositions. Agreement on (2) does not exclude debate of it.

The grammar of the word 'morality' differs from that of words such as 'chess' or 'Euclidean geometry' in two significant ways. The latter are tied to a set of constitutive propositions which define the activity. A person simply is not playing chess or doing Euclidean geometry if he does not accept and act in accordance with these constitutive propositions. We cannot raise a significant doubt about whether in chess the knight ought to move the way it does or whether the knight ought rather to move the way the bishop moves, and so on; or whether we should, in Euclidean geometry, abandon the parallel axiom. If we want to raise this sort of doubt, we have to ask whether another game or other type of geometry might not be preferable or better adapted for certain purposes which would then have to be spelled out. It is not part of the meaning of 'chess' or 'Euclidean geometry' to imply that the constitutive rules of these enterprises are best suited for some underlying implicit purpose. In the case of 'morality,' however, this is implied, hence we can raise the analogous doubt. Whatever we now recognize as the constitutive propositions of the moral point of view purport to be best suited or adapted to some underlying purpose, or set of purposes. One task of moral philosophy, not yet satisfactorily accomplished, is to make clear what this purpose or set of purposes is.

The second and related difference is that 'chess' and 'Euclidean geometry' do not of course carry any implication about whether and when people ought or ought not to engage in the activities defined by these words, or whether it would be preferable to engage in slightly modified versions of these activities. By contrast 'morality' does carry such implications. When we look at some situation from the moral point of view, we arrive at conclusions which spell out what ought to be done by whom and at what time. It is, moreover, a point of view from which everyone always ought to look at his situation and one which, like Yahve, does not brook any rivals. If a case can be made for a modification of the constitutive rules of such a supreme point of view, then a case has *ipso facto* been made against the hitherto recognized constitutive rules of the moral point of view.

This leads us straight to Pincoffs's point (iii), that no one is qualified to debate any issue from the moral point of view, unless there are some things that count with him as reasons for, and certain other things as reasons against doing something.

As it stands, this claim is, however, ambiguous, for it may mean merely that he must have an internally more or less consistent set of practical reasons, or it may mean that his set of reasons must include a certain specified set of reasons. If it means merely the former, then it is uncontentious, since having some such set of reasons really would seem to be a condition of being a reasoner, arguer, debater. But in that case it does not support Pincoffs's conclusion that no man is qualified to debate moral issues unless he accepts certain specific propositions, such as 'cruelty is a bad thing.' However, if it means the latter, then it commits itself on the highly contentious issue of what the propositions are which a qualified debater or reasoner must subscribe to. Even then, however, this point does not support Pincoffs's conclusion. One may wish to assert that a person is qualified to debate moral issues if he is qualified to debate anything at all. He may, for instance, accept as reasons against doing something, a set of propositions, such as the fact that some proposed course of action would cause one pain, harm, or would make one's life less worthwhile than if one refrained from entering on it, or that the proposed course of action would have such consequences for someone one loved or at any rate cared about. One might argue that a person who accepted such propositions as 'cons' was rational and therefore qualified to debate anything that was debatable, hence also the question whether anything was a good or a bad thing. One might in other words maintain that it must be possible to argue with a person who did not accept all, perhaps any, of the propositions which constituted and were peculiar to the moral point of view. For otherwise, one might say, a theory of moral reasons would have no better epistemic support than a theory of a special moral sense or moral intuition. It seems to me that such an ethical theory is not itself undebatable and I for one would want to argue against it.

Lastly, then, I turn to Pincoffs's point (iv), that no person would be qualified to debate any moral issue unless the proposition 'that would be cruel', 'that would be dishonest' and other similar propositions (which he does not enumerate) counted for him as *moral reasons* against doing that.

Now, I can accept this point, provided it is not used to press the earlier points already rejected. It may well be necessarily true that a person is not qualified to debate the moral rightness or wrongness, the moral goodness or badness of a certain course of action, unless he accepts these very considerations as moral considerations. But it would be quite wrong to infer from this that therefore he cannot discuss, debate, or argue about the question of whether these are in fact moral considerations.

For suppose that the definition of 'morality' I took from Gauthier were defensible, then it might well be possible to show that, from the moral point of view, thus defined, 'that would be cruel' necessarily counts as a 'moral *con.*' Then Pincoffs's point (iv) would be sound. Nevertheless, its soundness or otherwise could still be argued about or debated. A pupil who had been taught this in such a way that he cannot argue about it with his tutor or with anyone else, would still have been indoctrinated, though as it happens correctly. He would still be in no better position than a Platonic Auxiliary.

It seems to me therefore that Pincoffs's argument is unsuccessful. He has not shown that there are moral 'doctrines' which no one can disagree with or argue about, without *ipso facto* showing that he is not qualified to argue about them. It is on the contrary reasonably clear that unlike a game such as chess or an axiomatic system such as Euclidean geometry, the constitutive rules of morality are not determined by the currently accepted meaning of the word 'morality' or 'moral point of view.' He has not shown that 'cruelty is a bad thing' or 'dishonesty is a bad thing' are such unarguable, undebatable 'moral doctrines.' It is on the contrary fairly clear that they are debatable and that it would therefore amount to indoctrination if one taught these 'doctrines' to one's pupils as if they were undebatable. (Perhaps some people find it plausible to say that such doctrines are not debatable because they have in mind a sense of 'debatable' namely, 'incapable of conclusive support,' in which they may well not be debatable. In this sense, the claim that 'Disprin' is more effective than 'Aspirin' is debatable, *ad nauseam*, whereas the claim that the Rolls Royce is a more comfortable car than the Volkswagen is not. Equally plainly, however, both claims are debatable in the sense under discussion. A person who was so trained that he had not become able to argue about the second issue had not been properly trained to think for himself, but indoctrinated by Rolls Royce advertising, even if he had been indoctrinated with the true doctrine.)

III

Nevertheless, in spite of all I have said, it seems to me that Pincoffs's basic idea is sound. I agree with him that it should be possible to formulate some doctrines which one can deny only at the cost of disqualifying oneself from moral debate, where morality is the sort of system of rules which, unlike a game, ought to be followed by everyone at all times.

Let us look once more at the case of dishonesty or lying. Pincoffs argues that 'only people who have a certain character . . . are free to disagree upon, to debate, matters of doctrine. For debate, there must be a certain degree of respect and trust' (p. 66). Now clearly, this degree of respect and trust need not be very high. A person who in debate refrains from dishonesty and lying to the extent to which he thinks it necessary for the maintenance of that degree of respect and trust which will ensure that he is believed by others, may well quite often engage in dishonesty and lying, namely, whenever he thinks it to his advantage. For it seems that a man's advantage is often better served by dishonesty and lying, even in debate, e.g., political debate, than by honesty and truth-telling. Thus, dishonesty and lying in debate may often be a good thing, not a bad thing. We cannot prove that they are good things by reference merely to the aims we have when engaging in debate.

We may now say that a person who argues like this is defeating himself. But this is not necessarily so, as long as he is not producing these arguments in the middle of a political or similar debate. In other contexts, such arguments need not be self-defeating. I do not imagine that my producing these arguments here will cast doubt on my veracity or honesty, at least in this debate. For what difference would it make to my arguments whether I believed in them or not?

It might, of course, be said now that by arguing in this way, I was not arguing from the moral point of view, but from a selfish point of view. But to say this without further argument would be to beg the question. We cannot at the same time argue that the doctrine 'dishonesty is a bad thing' is not arguable or debatable from the moral point of view, on the grounds that it is one of the 'axioms' or 'constitutive rules' of the moral point of view, and also argue that it must be such an axiom or constitutive rule because a person who rejects this 'doctrine' *ipso facto* disqualifies himself as a person arguing from the moral point of view. To avoid begging the question, we must define the moral point of view in a way which does not depend on any substantive moral judgment.

Here I can give only a brief sketch of how it might be done. We must begin by making clear what we actually mean when we call conduct 'morally wrong.' In my view we mean two things: that it is conduct which breaks a precept based on certain sorts of reasons or grounds, and that it is not solely the agent's business whether or not he follows or ignores a precept of this sort. When we tell someone that in talking to the Dean about his current research he had done the wrong thing, we mean 'morally wrong' if and only if we imply that he went counter to a precept which it was not solely his business to decide whether to follow or ignore. We imply in other words that it would be justified to have other people see to it that he followed such precepts. This account of 'morally wrong' says in different words what I have said before, namely, that unlike a game, morality is a system of rules and precepts which everyone must follow all the time, that it is not up to him to decide when it suits him to 'play,' that is, to do what the rules require. I believe that this is the peculiar sense of 'moral wrongness' which Kant tried, unsuccessfully, to capture by his concept of the 'Categorical Imperative.'

If this is what we mean, then we immediately face two further difficult questions. The first is whether we should ever employ such a system of concepts whose employment implies that people not following such rules and precepts may or perhaps ought to be *pressured* to follow them, if they do not do so voluntarily. This is not the question 'Why be moral?' as previously explained, but the similar question 'Why should there be a morality at all?'; 'Why should there be a set of rules which people are not merely encouraged but pressured to follow?' The second connected question concerns the nature of the reasons or grounds used in support of such rules or precepts: 'What must be these grounds if precepts based on them are such that it is not solely the business of those to whom they apply whether or not to follow or ignore them?' If we can answer this second question, then we can say what it is to be moral: it is to follow precepts based on such grounds.

It is not difficult to answer the first question, why we have to have a system of precepts which others may insist that we follow. For it is plain that in the absence of such a system of precepts, rational beings would tend to follow what I have called self-regarding reasons. These must not be confused with reasons of self-interest in the narrow sense. Self-regarding reasons include reasons of self-interest but also reasons relating to the pleasure and interest of others we love or care about, and reasons relating to the suffering and detriment of others we hate. Clearly, as has frequently been pointed out, the life resulting for people living in close proximity and interaction when they are guided by self-regarding reasons is unsatisfactory and could be vastly improved by the introduction of compulsory social rules overriding the individual's self-regarding reasons when such a modification of individual behavior would result in a vastly superior way of life for all concerned.

Given that it is desirable to develop a system of reasons which are to be regarded and treated as overriding self-regarding reasons, life for people living under such a system can be further improved by making these reasons as appealing to every individual as possible. This will decrease the need for sanctions, the waste of resources involved in administering them, and the amount of suffering caused by the need to administer them. We can make these reasons as appealing as possible by the application, in the formulation or reformulation of the compulsory social rules, of the principle of equity. For this principle ensures that compulsory social rules adjudicate between the conflicting claims of different individuals in such a way that the interests of all those involved are served equally.

Such an account of morality explains what we mean by 'morally wrong,' satisfies the requirement that everyone must always follow the precepts of morality, explains why there must be a system of reasons overriding self-interested and self-regarding ones, and explains why it is not enough that such reasons be simply taught as superior to all others, and why it is further necessary that conformity to such precepts be considered not solely the agent's own business. Such an account of morality also satisfies the conditions about the relation between reasons of self-interest and moral reasons which are stipulated in the theory I quoted from Gauthier. It therefore also satisfies the requirement that there be an answer to the question 'Why be moral?' It does in other words satisfy the main demands we can make on an account of morality, and it extracts from such an account some criteria in terms of which purported substantive moral rules can be tested for soundness.

We must mention a further practice, the practice of justifying oneself, which is part of the practice of calling people to account, which in turn is part of the social practice of seeing to it that the social rules, conformity with which is not solely the agent's own business, are always followed by everyone. The existence of the practice of justification further helps to raise the level of conformity to these rules, for it forces each agent to demonstrate the conformity of his behavior to the compulsory social rules or else suffer the sanctions. This practice also further helps to clarify the sense in which moral reasons really are superior to reasons of self-interest: for it is obvious that in the public forum of justification, no one could argue that when moral reasons (as defined) conflict with reasons of self-interest, the latter are superior to the former. But since everyone has an interest in the existence, the universal use and the efficacy of the practice of moral justification, and since in it only following moral reasons justifies, it is clear why they are and must be treated as superior to and overriding reasons of self-interest.

Given that this or a similar account of the nature of morality is correct, then there are many things which moral education can safely teach. For then there are many things which are necessarily involved in being a moral agent. If we teach these things, we are not committed to any substantive moral principles but only to framework principles involved in anything that can be called 'a morality.'

The most general principle is the principle that one ought to act only in such a way as can be justified, that is, shown to be in accordance with reasons suitable for the practice of justification, that is, reasons one can wish that everyone should be permitted to use in his defense. The universalization principle is sound if the practice of justification is sound.

We can teach that there are reasons, those we call moral reasons, which are such that we are required always to be guided by them rather than any others with which they may come into conflict and which may have greater psychological appeal to us, and that for this reason it is desirable there should be people entrusted with the task of seeing to it that everyone follow these reasons rather than his inclination.

We can teach that there is necessarily a difference between morality and self-interest, that the two may occasionally conflict though not always, and that when they conflict, moral reasons ought to be treated as superior to and overruling those of self-interest.

We can teach the consequent need for everyone occasionally to set aside his own best interest for the protection of the rights of others, i.e., those interests of theirs which have a better claim, whether or not he has a natural inclination to do so.

We can teach the related need for everyone to cultivate in himself the good will and the respect for other persons, that is, carriers of rights, and not merely possessors of abilities and dispositions one can use for one's own purposes.

We can teach the respect due to the compulsory social rules of our society (the laws) which purport to spell out or at least conform to the moral reasons whose nature we explained. And we can teach the condition on which the obligatoriness of these rules depends, namely, that they embody the principles of equity whose embodiment alone gives everyone an equally good reason for supporting the enforcement of these compulsory rules.

Given that this is what is essential to a moral order, we can then establish some substantive moral doctrines without begging any question.

We can teach that dishonesty is a bad thing morally speaking, because it is not desirable that a person should be able to use 'I had to be dishonest to achieve my purpose' as a valid reason in justification. Teaching such a doctrine as certain or established is not, in this context, indoctrination, because it is not preventing the student from thinking for himself. On the contrary, it is showing him what sort of thinking moral thinking is and how this substantive doctrine can be established by moral thinking.

Of course, what I have just said presupposes that the account of moral thinking I have given is correct. In one respect, at any rate, I am confident that it is on the right track: it gives both a sketch of a way of practical reasoning and a defense of the claim that that way is moral reasoning. I believe that no teaching of substantive moral beliefs can escape the stigma of indoctrination unless it rests on a theory which has established this claim. We do not speak of indoctrination in the case of teaching chess or geometry because there we are only teaching how to do these things, which does not imply that, or when, or by whom they ought to be done; what place they should occupy in the scheme of things. But to call any method of thinking or reasoning 'moral' does have such implications. Hence if moral teaching is not to be indoctrination, it must not only show that some moral doctrines are derivable by some mode of reasoning, but also that this mode is moral reasoning, i.e., reasoning whose conclusions everyone always ought to follow. But when that is done, then teaching this method of reasoning is not indoctrination; nor is teaching the very young some of the doctrines provable by these methods without giving them the proofs; nor is inculcating in them the psychological attitudes, such as good will and respect for persons or for the law, which are involved in morality itself.

Part 3

The aesthetic dimension of education 6

H. S. Broudy

The educational situation

Although aesthetic values (especially the beautiful) are dutifully listed among the higher goods to be achieved in life and education, they have a low priority in both. This estimate has to be qualified because of a certain ambivalence in the public's attitude toward the aesthetic. The low priority of the aesthetic in life refers to the fine arts or high art or serious art, or, if you like, art produced by people primarily concerned with aesthetic values. There is evidence that this is so despite alleged culture explosions.[1] In everyday life, by contrast, the aesthetic has a high priority indeed, as numerous phenomena ranging from the use of imagery in the making of a president to the selling of soap flakes by television can attest. This ambivalent attitude toward the aesthetic becomes socially significant if one considers the power of the mass media to utilize aesthetic means to influence thought and choice. And this fact raises in a crucial form the educational question: Is there merit in the argument that serious art, high art, etc., will order feeling 'better than' the popular, commercial, mass media arts? Should aesthetic education therefore cultivate a mass public for serious art? Or should aesthetic education adopt a different gambit?

So long as the education of the elites and the masses was sharply distinguished, an affirmative answer to the first question was taken more or less for granted; the second was not seriously entertained. For it was also taken for granted that the masses needed only literacy, political docility, and vocational training—their aesthetic needs would be met adequately by folk and popular art, which required no special training to appreciate. If serious art figured at all in the schooling of the masses, it was only to remind them that there was such a thing and that their betters would serve as its custodians and cherishers. The masses were to respect the tastes of the elites, but they were not expected to share them.

In the American high school this respect was translated into a conventional, often merely verbal, admiration for small samples of familiar classics in the various arts. A small and persistent repertoire of these showpieces of the higher culture was included in the college preparatory curriculum, but in literature alone were they accorded anything more than perfunctory attention. Even this modest exposure to serious art was thought to be unnecessary for the working-class child in order to fulfill his destiny on the farm or in the factory.

The rising economic and political power of the masses and the mass media changed all this. One wonders whether high-grade aesthetic experience, no less than high-grade cognition, for the bulk of the population is being recognized even now as a necessary condition for an enlightened mass society. Some, of course, deny the possibility of a mass society being enlightened, but if technology has anything really redemptive up its sleeve, it is this possibility, and for a free society it is a necessity.

New expectations

In American education a cluster of developments dating from the mid-sixties shifted attention from an almost exclusive concern with intellective attainment to what the school might or ought to do in the affective and volitional domains.

1. Poverty and racial discrimination in American society were 'rediscovered' and therewith the problem of educating children suffering from acutely depressing environments. From 1957 to 1965 excellence in schooling meant teaching more and more 'good' science to more and more good students; from 1965 on, schools have been called upon to diminish the wrath of the militants, black and white, the misery of the indigent, and the violence of the revolutionaries and their suppressors alike.

2. The campus cauldron has been kept bubbling by a widespread irritation with science and science-based technology. These were blamed for war, the rising power of the military, and pollution of the environment. The drift of Merit scholars away from the study of physics has been a serious blow to the scientific establishment. Along with these anti-scientific sentiments has developed a mistrust of all rational processes in social reform; these processes were construed to be procedural means developed by the establishment to postpone or to dilute efforts at reform.

3. The challenge to the sexual and sartorial mores of the middle class prodded parents, editors, and legislators to call upon the school—even more vociferously than usual—to do something about value or character education. Disappointed by the standard approaches to moral training—admonition and parental pressure—some of the parents and editors have asked for a return to the study of the humanities and the arts as part of the humanities.

94

Possibly the unsightly symbols of youthful revolt created a fresh awareness of the relation between the aesthetic and moral dimensions of life. 'Unsightly' and 'unseemly,' just as cleanliness and godliness, seemed to coalesce in their import. But here also there is an ambivalence. If art is to save the young, then it cannot be the 'new' art that allegedly depraves them.

Although the schools have made a wide variety of responses to these developments, it is to a possible aesthetic response that this paper will give major attention. The general name of that response might be 'aesthetic education' in the form of courses in the humanities and related arts in the elementary and secondary schools. These courses, struggling to define their content and mission and creating about as much resistance as enthusiasm, are expected to meet current educational difficulties in at least the following ways.

For one thing, they are to serve as a surrogate for the linguistic studies that have formed the backbone of the school. With a strong assist from Marshall McLuhan, the social reformers have branded the book as the arch villain that makes the school the oppressor of the black child and indeed of all save middle-class W(hite) A(nglo) S(axon) P(rotestants). The arts are expected to liberate the creativity of these children, which is thought to express itself in feeling and image rather than linear verbal discourse.

The arts are also expected to convey persuasively the norms of conduct and the ideals of the culture, especially insofar as they are expressed in the humanities, i.e., moral philosophy, literary history, poetry, drama, painting, sculpture, and architecture of the classic periods. A return to the humanities is urged on the ground that neglect of them in favor of the sciences has weakened the allegiance of recent generations to the virtues and ideals celebrated in these studies. Because the classics are held to stress excellence of form as well as content, their appeal is believed to be more direct (because of the immediacy of perception) than that of ordinary studies. This is quite a burden to place on aesthetic education.

The advocates of aesthetic education seem to be saying that there is something missing in the standard curriculum which, if aesthetic education will supply it, may order feeling as the intellectual studies order thought. Obviously the merits of these claims and expectations depend on how one conceives of the aesthetic experience and its role in life and education. Does aesthetic experience utilize contents and activate processes that are missing from other modes of experience and education?

Traditionally, both philosophy and education have concentrated on the obligation of rational cognition and moral reflection to influence human action in the right direction. No less traditional is the hiatus between thought and action, the failure of thought to meet its obligations. Can this hiatus be bridged by the imagination? The imagination has been thought to relate thought and action by creating images not only of possible experiences but also of their potentialities for pleasure and pain. The aesthetic or the artistic imagination objectifies human import in images. They thus make value intimations *perceptible*—a mode of being not native to values or the feelings that attend value experience. Seas are not literally tranquil or angry; music is not literally sad, nor is sadness ordinarily a pattern of sound or colors. Because of this metaphorical character, the aesthetic object always requires imagination for both its creation and reception. The distinctive function of aesthetic experience and of aesthetic education therefore would seem to be the apprehension of value via the perceptive imagination or the imaginative perception, a view not unlike that of Santayana.

If the existence of such a faculty be granted, then the aesthetic aspects of experience, whether employed upon natural or contrived objects, may provide an important access to feeling and therewith to choice and action. I think there is little reason to doubt this. Further, I think it can be said that the standard curriculum of our schools—at least in the United States—is primarily concerned with cognitive content and intellective powers. The imagination, especially the aesthetic imagination—is not the objective of systematic cultivation.[2]

Justification of aesthetic education

Granted that the imagination has a potential influence on feeling and action, is it necessarily a benign influence? Rationalists have always been suspicious of *imaginatio* precisely because of its susceptibility to emotion. On what grounds then can development and cultivation of the imagination, especially the aesthetic imagination, be urged?

In one sense it is odd to ask for a justification of aesthetic experience because it is often believed to need none. It gives pleasure, a special rarefied sort of pleasure, to be sure, but nevertheless unmistakably pleasure. Two difficulties arise here. First, to say that aesthetic experience is pleasurable, or more broadly with D. W. Gotshalk, to say that it is 'intrinsically interesting to perception,' does not guarantee that it will make our lives better in other ways or on the whole. Hedonism, as an ethical theory, usually ends up by preaching a higher hedonism on some basis other than pleasure or interest. For it simply is the case that aesthetic satisfaction is sometimes experienced—and often in refined forms—by criminals, sadists, and scoundrels. The intrinsic satisfactoriness of aesthetic experience is no guarantee of moral or intellectual or religious 'rightness.'

Nevertheless, the intrinsic phase of aesthetic value remains at the heart of the matter. Unless aesthetic pleasure or interest is phenomenologically distinguishable from other value experiences it would be impossible to identify it either for discussion or development. Whatever its biological origin and function, the aesthetic quality can achieve 'functional autonomy' and be experienced in its uniqueness. Indeed, aesthetic education would regard this achievement as a necessary and *almost* sufficient condition for its success.

Moreover, unless the capacity for the intrinsic enjoyment of the aesthetic is developed, it may be difficult for the individual to realize such instrumental values as might be claimed for it. And the instrumental potency of the aesthetic is a more telling justification for aesthetic education than the intrinsic values it may engender. This is so because as a social institution the school justifies itself by its contribution to the maximization of *all* values. Does the imaginative perception exercised in aesthetic experience make such a contribution to human welfare?

Unfortunately, the imagination, while it seduces the will by its representations, is an unreliable guide to truth and goodness, and in education as in philosophy it is dangerous to take the deliverances of imagination as descriptions of reality or prescriptions for conduct without further tests. The unique value of the imagination, therefore, is as a source of potentiality not as a description of or prescription for actuality. At a time when actuality seems to have outdistanced our powers to control it; when despite our technological sophistication, life seems frustrating or pointless, it is understandable that we should look to the imagination for new possibilities. It is common gossip that we live in such a time.

It can be put in this way: science and technology have enlarged the volume of possibility of knowledge, action, and moral obligation. Contrary to the common assumption, science is not confined to means for which the humanities specify the goals. Science can create new goals. For example, the eradication of cancer and poverty can become moral ends only when the possibility of voluntary action respecting them arises, and excuses for not so acting are absent. The rapid expansion of the possibility of action by technological advance has frustrated our moral reflection; we simply cannot foresee fully and rapidly enough the consequences of our choices—e.g., proliferating problems of ecology, nuclear fission—to enable us to make rationally defensible choices, let alone emotionally satisfying ones.

This does not command any profound transvaluation of values or the abandonment of the traditional virtues or even our 'essential human nature.' Rather it seems more as if we are trying, more rapidly than ever before, to find life styles or behavioral forms that would embody these values so that they can withstand moral scrutiny and yield the subjective satisfaction without which no life is accepted as good. In such a situation, assistance may be sought either from computers scanning all conceivable combinations of elements that we can feed into them, or from a fortuitous stroke of the creative imagination. Both solutions have their advocates. The first reaffirms a faith in rational calculation, whereas looking to the aesthetic manifests a belief that our crisis is caused by a failure of the imagination rather than a failure of either reason or of will. On the latter view we should look to art for the new life forms.

In its originative role art extrudes any number of forms, and there is no way of predicting which of these, if any, will capture the imagination of people seeking a new life form. Indeed, the artist is not consciously concerned with such possibilities. If we could predict, even in general terms, the characteristics of the successful forms, we could program computers to find the combinations that would satisfy the formula. The uniform distrust of logical extrapolations to find new life forms is witnessed by the animadversions on Orwell's *1984* and Skinner's *Walden II*, and more recently on his book *Beyond Freedom and Dignity*.

One may say it is to art that many are looking for the life-style of the liberated woman, the new patriot, the new youth, and the new parent, and perhaps even of the new state. Art, for its part, cannot deliberately manufacture such forms, but, driven by its own dynamic of expressing life import aesthetically, it may turn up images of life that invite widespread imitation and capture commitment. For example, the 'new' poetry, music, and theatre have already found devotees by the thousands, not for any special ideas, but rather for a generalized attitude toward life. Some characteristics of the new life forms have remained esoteric; some have had a fairly wide acceptance, e.g., general increase of hirsuteness, but in general there is an attempt to externalize belief into appropriate appearance. That art created these attitudes may be debatable, but that it provided images for their expression seems obvious.

The originative power of art is not its only power. While art may, and perhaps has, captured some intimations of reality and value that create possibilities for new life forms, it also celebrates what the group or race has found to be significant. On the one hand, there is the well nigh universal tendency to ritualize, mythicize, stylize, and formalize those events the group regards as important—from weddings to wars. Art in this way summarizes the value experiments and adventures of the group into convenient mnemonic devices. Popular art may be thought of as the aesthetic version of the mores.

On the other hand, a continuous critical tradition assesses those works of art that are especially significant in expressing the group's value quest in aesthetic terms: the masterworks that in some sense are summative, bridging, or (in hindsight) prophetic of things to come.

For aesthetic education, both functions of art are important. The originative function requires a public with a highly developed aesthetic receptivity; the celebrative function of serious art asks allegiance to a critical tradition by which the young are to be inducted into selected modes of perception and feeling.

The originative function calls for the cultivation of the imaginative perception or perceptual imagination in a nonprescriptive way, except in the sense that expertise is prescriptive; the celebrative function is prescriptive in that it is selective. The current press for aesthetic education does not always distinguish these functions. Those who stress creativity, diversity and freedom fear the 'imposition' of traditional norms; those who are dismayed by the disorder of our times look for an ordering of feeling by 'great' works of art, inspired presumably by a vision of the nature of things vouchsafed to genius.

Aesthetic education as cultivation of aesthetic perception

If we accept the imaginative perception of import-bearing images as the distinctive characteristic of aesthetic experience, we can formulate a fairly straightforward approach to aesthetic education with emphasis on descriptive rather than judgmental criticism.[3] On this approach the emphasis is on disclosing, first of all, the sensory contents and differentiations in the object. Here I intend nothing more profound than what is meant by the expert when he says that the naive observer rarely perceives all of what is there. As Croce observed, we ordinarily perceive indices of our purposes in the object rather than its full perceptible content.[4] For action this is enough, just as for understanding what we read, it is sufficient to perceive only a quite small upper left-hand portion of each printed work. For perception of the particularity and individuality of the aesthetic object this is not enough—the full content has to be perceived. Indeed, on some theories of criticism the absence of the slightest detail would change the aesthetic character of the aesthetic object. Aesthetic perception presumably is not selective.

The second aspect of the aesthetic experience to which one can

99

direct instruction is the formal. Here the emphasis is on becoming sensitive to design after the manner of an artist working in a given medium. Paintings, for example, often have a compositional design in terms of geometrical shapes and balances, but balance in terms of color values, volumes of space, or even the interest potential of subject matters also constitute valid aesthetic designs. The important outcome of instruction is to form the habit of perceiving in terms of pictorial design or musical design or poetic design as an artist does. This does not require that agreement be reached as to *the* design of the work of art. There is some reason to believe that young children are nearer to the artist in this respect than they are later when cultural demands stereotype their perception.

Third is instruction in some of the technical factors used in achieving certain aesthetic effects. This aspect is perhaps less important in aesthetic theory than in aesthetic education, although Bosanquet makes much of the role of the medium in the final work of art.[5] In aesthetic education, technique plays a dual role: First, it helps to educate the expectations of the perceiver. If certain effects cannot be achieved in certain media, it is 'uneducated,' so to speak, to look for them, e.g., the limitations of stained glass, tapestries, water colors, or the orchestra of Mozart's day. In the second place, the technical aspect of art production is closely related to the studio training in the arts in which performance rather than appreciation is the primary objective. Artists' contempt for the mere appreciator—unless their own works are the ones being appreciated—is notorious. Nonetheless, one wonders whether one can learn to perceive as an artist does without making some effort to work in his medium. In any event, admiration of technical competence, while no substitute for aesthetic perception, is not a bad introduction to it.

Finally, there is the expressive aspect of the work of art or the aesthetic object. Whereas the first three dimensions or aspects are fairly easy to identify and teach, expressiveness is not easy to identify or teach. It is precisely in this dimension that most of the abuses of art appreciation courses are likely to occur. For it is when we try to teach what the work of art expresses that we are most likely to make strange guesses about the message or lesson that allegedly the artist intended to convey and which the pupil *ought* to apprehend.

Now it may well be that the artist did have such an intention and that the work of art does in fact teach a lesson or a moral. For example, few Americans escape some constriction in the throat at the first sight of the Statue of Liberty after a long trip abroad. But to be relevant, the lump in the throat must be a response to the aesthetic properties of the statue and not merely to one's own psychological history. And for these properties to count aesthetically, they must be perceived. If, however, the pupil is told that the properties are there whether he perceives them or not, he may forever after repeat dutifully that the Statue of Liberty expresses the sentiments inscribed on its pedestal. This is the conventionalization of judgment that nobody wants.

Even less global qualities, such as cheerfulness, sadness, emptiness, turbulence, that art objects are often said to express are sufficiently variable to warrant caution about teaching anyone that they are there, unless we are prepared to point out for perception those qualities in virtue of which the attribution is made. And yet we should all agree that if aesthetic experience is not merely an idle contemplation of purely formal arrangements of sensory materials, there must be some aesthetic objects that do express what is humanly relevant. That they express human import in a metaphor via an image, i.e., that they represent a meaning or a value as embodied in an image, is what makes art a resource for human experience that is not identical with history, science, mathematics, philosophy, or religion. Indeed, an object not perceived as expressive at some level is not aesthetically perceived at all on the view I am defending.

On the perceptual approach, therefore, the most important component of aesthetic experience—that which in artistic parlance gives life to the painting or the music—is treated (at least in the initial stages) as a concomitant of instruction in the other three dimensions. However, pupils can discuss it without raising the question as to what is 'really' expressed. If, as I am inclined to believe, expressive properties of the object depend on the multilevels of meaning that sensory images can and perhaps always do bear, then to say that a given work expresses more than one meaning and that the meaning is *in* the work are not inconsistent with each other. The important thing, it seems to me, is not that all pupils agree on the content of the expression, but rather that whatever the pupil *says* is expressed be related by him to something he has perceived in the object.[6]

Development of aesthetic perception is at the present time a good strategy for making aesthetic education an integral part of general education for these reasons.

1. This approach reassures the educators who are norm shy. Especially sensitive are those teachers who equate aesthetic education with education for creativity, individuality, and freedom from conformity. It also frees the teacher to use a wide variety of materials without worrying whether or not they are 'good' art by conventional standards. Some materials need not be art objects at all; some may be contrived to bring out the formal properties, others the sensory ones.

2. The perceptual approach also smoothes the feathers of artists which are ruffled by the proposal to teach anything about the aesthetic to anyone. Doing art is for them the only important thing. Telling artists who feel this way that we are trying to get pupils to perceive as artists do disarms them a little, for their complaint against the amateur is that he perceives the wrong things and consequently values or disvalues them for the wrong reasons.

3. The language of aesthetic perception is about as close as we come to a *lingua franca* of all the arts. All works of art can be discussed in the four dimensions, and I have some evidence for believing that one can learn to discern these dimensions in a number of media without becoming an expert in them. This is important in recruiting staff for aesthetic education and for the strategy of instruction. Teachers who are competent in no art or even in one have to be reassured that they can learn to perceive and teach others to perceive in other arts.[7]

4. The perceptual approach is to be preferred to two alternative approaches: that of studio training in performance or some version of it, on the one hand, and appreciation courses, on the other. The performance approach in the schools customarily has taken the form of teaching music and art or drawing during the elementary grades (see footnote 2). In the secondary school they are available as electives. The fact is that they are not widely elected in American high schools, so that we must presume that the elementary work did not create a universal appetite for further experience in performance. Nevertheless, inasmuch as performance gives one a feeling for the medium and its technical problems there is much to be said for the performance approach in the elementary grades. However, it is difficult to do performance training in more than one of the media, so that it leaves the pupil relatively 'illiterate' in most media. For the prospective professional, of course, there is no alternative to intensive performance training, but general education is not directed at the prospective professional or even the talented amateur.

The appreciation course customarily exposes the student to masterworks that illustrate periods, styles, historical significance, and biographical information about artists. Without in any way denigrating the value of such knowledge about the masterworks, one must point out that it is no genuine substitute for training in perception in a wide variety of media. Furthermore, so much of the instruction in these courses is judgmental that it fosters the introjection of highly conventionalized norms without the background of direct experience that makes such introjection defensible.

Although aesthetic education does not necessarily commit one to teaching about more than one art at a time, in practice the curricular time available for this work is so limited that a multi-media approach is almost imperative. For this reason one can be pardoned for speaking about 'aesthetic literacy' as the ability to use the concepts of aesthetic perception in discussing the various arts as a goal of aesthetic education.

Perceptual competence not only can be developed but it can also be kept from evaporating into vagueness by insisting that both pupil and teacher (as well as critics) point to that in the work of art which prompts them to predicate a given quality of it. And these requirements or ground rules fit quite well with two necessary conditions for experience to qualify as aesthetic. One is that the object be perceptible—as an image—and the other that, regardless of ontological or psychological considerations, the qualities of the object be perceived as being in the object (phenomenological objectivity). Thus if the music is perceived as sad, it must be so perceived by virtue of some properties or configuration of them that it is heard in the music.[8]

Aesthetic education as normative

I doubt, however, whether the merits of aesthetic education as the cultivation of aesthetic perception will of itself impress many school authorities sufficiently to grant it a place in the curriculum. A typical school board will want assurance that the development of aesthetic perception will have some beneficial effect on other modes of experience, e.g., the intellectual, moral, religious, social.[9] It would also want to be shown that aesthetic perception cannot be cultivated outside of the school, e.g., by the informal transactions with the arts, especially the popular arts.

Such assurance might come from the celebrative rather than the originative role of art. If it is held that 'good' art celebrates and vivifies the ideals of the group, preferably of the entire human group, then the instrumental role of art becomes clear. The argument for this view has two parts: that art can be and in fact is used to enhance any value experience. This is amply verified in ordinary experience when we use art to underscore religious rituals, wedding ceremonies and funeral rites. This fact, however, does not argue for any special attention to 'serious' art, however ill defined that term is. Popular art, commerce with which requires no formal tuition, also celebrates nonaesthetic values by aesthetic means, as in advertising. The case for formal aesthetic education requires that there be a type of art that can neither be enjoyed intrinsically or used extrinsically without deliberate cultivation of aesthetic sensibility.

This brings us back to what the perceptual approach to aesthetic education avoids, or at least postpones, namely, the question of norms, in two senses: first, whether the works of art selected for study embody approved moral, intellectual, religious, or civic values; second, whether the selected works are to be regarded as exemplars of aesthetic merit. Some works might be regarded as exemplary in both senses of norms, and there might be very good pedagogical reasons for selecting these for instruction. However, there are those who believe that one can make defensible judgments of better or worse as regards aesthetic or artistic merit regardless of non-aesthetic or extra-aesthetic norms that may be attributed to works of art.

One cannot predict in which of these camps a given school board hearing the pleas for aesthetic education might fall, but one can be quite sure that if it is argued that there are no norms either aesthetic or extra-aesthetic by which materials for instruction can be selected, or that the question of the existence of such norms is meaningless or misguided, the typical school board will spend no more time on aesthetic education.

If taste is beyond judgment and improvement, the board will say, then it becomes a private matter on which the school has nothing to say. It would also point out that as far as consumption of the popular arts is concerned, it needs neither encouragement nor tuition from the school. And, I think, the same response would be forthcoming to a plea for the study of science, if it were argued that there were no norms by which one scientific statement could be judged better than another. Similarly we would be told that there is little point in devoting time to the study of science in school, if the common-sensical, untutored explanation of phenomena current in the cultural milieu were not different from or better than those taught in scientific textbooks.

However, if school authorities are convinced that there are defensible norms in aesthetic matters, and that aesthetic education should teach them, they would encounter the argument that to impose these norms on defenseless pupils precludes any subsequent criticism of these norms; hence the pupil is giving up his chance for having authentic value norms. Is imposition of this kind compatible with education that aims at the moral and intellectual autonomy of the pupil?

Philosophical and educational criteria

This problem of imposition is not confined to aesthetic education. Every realm of experience is rooted in some intrinsic interest. The pupil will learn naturally and readily what is necessary to satisfy such interests. This fact has always impressed educational reformers who point to the ease with which children learn the statistical data about athletic heroes, but cannot or will not learn school arithmetic. There is little evidence that the young spontaneously or naturally are ever eager to learn what the school thinks it important for them to know as adults. Motivation, accordingly, is the major problem of pedagogy; of imposition, direct or indirect, the school is easily convicted.

There is a gap between common sense science and sophisticated (educated) science; between common sense moral judgment and the subtle reflections of the ethical theorist; between the simple religious faith of the common man and the refinements that supervene on these feelings in the experience of the theologian or the saint. In all of these domains the simple form of the experience requires little if any formal training. One learns it by living in a culture, and motivation is no problem. It is the sophisticated version of these modes of experience that needs justification in life and in formal education. The distinction between connoisseur and the layman can be found in all kinds of activity. The moment one becomes a 'buff' of anything—antique automobiles, opera records, jazz, folk songs—the spontaneous untutored response is subjected to scrutiny and ever finer discrimination, and from that moment on the 'right' to judgment in the field is limited to those who have cultivated their tastes, i.e., members of the cult.

There is relatively little trouble when the schools 'impose' educated science, mathematics, and language usage on the pupil without first securing his consent, although in some quarters there is a growing resistance to such prescription even in the cognitive disciplines on the grounds that they are the product and instrument of middle-class ideology.

In matters of value, however, imposition is condemned because there is no agreement (let alone scientifically validated agreement) on moral and aesthetic norms, as there is in science or mathematics. Aesthetic education, therefore—and moral education as well—is either rejected entirely or some form of it that leaves the individual free from 'imposition' is stipulated. In other words, imposition is never good, but it is defensible only if there is agreement as to what is to be imposed.

Plausible as the distinction seems, I believe it rests on a confusion between a philosophically valid criterion and an educationally viable one. Philosophically, any conceivable counter instance is sufficient to impugn the validity of a criterion—any first-year student in philosophy can make a shambles of any proposed criterion, even of skepticism itself. Educationally, or, if you like, institutionally, the operative criterion is the *consensus cognoscenti* or the consensus of the credentialled members. These members lay down, or at least recognize among themselves, the rules for judging the merit of any work in their purview. Sometimes the rules have a methodological base, e.g., the scientific method, but more often evidence of experience in a field under the tuition of a credentialled member is the source of the credential. 'Good' physics is what members of the official physical society say it is, and good philosophy is what members of philosophical associations say it is. That the view changes from time to time does not change the nature of the criterion group.

May I reiterate that this mode of credentialling will not withstand philosophical scrutiny or the reformer's righteous indignation. This is why in a healthy society there is a continuous rebellion against the Establishment, but also an Establishment against which one can rebel; one which inducts each generation into a tradition of disciplined criticism. This is the *de facto* source of educational authority whether it is in the sciences or the humanities, and inasmuch as the school is itself not primarily a research agency, this could also be the source of its authority *de jure*. Certainly under no other banner can it stand up against political pressures nearly so well.

The strength of that authority does not lie in agreement as such because the views of the 'academy' change from time to time, and even at the same time no active discipline is free from controversy among equally credentialled members. The authority stems from the agreement as to what constitutes competence within a field of inquiry—only a major assault assisted by fortuitous circumstances ever breaches this agreement. For the most part, even successful challenges to the consensus must first find allies from within the credentialled group.

The induction of the young into the critical tradition of the arts, therefore, has the same motivation and justification as the induction of the young into the intellectual traditions. It is to help them perceive human experience through the artistic images which, in the judgment of the tradition, were of special significance. That this is worthwhile rests on the more general argument for cultivation of human powers to which allusion has been made, but more importantly on the belief that such induction defeats the negative import of imposition and lays the foundation for enlightened autonomy. As Michael Polanyi has put it:[10]

The assimilation of great systems of articulate lore by novices of various grades is made possible only by a *previous act of affiliation*, by which the novice accepts apprenticeship to a community which cultivates this lore, appreciates its values and strives to act by its standards. This affiliation begins with the fact that a child submits to education within a community, and it is confirmed throughout life to the extent to which the adult continues to place exceptional confidence in the intellectual leaders of the same community.

However, even as a mode of induction, aesthetic education need not and should not be a branch of intellectual or cultural history. One can still insist that the induction be through imaginative perception. The difference between this approach and that previously described as perceptual lies not in the method of teaching but in the materials chosen for study. In choosing works that the tradition has already validated as significant, we are doing more than merely training perception; we are exposing the pupil to normative decisions made *for* him rather than *by* him. In the former approach no such selection is needed, and in strictly contemporary art no such selection is possible.

Either approach is a way of acquainting the pupil with the canons of the credentialled group—both give the pupil a sample of the way the expert perceives and judges. Whether development of imaginative perception is as far as we need to go in aesthetic education is not altogether clear. To do so would be a departure from the mode of induction into the disciplines that order our other modes of experience. And whether the perceptual approach is really as neutral as it purports to be is also something that needs careful scrutiny. However, the process itself seems to me a necessary condition for any conception of aesthetic education as a distinctive ingredient in the curriculum.

Summary

The problems to which this paper is addressed have to do with the understanding of the current demands for and the justification of a program of aesthetic education as part of general education. This includes an attempt to find a distinctive function that is not now being adequately performed in standard curricula. Both of these requirements are filled by regarding aesthetic experience as imaginative perception of human import by means of sensory image.

In arguing for the value of the arts as producers of such images, one may point to their originative role as a source of possible new life forms, a dearth of which may be regarded as a result of our technological advances outstripping our capacity to translate them into life styles that will bear moral scrutiny. Art in its celebrative role objectifies significant values of the group in image.

These functions impose somewhat different tasks for aesthetic education. To exploit the originative function of art the emphasis is put on discerning, and discriminating among, the sensory, formal, technical, and expressive properties of the aesthetic object. Training with respect to the first three types of property presents no special problem, but response to the expressive properties cannot be taught directly. The perceptual approach has many advantages over its rivals. Nevertheless, these advantages may not be sufficiently persuasive for those who seek reinforcement of norms in aesthetic education. Teaching selected works of art as great or good art or as exemplifying extra-aesthetic norms runs into the problem of imposition of norms as a threat to the autonomy of the pupil. It was argued that the problem of imposition is not unique to aesthetic education; that it rests on a confusion between philosophical criteria for value norms and institutional criteria. The latter are provided by a consensus of credentialled experts who constitute a living tradition into which the young are inducted. This, it is held, deprives 'imposition' of its negative import. In any event, development of imaginative perception is to be regarded as a necessary if not sufficient requirement for aesthetic education.[11]

Notes

1 Alvin Toffler, *The Culture Consumers: Art and Affluence in America*, Penguin, 1964; and a less optimistic interpretation in William J. Baumol and William G. Bowen, *Performing Arts: The Economic Dilemma*, A Twentieth Century Fund Study, 1966.
2 In the United States music and drawing (art) are required in the first six grades but are given in small doses by an art specialist or by a generalist who is usually uncomfortable in either medium. At the secondary level, the arts are usually elective. At both levels, the instruction approximates a simplified version of studio training in performance. Except among the most rigid of the specialists, it is generally agreed that this sort of instruction does little to develop the aesthetic perception or imagination, as they would like to have it do. Even less enthusiastic are they about conventional courses in art appreciation, which tend to reduce the aesthetic experience to illustrations of program notes about familiar works of art.
3 Monroe Beardsley, *Aesthetics: Problems in the Philosophy of Criticism*, New York, Harcourt, Brace and World, 1958, ch. I.
4 Benedetto Croce, *Aesthetics*, trans. Douglas Ainslee, 2nd ed., New York, Macmillan, 1922.
5 Bernard Bosanquet, 'The Aesthetic Attitude and its Embodiments', in *Three Lectures on Aesthetic*, Macmillan, 1915.

6 Whether aesthetic education as a distinctive type of instruction is possible and necessary depends somewhat on whether aesthetic experience is itself identifiable as a distinctive mode of experience. While I am impressed by the difficulty of arriving at a fixed genus-differentia definition of aesthetic experience, I am not convinced that it is not useful to try to demarcate the aesthetic domain. For example, Morris Weitz in 'The Role of Theory in Esthetics', *The Journal of Aesthetics and Art Criticism*, vol. 15, p. 1056, argues against the possibility of a closed or fixed definition of art. However, in commenting on Wittgenstein's metaphorical use of family resemblances as a substitute for definition by common and essential properties, Mandelbaum notes that taken literally, family resemblances are based on really common genetic ties which, of course, are not observable in physiognomic resemblances. Similarly in games the purpose of a game may contain a genuinely common characteristic with other games that is not obvious when we note only how games are played. Maurice Mandelbaum, 'Family Resemblances and Generalizations Concerning the Arts', *American Philosophical Quarterly*, vol. 2, no. 3, July 1965.

7 The evidence on which this optimism is based comes from having taught for many years a seminar in the foundations of aesthetic education to a collection of students from the various arts; from participation in workshops with teachers at the elementary and secondary level. In relatively short periods of time they learned the things to look for in the various media and a vocabulary in which to discuss them.

8 For a helpful note on this aspect of aesthetic education, see Virgil C. Aldrich, 'Education for Aesthetic Vision', *The Journal of Aesthetic Education*, vol. 2, no. 4, October 1968, pp. 101–8. The objection is some-times raised that perceptibility is not a necessary condition for the aesthetic object and the elegance of a mathematical formulation is cited as a counter-example. I find it difficult to 'imagine' what one would be admiring if not some image of perfection, symmetry or the like. In any event the objection, even if it could be sustained, would not, it seems to me, impair the advantages of the perceptual approach to aesthetic education.

9 D. W. Gotshalk, *Art and the Social Order*, University of Chicago Press, 1947, explores these possibilities in detail, but above all makes clear that this does not destroy the autonomy of aesthetic experience.

10 *Personal Knowledge*, University of Chicago Press, 1958, p. 207.

11 For a somewhat different approach to the justification of aesthetic education, see R. A. and C. M. Smith, 'Justifying Aesthetic Education', *The Journal of Aesthetic Education*, vol. 4, no. 2, pp. 37–52, April 1970.

The aesthetic dimension of education: A reply

7

Kingsley Price

I

The arts, Professor Broudy holds, embody values that are appropriate to all men, but they have never been presented seriously in public education in America. They have been retained in its curriculum on a small scale to salve the conscience of educators rather than to advance the higher culture. Since the mid-sixties, their place in the curriculum has become even less secure. It has been undermined by the youth revolution's contempt for the establishment and magnification of popular culture, praise of their own arts by minority groups, and growing sentiment against the life of intellect. Aesthetic education, Professor Broudy suggests, will bring the youthful revolutionary to an allegiance to the arts that will enlighten his criticism of the establishment, will show minorities that there is something in the higher culture worth possessing that will not dissipate the enjoyment of their own, and will raise a barrier that will protect the life of intellect against the destructive flood of contrary sentiment.

Aesthetic education is cultivation of aesthetic perception of the arts. This perception is intrinsically good; and for that reason, the revolutionary, the minority member, and the anti-intellectual will want to engage in it. But it possesses two other traits that make it useful. From it, new ideals of human conduct may be derived; it is 'originative.' In it, events that are important to human life are praised and commemorated; it is 'celebrative.' Aesthetic perception of the arts is valuable both intrinsically and instrumentally; and for this reason, giving the arts a wider and more stable place in the curriculum will help to solve the problems attendant upon the youth revolution, the clamor for equality of minority groups, and the swelling tide of anti-intellectualism.

The cultivation of aesthetic perception consists in four distinct tasks. The first is to foster in the student the ability to perceive art in all its sensory individuality. This task requires that the student be taught how to suspend interests such as the economic and moral, that would lead him to overlook or to distort the sensory character-

10

istics of art. Secondly, the student must be accustomed to look for form or design. Thirdly, he must be brought to an acquaintance with the various techniques for producing art. And fourthly, he must be made able to perceive the expressiveness of art—the most difficult and unformulable of the four tasks. Art's sensory individuality, its form, its technique, and its expressiveness—all these are sources of its value; and if aesthetic education is thoroughly successful, it will teach the student to find them all.

The aesthetic dimension of education, as I understand Professor Broudy, is the possibility, outlined above of channeling the discontent of alienation toward traditional values without destroying its creative and innovative impulse. I want now to raise the question whether the four tasks involved in aesthetic education are adequate to this redirection of energetic discontent.

II

There is a distinction that runs throughout the arts that must be mentioned. Some of them are performing arts, such as those of music, of drama, and of dance. The others are creative arts; and they are typified by sculpture and architecture. And within the creative arts, there is a three-fold distinction which is also fundamental. Each may be thought of as an ability; the art Cézanne acquired was his ability to paint pictures. Each may be thought of as an activity; when Cézanne was painting, he was exhibiting his art. And each may be thought of as a set of works—the works of art that result from the activity; Cézanne's art is found wherever his works are shown. But the performing arts do not contain this three-fold distinction. The musical performer, in distinction from the composer, possesses an ability; his ability to perform musical compositions. And he engages in an activity—the activity of performing compositions. But there is nothing of his art of performance that results from his activity of performing like the Clarinet Quintet that resulted from Mozart's activity; or the Laocoön that resulted from Agesander's: the creative arts are abilities that manifest themselves in activities that result in works of art such as musical scores, sculptures, and buildings. But the performing arts are abilities that manifest themselves in activities of performances that have no results—in activities that make evident, simply, the content of works like the Clarinet Quintet that result from creation.

We must notice a second distinction. This is the distinction between appreciating, on the one hand, and creating and performing on the other. A work of art is created by its artist; and his attitude toward it, is that of a creator toward what results from his activity. For the sculptor, the sculpture is something to be brought into existence; and his activity of sculpting is pervaded by the intent of altering his material until it falls into a condition he finds satisfactory. For the performer, a work of art is something to be performed; and his attitude is the intent to follow the score, the manuscript, or the choreographic notation in such a way that each is properly manifest in his performance. In the one case, the creator deals with his material in such a way as to produce something that may remain after his activity has lapsed—the work of his art. In the other, the performer looks to do something already created— the score, the play, or the dance notation—as the governor of his activity of performance. But the activity of appreciating is quite unlike that of creating and of performing. It looks neither to a future result as its product, nor to a past accomplishment as its guide. When we appreciate a work of art, we do nothing that can be determined by a future possibility or a past achievement. We simply open the doors of perception, however complicated an act that may be, to what is before them, guiding our actions only by clues that are found in what is present. To create is to bring something into existence; to perform is to act in accord with a set of instructions laid down in the past. But to appreciate is neither of these. It is, simply, to be aware (with favor or disfavor) of what now exists before the mind.

III

We must now ask whether the aesthetic perception of the arts that aesthetic education cultivates is perception of the creative or performing arts, of abilities, activities, or works; and whether it is appreciation, creation, or performance.

A consideration of the four tasks in which aesthetic education consists yields a part of the answer. The first, to cultivate awareness of sensory individuality cannot be directed upon abilities, creative or performatory; abilities have no sensory characteristics. Nor can it be directed upon creative activities. For even though creative activities may be individual, they have largely vanished into the past like those of Mozart and of Michelangelo. Besides, Professor Broudy can hardly be supposed to hold that aesthetic education is the cultivation of our perception of creative artists at work. Such cultivation would foster not aesthetic perception, but surveillance of creators.

But aesthetic perception is directed, *inter alia*, upon activities of performance. These are exemplified in a performance of the Clarinet

Quintet, a performance of the *Tempest*, and a performance of *Swan Lake*. These performatory activities clearly possess sensory individuality; and the awareness of it in them and in their fellows is surely included in the aesthetic perception Professor Broudy would have us cultivate.

But is aesthetic perception the appreciation, the creation, or the performance of compositions, of plays, and of dances? Professor Broudy describes it as the perception of import-bearing images. Now it is evident that creation of an image must differ from the perception of it. The creation of an image is the process that brings it into existence, and that must lapse when it comes to life; so that since it does not exist, when its product does, it cannot be the perception of the image. But the activity of presenting an image in a performance also cannot be the perception of the image. For the performer does something; he does not perceive the image despite the fact that he reproduces it. And the perception of import-bearing images, presented in performance, that aesthetic education cultivates must be the appreciation of them—the holding of the images before the mind in all their sensory individuality. It is the audience's perception.

It includes, also, the appreciation of works that cannot be performed. It is clear that their perception is not their creation, and that the notion of performance is quite inapplicable to them. To perceive a statue cannot be to create it, and to perform a statue is an absurdity. Hence the perception of works that cannot be performed, as well as that of performances, is the appreciation of them that an audience engages in.

The first task of aesthetic education is the cultivation of aesthetic perception of the presentation in performance of import-bearing images, and of the works of art, like sculptures, buildings, and paintings, which are not activities as performances are, but things that result from activities of creation.

The other three tasks—the cultivation of the perception of form, of technique, and of expressiveness—are clearly directed also, upon performances and upon works that cannot be performed, rather than upon artistic abilities and creative activities; and it is clear that the aesthetic perception that each would cultivate is the appreciation of performances and works rather than the performances themselves and the creation of the works involved. For the characteristics whose perception these tasks further either cannot attach to abilities and to the process of creation on pain of absurdity, or where they can, they are not among those things, the cultivation of whose perception would be furthered. What could be, for example, the technique or the expressiveness of an ability or a process? And how could anyone regard the form of an ability as something to be perceived aesthetically even though there may be a sense in which abilities may be described as possessed of form? And the perception of form, of technique, and of expressiveness in performances and works cannot be thought of as identical with the performances that have these traits, or as identical with the processes of creation from which the things that have them result. It is appreciation; and all the four tasks into which aesthetic education is resolved are directed toward the cultivation of the audience's appreciation of performances and of works, like buildings, to which the notion of performance cannot be applied.

IV

It is quite likely that the four tasks of aesthetic education, should they be taken seriously, might succeed. It is quite likely, that is to say, that if those who are alienated from the performances and works of the traditional arts were seriously exposed to them, they might come to appreciate their sensory, formal, technical, and expressive qualities. But we must notice that the success of the four tasks would consist in the student's opening the doors of his perception to these performances and works, and viewing them with enlightened enjoyment. But this act of opening the mind is passive; and while it might alter greatly the things upon which the student focuses his enjoyment, no more than that might result. The intrinsic value that art possesses might eventuate in no change in the student's interests other than a change in taste.

For in appreciating something, one is doing nothing: but it is the doing of things that establishes those habits of mind that constitute character, and that constitute, when new, a change in character. Plato held that of the two forms of literature, narration and imitation, the former is less likely to be troublesome. For telling a story of bad character leads, at the worst, to the appreciation of such things; while the imitation of bad character—its portrayal in dramatic action—leads to the establishment in the actor of the bad habits enacted. And we may interpret his discussion in the *Republic* (Book III) as holding that to establish a good character, the student should be brought not merely to appreciate the good in human life, but through performances that display good character, to the possession of its ingredients.

But Professor Broudy wishes, I believe, to do more than to improve taste. He points to the originative and the celebrative traits of performances and works; and in them (especially in the originative), he points to the power that great performances and works may have to inspire new ideals of conduct. If these are to be generated by aesthetic education, the conception of its four tasks must be broadened a little. We must think of it as directed toward the cultivation of aesthetic perception, as he suggests; but we must think of it, also, as the fostering of the impulse to create works that cannot be performed, like buildings, cities, national societies, and even an international community; and the creation and performance of performatory works like plays and dances. The exercise of these abilities, and the performance of these works may establish habits of loving the good that go beyond appreciation to direct the energies of alienation to a positive construction.

Aesthetic education, if it is to accomplish the objective laid down for it, should be conceived as the cultivation of aesthetic creation and performance as well as that of aesthetic perception.

Part 4

Freedom and the development of the free man[1] 8

R. S. Peters

Introduction

There is a presupposition implicit in the writings and practices of educators which is of interest in its own right and to educational theory generally. It is that some desirable state of mind or character-trait will be best developed by an institution whose workings reflect the principle, which is thought desirable when personalized as a character-trait. Thus Plato assumed that justice in the individual soul would flourish in a society whose organization satisfied the conditions required by this principle. The institution of punishment has been defended on similar grounds. It is claimed that it is a manifest exemplar of justice and that children who witness its operation will receive the imprint of justice on their minds. Alternatively it is assumed that if certain procedures characterize the working of an institution (e.g., rules decided by appeals to authority, by democratic discussion, etc.) corresponding attitudes of mind will be fostered amongst its members. A. S. Neill, for instance, assumes that his ideal of self-regulation or freedom of the individual will be best developed in an institution in which external regulation is at a minimum, and in which such regulation as there is does not stem from the authority of adults.

It is this type of assumption which, in my view, lies behind the intuitive plausibility of so much educational argument. A. S. Neill is actually very guarded in his claims for the long-term effects of Summerhill on its inmates. And what he does claim is based purely on selective impressions. He has conducted no surveys to find out how many of his previous pupils have succumbed to the 'fear of freedom', and ended up as members of the Communist Party, the Catholic Church or as conformists. Nevertheless, he persists with his type of school and, I suspect, would be absolutely unconvinced by negative evidence of this mundane sort. He would offer some special explanation of cases in which children of servile dispositions issue forth from an institution in which freedom, as a social principle, is 'writ large'.

There are, as far as I know, no empirical studies which can be produced to test this assumption. Yet the interesting point is that considerations can be produced to support or to cast doubt on its plausibility. By examining what is meant by 'freedom' in a social context, like that of a school, and what is meant by a 'free man', some suggestions can be made about the connexion between the two. To connect them some assumptions would also have to be made about human learning. But I must not, by developing this point any further at this stage, anticipate one of the main points which I want to discuss in this paper. For it has a three-fold intention behind it. I propose to take 'freedom' as an example of the general assumption about the fit between institutions and states of mind. To develop my general thesis I will first examine the concept or concepts of 'freedom' in education and distinguish the various things that might be meant. Secondly I will explore what is involved in learning to be free, including the status of the presupposition about the influence of institutions on learning in this sphere. This will lead, finally, to a few general reflections about human learning arising from this particular case of it.

I The analysis of 'freedom'

In approaching these questions I shall attempt no new analysis of 'freedom'. In the main I shall rely on the distinctions already worked out by Stanley Benn[2] and William Weinstein: (i) freedom as a social principle, (ii) man as a chooser, (iii) autonomy, which are particularly helpful in an educational context. My use of their analysis, however, will be strictly tailored to its relevance for discussing how individuals learn to be free.

(i) Freedom as a social principle

If we say that a man is not free to do something we are suggesting that there is something or somebody that is stopping him. We assume that there is something that he might want or choose to do and we suggest that there is some closing up of the options available to him. The most obvious way of closing up a person's options is to restrict his bodily movements by tying him up or imprisoning him. But more usual ways are the making of laws and regulations, giving him commands, and subjecting him to a variety of social and personal pressures.

It is common-place of political theory that the state of natural freedom is an illusion. If there are no levelling constraints like those of law and custom, men do not in fact live unconstrained lives. Those who are physically or psychologically weak are constrained by those who are strong. In spheres, therefore, in which people care what others do and in which it is possible for them to interfere with them, freedom in fact prevails only if there is a general system of regulation which safeguards these spheres against interference from others. This is an empirical generalization derivative from certain facts about human nature and the conditions under which men live. It is not, as many enemies of freedom have argued, a conceptual truth about the meaning of 'freedom'. For 'freedom' manifestly does not mean the acceptance of constraints. It is just a general empirical fact that the acceptance of some forms of constraint by all is necessary for the avoidance of more grievous forms of constraint by some others. This so-called 'paradox of freedom' is extremely relevant to a school situation; for the constraints of the bully or the peer-group take over if the more explicit levelling constraints issuing from the staff or from the community as a whole, are withdrawn.[3] There are also more subtle forms of social pressure—e.g., those issuing from a charismatic teacher who may believe fervently in freedom—which may be more damaging to freedom in a more fundamental sense, than the straightforward exercise of authority. What, then, is this sense?

(ii) Man as a chooser

Presupposed by this analysis of 'freedom' as a social principle is the notion of man as a chooser who can have his option closed up in various ways by the acts of other men. We speak of various spheres of authority as being spheres where individuals are not free to do as they please. Yet there is also an important connexion between 'authority' and 'consent' or 'choice' as many writers in political theory have pointed out. We often, though not always, obey a command because we accord its author a right to tell us what to do. In the case of a voluntary club or association we do actually commit ourselves to its constitution and rules when we join it and we can leave it if we so choose. And in other spheres of authority, even if we have not explicitly committed ourselves in this way, it is open to us to reject the system as binding on us. Similarly if a person is playing football his freedom of action is limited by the rules and by the referee's decisions. But he can choose not to play football. There are difficulties, of course, about obedience to a state if there is nowhere to live that is not under the jurisdiction of some state. There are difficulties about leaving a place of employment if the alternative is the dole. But even in these dire extremities a person still remains a *chooser* even if the alternatives open to him are such that we might say that he has no choice or Hobson's choice.

In a school situation there are plenty of cases in which we would say that a student is not free to do certain things but that he still remains a chooser. For instance, he may not be free to run in the corridors, but he may, in fact, do so, knowing full well the penalty if he is caught. Indeed he may defy the whole system of rules and end up by being expelled. These situations of explicit subordination, or of refusal to be subordinated, need to be distinguished from those in which the notion of choice seems out of place. Suppose that a girl has an obsessive passion for a master. To do anything which he forbad, or of which he disapproved, would never enter her head. Indeed she might constantly look for things to do of which he approved and, if he told her to fast for a week or to steal, she would fall in with his wishes. In respect of her dealings with him she cannot really be described as a chooser; for alternatives that are presented to her are not really alternatives if they involve in any way going against his wishes. Like a person under post-hypnotic suggestion she may conjure up other alternatives and invent other reasons for doing what she is bent on doing anyway; but this is a mere shadow-play. She is really programmed to do what he wants. This kind of situation can exist in a school which has a normal authority structure; or it may exist in a progressive school that prides itself on the absence of such a structure. The lack of freedom involved is perhaps more dire than that of a situation structured by explicit regulation; for the girl is unfree in a more fundamental sense than are those who keep or break rules in a more straightforward way.

This type of case is a mild and usually short-term example of a range of cases about which we might say that an individual is no longer a chooser. They differ from the first application of 'freedom' to social situations in which what Benn calls the *objective* conditions of choice are interfered with or loaded in various ways—e.g., by threats, imposition of sanctions, etc. In this second type of case, in which we sometimes speak of 'unfreedom', men cease to be choosers, because there are various defects or interferences with the *subjective* conditions which are necessary for choice.

The forms of impairment to subjective conditions can roughly be indicated by setting out what we normally assume when people are in what I have elsewhere called a situation of practical reason, when they ask themselves the question 'Why do this rather than that?'[4]

(a) We assume that there is more than one type of end which can function for them as a goal. They do not, as it were, veer towards 'this' rather than 'that' like a moth towards a light. A man who had been starved for a week would probably not satisfy this condition. He would be 'driven' towards a goal. Drug addicts and alcoholics do not satisfy this condition in relation to a whole range of their deliberations.

(b) We assume that people are capable of weighing the pros and cons of the alternatives before them without being paralysed by indecision or going out of the field in some other way. Some hysterics would not satisfy this condition.

(c) We assume that the weight which people attach to different alternatives can be influenced by information which is relevant to the validity of their beliefs. Paranoiacs, or people suffering from other sorts of delusions or obsessions, would not satisfy this condition. For they hold on to beliefs in the face of relevant evidence, because their beliefs cannot deviate from the lines dictated by some irrational wish or aversion.

(d) We assume that changes in people's beliefs about 'this' or 'that' can modify their decisions. A psychopath, for whom the future has a kind of unreality and who is unmoved by the unpleasantness which he sees to be the probable consequences of his actions, and which he wishes to avoid, would not qualify in this respect.

(e) We assume that people's decisions can be translated into appropriate actions. A compulsive would fail to satisfy this condition.

(*iii*)   *Autonomy*

Our normal expectation of a person is that he is a chooser—that he can be deterred by thoughts of the consequences of his actions, that he is not paranoid or compulsive and so on. But such a person might be a time-serving, congenial conformist, or an easy-going, weak-willed, opportunist. Being a chooser is a standard expected of anyone— which is related to norms of rationality or mental health;[5] it is not an ideal of conduct or of education. Certainly progressive educators, such as A. S. Neill, who equates freedom with self-regulation, have been concerned with more than this limited objective. What, then, has to be added for a chooser to develop into an ideal type of character in which being free features? To ask this is to ask for the criteria for calling a person 'autonomous'.

Authenticity

Etymologically 'autonomy' suggests that a person accepts or makes rules for himself. This is clear in what it denies but not altogether clear in what it asserts. It denies that the individual's code of conduct is simply one that he has picked up from others or adopted in any second-hand way. The rules which he lives by are not just those that are laid down by custom or authority. Hence the stress on authenticity going right back to Socrates' 'care of the soul'. This asserts positively that there must be some feature of a course of conduct, which the individual regards as important, which constitutes a non-artificial reason for pursuing it as distinct from extrinsic reasons provided by praise and blame, reward and punishment, and so on, which are artificially created by the demands of others. But beyond this point it is a matter of controversy as to what is asserted by the stress on autonomy. Presumably it would be consistent with a doctrine sometimes put into the mouth of D. H. Lawrence's characters that a course of conduct should be pursued that is congenial to the 'dark god' within, namely sex, which determines the lines of individual self-assertion. For this is represented as what the individual really wants as distinct from what conformity dictates. Or it would be consistent with some existentialist doctrine of 'criterionless choice', in so far as this can be rendered intelligible.

Rational reflection

More usually, however, autonomy is positively associated with assessment and criticism, as in Stanley Benn's account in his paper on *Conditions of Autonomy*. The individual is conceived of as being aware of rules as alterable conventions which structure his social life. He subjects them to reflection and criticism in the light of principles and gradually emerges with his own code of conduct. This is the Kantian conception of autonomy in which the 'subjective maxims' of the individual are subjected to critical examination in the light of principles such as those of impartiality and respect for persons. This does not mean that he must always reflect before he acts and ponder on the validity of a rule which he is applying; for such a man would be a moral imbecile without settled principles. It only means that he has thought about rules in this way and has a disposition to do so if he finds himself in a situation where changed circumstances intimate some adaptation of his code.

Strength of will

It is possible for a person to have a code of conduct which he has worked out for himself but to be too weak-willed to stick to it. Usually, however, when people speak of a person being autonomous they mean that he not only has thought out his own code but that he is also capable of sticking to it in the face of counter-inclinations. Autonomy, in other words, also suggests executive virtues such as courage, integrity and determination. It is revealed not simply in the refusal to adopt second-hand beliefs or rules, but also in holding steadfast in *conduct* against counter-inclinations which also incline an individual to be heteronomous in his point of view. For the counter-inclinations, which are relevant to weakness of will, are often those springing from types of motivation that make 'authenticity' in belief difficult. The strong-willed man, like the independently minded man, sticks to his principles in the face of ridicule, ostracism, punishment and bribes. There is thus a close connexion between autonomy and strength of will but the connexion is probably a contingent one to be explained in terms of the group of counter-inclinations that are necessary to give application both to the notion of authenticity and to that of strength of will.

There is thus a gradation of conditions implicit in the idea of autonomy. The first basic condition is that of authenticity, of adopting a code or way of life that is one's own as distinct from one dictated by others. The second condition of rational reflection on rules is one espoused by most believers in autonomy. To discuss whether it is essential to autonomy would involve discussing the intelligibility of romantic and existentialist alternatives, which is beyond the scope of this paper. For the purpose of this paper, however, it will be assumed to be a necessary condition of autonomy. The third possible condition, that of strength of will, seems to be much more contingently associated with autonomy, and will be ignored.

II The development of the free man

So much, then, for the different ways in which 'being free' can be understood. The lynch-pin of the analysis is the notion of man as a chooser, a rational being placed in what I have called the situation of practical reason. This is a presupposition of 'freedom' as a social principle; for a man who is 'not free' is one who has his options closed up in one way or other and this presupposes a being of whom it makes sense to say that he has options, i.e., that he is a chooser. In education, however, we are usually concerned with more than just preserving the capacity for choice; we are also concerned with the ideal of personal autonomy, which is a development of some of the potentialities inherent in the notion of man as a chooser. The concept of 'freedom' has now been sufficiently analysed to permit us to say a few things about the development of free men. Manifestly, in a paper of this length, there cannot be a massive marshalling of empirical studies which throw light on the conditions under which free men emerge. There is point, however, as will later be substantiated when something is said about the role of philosophy in the study of human learning, in giving an indication of the sorts of conditions that seem obviously relevant. For when we talk about the 'development' of free men we surely have in mind some process of learning, rather than some causal process such as is involved in the development of a photograph or of a plant. What, then, could be meant by 'learning' if it is suggested that human beings learn to become choosers or autonomous human beings?

There is a general concept of 'learning' used by most psychologists to draw attention to changes of behaviour that are not the product purely of maturation. I am not concerned with this general concept but only with the more specific one in which the changes in question are the result of past experience. At the centre of learning in this specific sense is some content that a learner makes his own by various processes of assimilation. He may copy it, grasp it, imitate it, memorize it and so on, depending on the type of content that it is. And what he can make his own depends largely on the existing state of his cognitive structure, 'structure' being understood as referring not just to what he has already assimilated in the way of content but also to how that content is conceived. For instance, for most of us so-called 'instrumental conditioning' operates only because we are capable of discerning a link between doing something and being rewarded, even though the link may be one of the extrinsic type referred to in the previous section. Similarly once a child has grasped the concept of a 'thing' he can quickly learn to recognize a variety of things such as bricks and balls by being presented with instances of them and having their features pointed out to him.

Now there are some concepts, such as that of 'thing' in the latter example of learning and 'means-to-an-end' in the former example, which are of particular importance in mental development in the theories of psychologists such as Piaget and Kohlberg, who have been much influenced by Kant. For they are categoreal concepts marking stages in the development of the human mind in that they define forms of human understanding and hence set limits to what can be learnt by imposing a framework for the assimilation of content. These fundamental types of concept, they argue, cannot therefore be taught by any process of direct instruction; rather they emerge as a result of the interaction between a mind equipped with potentialities for ordering and selecting and an environment which has invariant features which are there to discover. This kind of development, however, can be aided by what Kohlberg calls 'cognitive stimulation', which he contrasts with explicit instruction (see Kohlberg, 1968, 1969).

It is, surely, the learning of forms of understanding such as these (e.g., seeing something as a 'means to an end') rather than the assimilation of any particular content of experience that is crucial for the development of free men. Let me try to illustrate this contention briefly in the case of the development of the capacity for choice and in that of the achievement of autonomy.

(*i*) *Becoming a chooser*

An account of becoming a chooser was sketched in section I (ii) by reference, mainly, to various forms of impairment in what were called, following Stanley Benn, 'subjective conditions'. But these themselves presuppose certain standing conditions without which they would be unintelligible. Being able to weigh up the pros and cons of alternatives and to act in the light of such deliberation presupposes that the individual can think in terms of taking means to an end. He appreciates, to a certain extent, the causal properties of things and can distinguish consequences brought about by his own agency from things that come about independently of his will. To do this he must possess the categoreal concepts of 'thinghood', 'causality', and 'means to an end'. These enable him to think 'realistically' in contradistinction to small children and paranoiacs whose consciousness is dominated by wishes and aversions. It presupposes, too, that he has a view of the world as an orderly system in which his confidence in his own powers and his expectations about the future will be confirmed. This is particularly important if his choice involves the delay of immediate gratification. Unlike the psychopath, the future is real to him and he has a steady disposition to take account of facts—both future and present. To regard himself as, to a certain extent, a determiner of his own destiny, which he must do if he is a chooser, he must have a sense of his own identity and that of others.

In developmental psychology there are two complementary approaches which throw light on these preconditions of choice. Piaget and his followers have mapped the stages at which this categoreal apparatus emerges; Freud and his followers, on the other hand, though allowing for the development of this apparatus in the doctrine of the 'ego', have concentrated more on the conditions under which it fails to emerge. They have shown the extent to which infantile, primary processes of thought persist in the mind of the adult and prevent it working rationally according to the principles dictated by this categoreal apparatus.

Piaget and Kohlberg, as has already been explained, argue that the development of this categoreal apparatus is the product, not of explicit teaching, but of cognitive stimulation. I will leave aside problematic Chomsky-type questions of the extent to which the emergence of this cognitive apparatus is innately determined; I will also leave aside the problems in the distinction made by Kohlberg between 'teaching' and 'cognitive stimulation'.[6] For, whatever allowance is made for other variables, the role of social influences which are connected with such 'stimulation' can be inferred from the fact that failure to develop such an apparatus has been shown by psychologists more interested in the Freudian type of approach, to be connected with certain types of socialization or lack of it. Most pathological states can be described in terms of the absence of features of this apparatus and these defects can be correlated with typical conditions in early childhood. It is generally agreed, for instance, that psychopaths who live on their whims and impulses for whom the future has little reality, and who have a way of thinking about the world rather like that of a young infant, are largely the product of homes which are rejecting towards the child and which provide a very inconsistent type of discipline.[7] Schizophrenics, whose belief-structure, especially in regard to their own identity, is deranged, are thought by some to be products of discrepant and irreconcilable attitudes towards them before they developed a secure sense of reality. They lack what Laing calls the 'ontological security' of a person who has developed the categoreal apparatus which is definitive of being a rational being or a chooser. As Laing puts it (1965, p. 39):

> Such a basically ontologically secure person will encounter all the hazards of life . . . from a centrally firm sense of his own and other people's reality and identity. It is often difficult for a person with such a sense of his integral selfhood and personal identity, of the permanency of things, of the reliability of natural processes, of the substantiality of others, to transpose himself into the world of an individual whose experiences may be utterly lacking in any unquestionable self-validating certainties.

There is no need to multiply examples of failures to develop the apparatus necessary for becoming a chooser and to attempt to relate them to various types of defects in 'normal social conditions'. To do this thoroughly would necessitate writing a text-book on psychopathology. Of equal interest, however, from the point of view of educators, are cases of people who could be termed 'unreasonable' rather than 'irrational',[8] and whose way of life bears witness to the limited development of the capacities necessary for being a chooser, which again seem to be the product of a certain type of socialization. An example of such a limited form of development is given by Josephine Klein in her book *Samples of English Culture* (1965). She singles out certain abilities which are presupposed in the account of being a chooser given in section I (ii) above. They are the ability to abstract and use generalizations, the ability to perceive the world as an ordered universe in which rational action is rewarded, the ability to plan ahead and to exercise self-control. She cites evidence from Luria and Bernstein to show that the extent to which these abilities develop depends on the prevalence of an elaborated form of language which is found in some strata of society but not in others. She also shows how the beliefs and conduct of some working class sub-cultures are affected by the arbitrariness of their child-rearing techniques. Such happy-go-lucky people have a stunted capacity for choice because the future has only a limited relevance for them and because they are prejudiced, myopic, and unreflective in their beliefs.[9]

So far examples have been given of the capacity for choice being impaired or stunted by others who, usually unwittingly, treat children in ways which bring about these results. It need hardly be added that these capacities can be neutralized, perhaps permanently impaired, by more conscious techniques which are combined together in brain-washing. The individual's categoreal apparatus can be attacked by making his environment as unpredictable as possible; his sense of time and place and of his own identity can be systematically undermined. He is gradually reduced to a state of acute anxiety, perhaps of mental breakdown, in which he is in a receptive state to being dominated by another who becomes the sole source of pleasure and security for him. He becomes suggestible and willing to accept beliefs, which, in his former life, he would have rejected out of hand. He becomes more or less a programmed man rather than a chooser. Domination by another can also take less dramatic and more temporary forms, as in some case of being in love which in Freud's view belongs to the same family as being hypnotized. There are some people, who sometimes find their way into the teaching profession, who seem to have this kind of hypnotic effect on others. These kinds of influence, which neutralize the capacity for choice, must be distinguished from others such as manipulation by bribing and threats, or feeding people with false information, which presuppose it. For these techniques rely on manipulation of the objective conditions of choice; they do not constitute an assault on the subjective conditions which are definitive of being a chooser.

It is not difficult to surmise why the most consistent finding from studies of child-rearing practices is that sensible children, who are capable of rational choice, seem to emerge from homes in which there is a warm attitude of acceptance towards children, together with a firm and consistent insistence on rules of behaviour without much in the way of punishment. An accepting attitude towards a child will tend to encourage trust in others and confidence in his own powers. A predictable social environment will provide the type of experience which is necessary for guiding behaviour by reflection on its consequences and so build up a belief in a future which is in part shaped by his own behaviour. Inconsistency in treatment, on the other hand, will encourage plumping rather than choosing and attachment to instant gratification; and a rejecting attitude will inhibit the development of the self-confidence which is necessary for being a chooser.

(*ii*) *The development of autonomy*

It could well be that teachers should be much more mindful than they are of the possibility that many children come to them impaired or stunted in their capacity for choice, and that they should be more mindful of providing an environment which encourages it. In particular, perhaps, they should be chary of imposing a 'self-chosen curriculum' too quickly on children from homes in which there is little encouragement for children to be choosers. The fact is, however, that when teachers talk of 'freedom' as an educational ideal they usually have in mind the development of autonomy or self-regulation which is a far more ambitious ideal.

In thinking about a child's progress towards this ideal the work of Piaget and Kohlberg, which is confirmed by that of Peck and Havighurst, is most illuminating. There is a general consensus that children pass through various stages in their conception of rules which is independent of the content of the rules concerned. They pass from regarding conformity to rules purely as a way of avoiding punishment and obtaining rewards to a level at which rules are regarded as entities in themselves that are just 'there' and which emanate from the collective will of the group and from people in authority. They finally pass to the level of autonomy, when they appreciate that rules are alterable, that they can be criticized and should be accepted or rejected on a basis of reciprocity and fairness.[10] The emergence of rational reflection about rules, which in section I (iii) was regarded as central to the Kantian conception of autonomy, is the main feature of the final level of moral development. Kohlberg produces cross-cultural evidence to support the general claim of the Piaget school, already mentioned, that these stages of development in the conception of rules are culturally invariant. He emphasizes that the explanation of this is that the levels of conceiving of rules is in a hierarchical logical order; so there could be no other order in which development occurs. Though cultures differ in the content of rules, there is thus an invariant order in the way in which rules are conceived, although, of course, in many cultures there is no emergence to the autonomous stage.[11] Kohlberg makes the same claim about the limitations of teaching in this sphere as he makes with regard to the teaching of categories for thinking about the physical world such as causality and conservation. He argues that, though the content of rules is learnt by teaching or imitation, the form of conceiving of them is the product of interaction with the environment that can be accelerated or retarded by the amount of cognitive stimulation available.

Here again there are findings which emphasize the importance of the social environment, provided that we do not enter into niceties as to what is to be called 'teaching'. Kohlberg himself stresses the difference in rate and level of development towards autonomy of those who come from middle-class homes, in which there is plenty of 'cognitive stimulation'; and those who come from working-class homes. There is, too, a series of investigations by Bruner and his associates which are more far-reaching in their implications. He conducted experiments into ideas about conservation with the Wolof, a tribe in Senegal, and found that those who had not been exposed to Western influences embodied in schooling were unable to make distinctions such as that between how things are and how the individual views them. They had not the concept of different 'points of view'. He suggests that animistic thinking, in which individuals project their own agency into external nature, is the product of cultures in which attention is paid to satisfying the whims of individual children. Also the concept of conservation is achieved much earlier by the Tiv, who are encouraged to manipulate the external world, than by the Wolof who adopt a more passive attitude towards it. Bruner and Greenfield argue that amongst the Wolof the motor competence and manipulation of the individual is not encouraged. The child's personal desires and intentions, which might differentiate him from others, are not emphasized. What matters for them is the child's conformity to the group. Thus their concept of a child is of a being who starts off full of personal desire and intention, but who has increasingly to subordinate such desires to the group. He thus becomes less and less of an individual because he is discouraged from thinking of himself as one. In cultures such as these, therefore, there is no encouragement for the individual to explore the world 'for himself' and find out what is true. What is true is what the group or the authority figure in the group says.[12]

We are, of course, familiar with this phenomenon in a less thorough-going form; for the appeal to the authority of the leader, parent, teacher or group, and the discouragement of individual testing out, is one of the main characteristics both of the second main developmental stage in the Piaget-Kohlberg theory and of traditionalist and collectivist types of society. But this attitude towards rules need not be just the product of vague social pressure and expectations; it can also be produced and perpetuated by the conscious techniques which we now call 'indoctrination'. For 'indoctrination' involves the passing on of fixed beliefs in a way which discourages questions about their validity. Societies, like the USSR, in which indoctrination is widespread, are not necessarily societies in which reasoning is altogether discouraged. They do not aim to undermine fundamentally people's capacities as choosers. The Russians are encouraged to calculate and to plan practical projects. Indeed they are renowned for their chess-playing and for their technology. What they are discouraged from doing is to question the validity of their moral and political beliefs and to place any emphasis on the role of the individual in determining his own destiny. They thus allow plenty of scope for the attitude to rules which is characteristic of Piaget's second stage but actively discourage any movement towards the autonomous stage, which they regard as an aberration of individualistic societies.

In the USSR Makarenko achieved considerable success in dealing with delinquents by reliance mainly on group projects and on identification with the collective will of the community.[13] As presumably most of these delinquents were either at the first egocentric stage or suffering from various pathological conditions, it was a distinct sign of moral advancement for these individuals to function at the second level of morality at which the individual does the done thing, which is determined either by the group or by those in authority.

If Piaget and Kohlberg are right, however, in their assumptions about the logical sequence of stages in development of autonomy, *every* individual has to go through these stages of what Kohlberg calls 'goodboy' and 'authority-oriented' morality before he can attain to the autonomous level. The Public Schools, who specialized in character-training, implicitly acknowledged this; for they combined an appeal to team spirit and to authority-based rule-conformity for all, with an emphasis on independence of mind and sticking to principles for those more senior boys who were singled out to command rather than simply to obey. It is questionable whether progressive educators have been sufficiently aware of the importance of this second level of development. They have, on the one hand, been reluctant for the staff to impose the rule of law but have been embarrassed by the fact that, if this is withdrawn, bullying and peer-group pressures take its place. On the other hand, they have emphasized the importance of individual choice without paying enough attention to the developmental stage which individual children have reached. Unless a child has been through the second level of morality, at which he is made to understand what an externally imposed rule is and to have some feeling about the inviolability of rules, it is dubious whether the notion of accepting or rejecting rules for himself is very meaningful to him. Decisions which are important in the shaping of character arise out of conflict situations. And how can a child go through any kind of existentialist agony if he is not acutely aware of the force of rules between which he has to choose?

So much, then, for general issues connected with the emergence to the autonomous stage of morality in so far as this involves rational reflection on rules. Some brief comments must now be made about the other aspect of autonomy which was thought to be essential to it when the notion was introduced in section I (iii) above, namely authenticity.

For this aspect of autonomy to be operative, namely the proclivity of the individual to be moved by considerations intrinsic to the conduct concerned rather than just by extrinsic considerations such as rewards and punishment, approval and disapproval, two conditions have to be satisfied. Firstly the individual has to be sensitive to considerations which are to act as principles to back rules—e.g., to the suffering of others. Secondly he has to be able, by reasoning, to view such considerations as reasons for doing some things rather than others. How individuals develop the required sensitivity is largely a matter of speculation. Obviously identification with others who already possess it is an operative factor; perhaps, too, a degree of first-hand experience is also necessary—e.g., not shielding young people but encouraging them to take part in practical tasks where there is suffering to be relieved. This kind of development can start very early; for Piaget and Kohlberg have shown not that children are incapable of such sensitivity when they are very young but that they are incapable of appealing to it as a backing for rules. In other words it does not function for them as a principle.

What then, can be done about encouraging the development of reasoning of this sort so that rules have the backing of authentically based principles? Presumably reasons for doing things can be indicated quite early on, even though it is appreciated that the child cannot yet think in this way. For unless there is this kind of 'cognitive stimulation' in the environment it is improbable that the child will emerge to the autonomous stage Obviously an atmosphere of discussion and criticism, especially amongst children who are a bit older, will help to stimulate this development. Language, too, which approximates to what Bernstein calls an 'elaborated code', is very important in aiding this development as well as non-arbitrary methods of teaching rules.[14] I am not saying, of course, that any sane parent or teacher will, in the early stages, make a child's acceptance of the reasons a condition for his doing what is sensible. All I am saying is that rules can be presented in a non-arbitrary way *before* children are capable of accepting them for the reasons given, to help them to get to the stage when they follow rules because of the reasons for them. But it does not follow from this that, on many occasions, parents and teachers may not have to insist on certain forms of conduct even though the children do not accept the good sense of it. Indeed this is a common feature of the 'good boy' and 'rule-conformity' stages of morality.

III   The influence of institutions

Kohlberg claims that, though the content of the morality of a particular community can be passed on by instruction and example, its form, which is defined by the way in which rules are conceived, cannot be so passed on. It is the product of interaction between the individual and his social environment which is merely assisted by 'cognitive stimulation'. How, then, if he is right, could an educational institution such as a secondary school, contribute to such development?

Obviously much can be done with regard to the appropriate *content* by instruction, example, and on the spot correction. In this boys and girls, who are a little more advanced in development, probably exert a more effective influence than the teachers themselves, as Thomas Arnold saw when he insisted that the older boys must bear the brunt of the responsibility for ensuring that rules of conduct are known and kept. But what about the form of morality, which is characterized by the prevailing attitude to rules? What can an educational institution contribute to this? Can it do much to aid development towards the autonomous stage?

No doubt much is contributed by a general atmosphere of discussion and by providing a backing of reasons for rules as well as insisting on them. A curriculum, too, which pays proper attention to those disciplines, such as literature and history, which provide a foundation for choice, is an obvious help. But of far-reaching importance, surely, is the general control system of the school and the motivational assumptions which support it. For Piaget's and

Kohlberg's stages of development are 'writ large' in these all-pervasive features of the institution. It is, surely, unlikely that autonomy will be widely encouraged by an authoritarian system of control in which anything of importance is decided by the fiat of the headmaster and in which the prevailing assumption is that the appeal to a man is the only method of determining what is correct. Similarly in the motivational sphere of authenticity students are unlikely to develop a delight in doing things for reasons intrinsic to them if rewards and punishment, meted out both by the staff and by a fierce examination system, provide the stable incentives to the discipline of learning; for the institution itself embodies an attitude to conduct which is appropriate to Piaget's first stage of development. These institutional realities are bound to structure the perceptions of the students. If an institution embodies an attitude to rules that is characteristic of an earlier stage of development, teachers who attempt to encourage a more developed attitude have an uphill task; for in their attempts at 'cognitive stimulation' they are working against the deadening directives of the institution.

The inference to be drawn from this is not that every school, which upholds an ideal of autonomy, should straightaway abolish its punishment and examination systems and introduce a school parliament which should direct the affairs of the institution in a way which is acceptable to autonomous men. Apart from the rational objections to the possibility of educational institutions being purely 'democratic'[15] it ignores the implications to be drawn from the Piaget-Kohlberg theory. For on this view children have to pass from seeing rules as connected with punishments and rewards to seeing them as ways of maintaining a gang-given or authoritatively ordained rule structure before they can adopt a more autonomous attitude towards them. Kohlberg has shown that many adolescents are still only at the first 'pre-moral' level; so the suggestion that an institution should be devised for them which is structured only in terms of the final stage is grossly inappropriate. Progressive schools, therefore, which insist *from the start* on children making their own decisions and running their own affairs, ignore the crucial role which the stage of conventional morality plays in moral development. The more enlightened ones in fact have a firm authority structure for the school which is arranged so that increasing areas of discretion and participation in decision making are opened up for the older pupils. This attempt to arrange an institution so that its control system is not out of tune with stages of development seems eminently sensible. In fact the Public Schools, at their best, have approximated to this. They have combined a great emphasis on decency, doing the done thing, and respect for authority with a pressure on prefects to develop some degree of autonomy. The criticism of this system is that the emphasis on a second level type of regulation was over done and that third level type of morality was encouraged only for the few who were singled out for positions of eminence.

It might, finally, be tentatively suggested that, though there are stages in character development which are 'writ large' in systems of institutional control, the arrangement is a hierarchical one. Earlier stages are not completely superseded; rather they are, ideally speaking, caught up in and transformed by the next stage. When a system maintained purely by naked force and the dispensation of rewards gives way to a system dependent on the belief in the sanctity of rules enshrined in tradition or laid down by authority, force and rewards are not abandoned. Rather they are placed in the background as palpable supports for the authority structure, which have to be employed if the support appropriate to an authority system becomes ineffective. Similarly when, with the advent of individualism and the belief in reason, traditional systems are challenged, and fundamental questions are asked about the institution of authority itself, authority becomes rationalized, not superseded. Its structure is adapted to the reasons for having it, people are appointed to positions of authority on relevant grounds, and their spheres of competence are carefully defined.

In a similar way the autonomous man is not a person who operates only at the level of a principled morality. He is not impervious to the promise of reward and punishment; he does many things because it is the decent thing to do or because they have been laid down by authority; but he is capable both of doing the same things because he sees their point as flowing from his fundamental principles, and of challenging certain forms of conduct that are laid down and acting differently because of his own convictions. He has, in other words, a rational attitude both to tradition and to authority. My guess is, however, that much of the conduct of autonomous people is governed by a second-level type of morality. They refrain from stealing and incest, because they do not regard it as the thing to do. They pay their debts, keep their promises, and adopt the principle of first come first served, when queuing for goods in short supply, without pondering much on the principles involved. Maybe they have thought about the ethics of such practices; maybe they are in part moved by considerations connected with their principles. But my guess is that they carry with them a solid precipitate from the conventional stage of morality whose motivation sustains the more mundane levels of their conduct. For unless a person has been solidly bedded down in this stage of morality he will not have the basic experience of rules as regulators of his impulses and as checks on the more calculating type of hedonism, deriving from the first level of morality. This provides a proper preparation for the autonomous stage of morality, and the attitude to rules remains with him even though the more rational attitude to rules, appropriate to the autonomous stage, is superimposed on it.

IV Assumptions about learning

Throughout this over-ambitious paper I have referred to various studies by psychologists and have indulged in what seem to be speculative sorties into the empirical which have sometimes been prefaced by remarks such as 'My guess is'. What justification has a philosopher for behaving like this, even though he is a philosopher of education and therefore necessarily has his ear closer to the ground than his less mundane colleagues in philosophy departments?

I could deploy a general thesis about the nature of philosophy to justify this procedure, in which I would try to show that the dividing line between philosophy and first order activities, such as science and morality, is not as easy to draw as many have thought. But there is no need, in this case, to appeal to such general considerations; for the justification lies in the nature of human learning, which, as I shall try very briefly to indicate, permits observations of this quasi-empirical character to be made.

In ordinary straightforward cases of human learning, in which some content is understood, memorized, imitated or made a person's own in various other ways, there is a sense in which the concept of 'learning' is neither monolithic nor concerned with anything that requires empirical investigation. For it draws attention to a range of achievements which are diverse and whose different criteria dictate the sort of thing that must be done if learning is to take place. Suppose, for instance, that one learns, in biology, what mammals are. 'Learns' here picks out the achievement of being able to classify animals in a certain way. The achievement involves being able to relate 'mammal' to other concepts such as 'mammarian glands' and to recognize cases of mammals. The so-called processes of learning involve being put in the way of both features of what it means to grasp the concept of 'mammal'. Examples are pointed out and the features which they have in common are explained. Learning a skill is different; for this involves, in the case of bodily skills like swinging a golf-club, the co-ordination of movements in a certain pattern. But here the relevant type of mastery dictates what learning must be like; for how else could such a pattern of movements be developed except by some kind of practice in moving the body in this way? Remembering similarly must involve some content which is accurately reproduced; so learning in this sphere must involve devices by means of which accuracy in reproduction is ensured. The type of achievement determines the general form of the process of learning.

This fundamental point about the concept of learning makes clear why the philosopher is intimately concerned with it; for it is a philosopher's task to explicate in general what is meant by 'understanding', 'knowing how to do things', 'remembering', etc. Anything that is to count as 'learning' in these spheres must be related intelligibly in some way to the achievement in question. By this I mean that there must be some relationship such as that of being logically presupposed to, or conceptually connected with, the achievement in question. Of course, the philosopher may not know all the *details* of the achievement. He may be rusty on his mathematics or ignorant about golf. But the details will be supplied not by empirical psychologists but by those who know a lot about the structure of the forms of understanding or skills in question. There are, of course, important empirical questions about aids to learning such as the influence of repetition; there are empirical questions about individual differences and about conditions which militate against learning. But the central core of what we call 'learning' depends upon making explicit criteria of 'match' and intelligibility of content in the various achievements of which human beings are capable.

In this paper, however, I have not dwelt at all on the learning of the *contents* of various forms of achievement. Rather I have been concerned with the development of forms of understanding, characterizing both a chooser and an autonomous person. In suggesting, for instance, that to become autonomous what is necessary is a predictable social environment, encouragement of the individual's attempts to manipulate things, and a general conviction that an individual's point of view matters, I have, in effect, been citing conditions that make the development of various components in the concept of 'choosing' intelligible. Brainwashing was explained as a process that undermines the categoreal apparatus necessary for choice by depriving the individual of a temporal framework and of a sense of his own identity. Similarly indoctrination was represented as a process that drastically discourages the fundamental questioning of the validity of rules which characterizes the autonomous stage. Unreasonable people were seen to be the product of a social environment embodying arbitrariness and a language that is concrete and weak on a syntax that aids thought in terms of universals. It was suggested that it is difficult to develop autonomy in an institution that is structured in terms of appeals to authority or in which rewards and punishments are the main incentives to learning. For it is such all-pervasive procedures that determine how an individual is likely to structure his experience. In proceeding in this way I am only sketching in some of the conditions of 'cognitive stimulation', which, on Kohlberg's view, encourage development from stage to stage or other influences that fixate people at a certain stage of development.

The question must be asked, however, whether in providing this kind of social setting for Kohlberg's speculations I am doing anything for which a philosopher is specially suited. There are parts of it, surely, which are eminently the concern of the philosopher. Piaget's and Kohlberg's basic claim is that the order of development of stage concepts is culturally invariant because it is based on logical relationships between levels of conceiving. If this is correct it has manifest importance in the moral sphere. It would dictate, for instance, the rather cautious conservatism in moral education set out in section III. For the purpose of this article I have assumed it to be a tenable view. But elsewhere[16] I have questioned it at least on the grounds that Kohlberg has not clearly spelt out the logical connexions.

Secondly it is a philosophical task to break down a notion like that of autonomy and to point out that some process of learning is required in relation to each aspect of the achievement of autonomy. This fits in with the general account of the philosopher's role in relation to learning set out at the beginning of this section. So does the attempt to indicate the *sort* of conditions under which forms of conception could be intelligibly learnt. For with these, as with any other concepts, one has to postulate both conditions in which they could be applied and some aids to conceptualization, even if they take the form of 'cognitive stimulation' rather than of direct instruction. It is an empirical question, of course, to determine the conditions which actually *do* have a marked influence. For instance, in the case of learning perceptual concepts of the sort that are involved in geometry—e.g., square, round—it is a philosophical point that some kind of experience is necessary for learning the concepts; for otherwise how could the concept be *applied*, which is part of our understanding of what it means to have learnt a concept? But it may be an empirical fact that a lot of manipulatory and visual experience is a great help in learning. This may not be the case with practical concepts such as that of 'toy' or 'tool'. And with the types of concept that are crucial in the development of autonomy, the case of the Wolof, studied by Bruner and Greenfield, suggests that both exploratory experiences and social influences are very important.

There are, of course, other discoveries in the developmental sphere about which the philosopher could have little to say—e.g., the importance attached to sexual and aggressive wishes in the Freudian explanation of why people do not develop along Piagetian lines and learn ways of interpreting things that lead to various forms of irrationality which even sometimes prevent them from achieving the status of choosers (see section I (ii)). But in these types of explanation, as well as in the types of explanation which have been used to account for the influence of institutions and social conditions, there are present some all-pervasive assumptions about generalization in learning, whose status is somewhat obscure. What is to be made, for instance, of assumptions such as:

> If human beings are exposed to a highly unpredictable environment, they will tend to lack confidence in their ability to predict and control events.

> If children are actively discouraged from asking questions they will acquire habits of unquestioning acceptance.

Assumptions such as these proliferate in the literature of psychology in general as well as in the particular speculations in which I have indulged in parts of this paper. All of them could be falsified in particular cases, though all of them have a kind of intuitive plausibility about them. Their plausibility derives from the fact that they all manifestly satisfy the basic condition of all human learning, namely that of an intelligent connexion between what is learnt and the conditions of learning. It is not the philosopher's task to explore the extent to which these common-sense assumptions are true. But philosophical points can be made about the types of condition which must be satisfied for different types of learning to take place. Assumptions such as these manifestly satisfy such conditions. We are, I think, only at the beginning of our understanding of what is a philosophical point about learning and what is an empirical point. This distinction applies to the content of experience as well as to its form, though I have mainly been concerned with the latter in this paper. It would, however, take another paper to begin to get to grips with this central problem in the philosophy of education. I have only introduced it briefly at the end of this one in order to defend myself against the charge that, because I have referred to things that go on in the world, I am necessarily bringing the Owl of Minerva down to the level of the cuckoo in the nest.

Notes

1 I wish to express my thanks to colleagues whose comments helped me to improve this paper – especially Stanley Benn and Geoffrey Mortimore of the Australian National University and Mrs P. A. White of the University of London Institute of Education.
2 Especially in Stanley Benn's paper on *Conditions of Autonomy*, which he read to a conference of the AAP in 1969 and which I discussed with him at length during my period as Visiting Fellow at the Australian National University. This paper was itself a development of ideas worked out, between Stanley Benn and W. Weinstein in their 1971 paper 'Being free to act, and being a free man'.
3 For development of such points see Peters, 1966, ch. VII.
4 See Peters, 1966; chs III, IV, V, VII especially.
5 See Peters, 1964, 1971a.
6 See Peters, 1971b.
7 See, for instance, Peck and Havighurst, 1960, pp. 109–11.
8 For distinction see Peters, 1971a.
9 See Klein, 1965.
10 Kohlberg actually breaks Piaget's three stages up into six stages with three levels. But it would be out of place to pursue these refinements.
11 See Kohlberg, 1968, 1969.
12 See Greenfield and Bruner, 1969.
13 See Lilge, 1958, especially pp. 25–6.
14 See Bernstein, 1961, 1969.
15 See Hirst and Peters, 1970, ch. 7.
16 See Peters, 1971b.

Bibliography

Benn, S. I. and Weinstein, W. (1971), 'Being free to act, and being a free man', *Mind*, vol. LXXX, pp. 194–211.

Bernstein, B. B. (1961), 'Social class and linguistic development: a theory of social learning', in Halsey, A. H., Floud, J. & Anderson, C. A., *Education, Economy and Society*, New York, Free Press.

Bernstein, B. and Henderson, D. (1969), 'Social class differences in the relevance of language to socialization', *Sociology*, vol. 3.

Greenfield, P. M. and Bruner, J. S. (1969), 'Culture and Cognitive Growth', in Goslin, D. A., *Handbook of Socialization: Theory and Research*, Chicago, Rand McNally.

Hirst, P. H. and Peters, R. S. (1970), *The Logic of Education*, Routledge & Kegan Paul.

Klein, J. (1965), *Samples of English Culture*, 2 vols, Routledge & Kegan Paul.

Kohlberg, L. (1968), 'Early Education: A Cognitive Developmental View', *Child Development*, vol. 31.

Kohlberg, L. (1969), 'Stage and Sequence: the Cognitive Developmental Approach to Socialization', in Goslin, D.A. (ed.), *Handbook of Socialization: Theory and Research*, Chicago, Rand McNally.

Laing, R. D. (1965), *The Divided Self*, Penguin Books.

Lilge, F. (1958), *Anton Senyonovitch Makarenko*, Berkeley and Los Angeles, University of California Press.

Peck, R. F. and Havighurst, R. J. (1960), *The Psychology of Character Development*, New York, John Wiley.

Peters, R. S. (1964), 'Mental Health as an Educational Aim', in Hollins, T.H.B. (ed.), *Aims of Education: the philosophical approach*, Manchester University Press.

Peters, R. S. (1966), *Ethics and Education*, Allen & Unwin.

Peters, R. S. (1970), 'Education and Human Development', in Selleck, R.W. (ed.), *Melbourne Studies in Education*, Melbourne University Press.

Peters, R. S. (1971a), 'Reason and Passion', in Vesey, G. (ed.), *The Proper Study*, vol. 4, Royal Institute of Philosophy, Macmillan.

Peters, R. S. (1971b), 'Moral Development: A Plea for Pluralism', in Mischel, T. (ed.), *Psychological and Epistemological Issues in the Development of Concepts*, New York, Academic Press.

The idea of a free man

Joel Feinberg

Professor Peters's admirable essay has two primary aims: (1) to articulate more clearly a widely prized ideal of character and (2) to consider how that particular personal excellence can be 'learned,' or at least fostered by a certain kind of institutional environment. The character trait in question is one that shares the glittering name of 'freedom' with a puzzling variety of other things that are *not* virtues of character, among them, a certain class of institutional arrangements and control systems. By analyzing the ideal of the free man, on the one hand, and the nature of a free social system, on the other, Peters hoped to be in a better position to illuminate the connection between the two in a way that will be useful for the purposes of educational policy and congruent with the results of psychological learning theory. I think that these purposes of Peters's have been largely achieved by his essay, and therefore I will restrict my comments to a related topic that he had to pass over.

When Peters writes that an examination of 'what is meant by "freedom" in a social context, like that of a school, and what is meant by a "free man,"' can lead to 'some suggestions ... about the connection between the two,'[1] he has in mind a connection of an instrumental kind. He is concerned to tell us how a free institutional environment can help *bring about* freedom as a trait of individual character. My intention is to complement his essay by considering the conceptual, rather than the instrumental, connection between the two kinds of freedom. I shall proceed by surveying the various things we might mean when we say of an individual person that he is free.

I   Free from ... and free to ...

'He is free' might, first of all, be an elliptical expression of a singular judgment that someone is, happily, without impediment or constraint to a desire that he has or might have to do, or omit, or be, or have something in particular. It is useful to interpret these singular judgments in terms of a single analytic pattern with three blanks in it:

——————————————is free from——————————————to do
(or omit, or be, or have)————————————————

Sometimes it is perfectly clear from the context *whose* freedom is under discussion. On other occasions, especially when we talk grandly about 'economic' or 'religious' freedom, relying on the adjective in the absence of any names or pronouns, the first blank in the schema will have to be filled in for the sake of clarity and the prevention of equivocation. On other occasions the speaker will be quite clear in his own mind what the subject of his assertion is free *to* do, but will be quite vague about what constraint he is now free *from*. Perhaps all he means to convey in his enthusiasm is that *nothing* now prevents him from doing X, in which case the whole intended emphasis of his remark is on the new option now open to him, and no specific descriptions of missing constraints are necessary to fill out his meaning. If, however, the X in question is something most of us are normally free to do anyway, we may be puzzled by the speaker's remark until he specifies more narrowly which constraint to his desire to do X, formerly present, has now been removed. But when this puzzlement does not arise, no description of specific missing constraints is required for clarity.

On other occasions, the primary or exclusive emphasis of a speaker's assertion of freedom may rest on a specific missing constraint. He may, for example, claim to 'be free' simply because one hated barrier to a given desire has been lifted, even when other barriers to that very same desire admittedly still remain. In that case, all of the emphasis of his remark is on the removed constraint, and his newly asserted freedom does not imply that he can yet *do* any more than he formerly could. He is free *from* one barrier to his doing X, and that may seem to be blessed relief from an oppressive burden, but he may still be unable to do X. In an extreme limiting case, a speaker may have no concern with future *actions* whatever, and the existence of new alternatives for choice may be no part of his intended meaning when he asserts that he is free *from C*. He may be exclusively preoccupied with the removal of some odious condition quite apart from any effect that removal might have on his *other* desires or options. He may simply hate his chains and conceive his 'freedom' to consist entirely in their removal.[2] In this not uncommon limiting case, freedom from . . . implies no new freedom to . . . other than the freedom to be without the thing one is said to be free from.

More typically, however, when we use the language of missing-constraint, we imply that there is something we want to do (or might come to want to do) that the constraint prevents us from doing, and that to be free from that constraint is to be able to do that which the constraint prevents us from doing. In the typical case, then, 'freedom from' and 'freedom to' are two sides of the same coin, each involved with the other, and not two radically distinct kinds of freedom, as some writers have suggested. Indeed, it is difficult fully to characterize a given constraint without mentioning the desires it does or can constrain (that is, desires other than the exclusive desire to be relieved of *it*). The man outside a divorce court who tells us that he is now free (presumably *from* the woman who was his wife) has not communicated much to us until he specifies which desires he can satisfy now that he could not satisfy when he was married. (It might be very bad public relations on his part to leave this entirely up to our ill-informed imaginations.) Without further specification, we know only that he is now without a wife and quite happy about it; but then, as we have seen, that *may* be all that he had in mind when he said that he was free.

It has often been said that there are two main concepts, or types, or ideals of freedom, one positive and the other negative, and that ideologies conflict in so far as they employ, or give emphasis to, the one, or the other, or both of them. The writers who have attached great importance to this distinction have often had an important insight, but even when that has been so, their insight can be preserved and expressed with greater economy in terms of the 'single concept' analysis given here. The writers to whom I refer argue that only one of the two allegedly distinct concepts of freedom, namely the 'negative' one, is to be analyzed as the absence of constraints. We may be free of all constraints to our desire to do X, these philosophers maintain, and still not be free *to* do X. Hence, they conclude, 'positive freedom' (freedom to . . .) is something other than the absence of constraint.

This way of making out the distinction between positive and negative freedom will seem plausible, I think, only if the idea of a constraint is artificially limited. In fact, however, two important distinctions between kinds of constraints, each cutting across the other, can be made, and once these distinctions are recognized, the apparent ground for the 'two concept' analysis vanishes. The distinctions I have in mind are between positive and negative constraints and between internal and external constraints. There is no doubting that some constraints are negative—the lack of money, or strength, or skill, or knowledge, can quite effectively prevent a person from doing, or having, or being something he might want. Since these conditions are absences, they are 'negative,' and since they can be preventive causes, they are constraints.

How we make the distinction between 'internal' and 'external' constraints depends, of course, on how we draw the boundaries of the self. If we contract the self sufficiently so that it becomes a dimensionless non-empirical entity, then *all* causes are external causes. Other narrow conceptions of the self would attribute to its 'inner core' a set of ultimate principles or 'internalized values,' or ultimate ends or desires, and relegate to the merely 'empirical self' or even to a world altogether external to the self, all lower-ranked desires, whims, and fancies. If the distinction between internal and external constraints is to be given a *political* use, however, then perhaps the simplest way of making it out is by means of a merely spatial criterion: external constraints are those that come from outside a person's body-cum-mind, and all other constraints, whether sore muscles, headaches, or refractory 'lower' desires, are internal to him. This would be to use a wide 'total self' rather than the specially intimate 'inner core' self in making the distinction.

The two distinctions described above cut across one another creating four categories. There are *internal positive* constraints such as headaches, obsessive thoughts, and compulsive desires; *internal negative constraints* such as ignorance, weakness, and deficiencies in talent or skill; *external positive constraints* such as barred windows, locked doors, and pointed bayonets; and *external negative constraints* such as lack of money, lack of transportation, and lack of weapons. Freedom from a negative constraint is the absence of an absence, and therefore the presence of some condition that permits a given kind of doing. The presence of such a condition when external to a person is usually called an opportunity, and when internal, an ability. Not every absent condition whose presence would constitute an opportunity or ability, however, is a negative constraint. Only those whose absence constitutes a striking deviation from a norm of expectancy or propriety, or whose absence is in some way an especially important consideration for some practical interest either of the subject or of some later commentator can qualify as constraints.

If only positive factors are counted as constraints, then a pauper might be free of constraints to his (actual or possible) desire to buy a Cadillac, and yet, of course, he is not free *to* buy a Cadillac. Similarly, if constraints are restricted to external factors, then the chronic alcoholic and the extremely ill man in a fever or a coma are both free from constraints to go about their business, but of course, neither is free *to* do so. Once we acknowledge, however, that there can be internal and negative constraints, there is no further need to speak of two distinct kinds of freedom, one of which has nothing to do with constraint. A constraint is something—anything—that prevents one from doing something. Therefore, if nothing prevents me *from* doing X, I am free *to* do X; and conversely, if I am free *to* do X, then nothing prevents me *from* doing X. 'Freedom to' and 'freedom from' are in this way logically linked. Thus, there can be no special 'positive' freedom *to* which is not also a freedom *from*.

Still, there is no harm, I suppose, in characterizing 'positive freedom' as the absence of negative constraints, and 'negative freedom' as the absence of positive constraints, *providing* (1) that both positive and negative freedom are held to be necessary, and equally necessary, to a man's freedom all told (without any adjective), and (2) neither is held to be 'higher' or 'lower' or intrinsically more worth having than the other, and (3) neither is analyzed as totally different in kind from the absence of constraints.

A final distinction between types of constraints can obviate still other difficulties in interpreting singular judgments of the form 'Doe is free *to* do X.' A speaker might mean by this judgment either of the following:

(i)   X is something Doe *may* do, i.e. something he is *permitted* (but not required) to do by someone in authority over him, or by moral or legal rules to which he is subject. (Another way of saying all of this is that Doe is *at liberty* to do X.)

(ii)   X is something that Doe *can* do, i.e. something he is *not in fact prevented* from doing (or required to do) either by coercion (direct or indirect) from others or by other kinds of constraints. (In this kind of case, talk of 'liberty' is not always interchangeable with talk of 'freedom.')

When commands or rules are not effectively enforced a person might well be able to do something that he is not permitted to do. Similarly, a person might be permitted to do something that he is unable to do because he is prevented from doing it by constraints other than rules backed by sanctions. Again, a person might be incapable of doing some act simply because the act is prohibited by commands or rules that *are* very effectively enforced. In that case, the enforced rule is itself a constraint.

Corresponding to the distinction between what may be done and what can be done is that between two perspectives from which singular freedom-judgments are made, namely, the *juridical* and the *sociological*. The former is the perspective of a system of legal or legal-like regulations itself. When I say that no one in New York State is free to play poker for money in his own home, I am simply reciting what the New York legal codes prohibit. My judgment is confirmable or discomfirmable by reference to those codes. In fact, of course, thousands of persons play poker for money in private homes in New York every night with little or no risk of apprehension by the indifferent police. When I speak from the sociological perspective, I might well say that everyone in New York, in effect, is free to play poker if he wishes. This judgment is subject to a different kind of confirming or disconfirming evidence, namely, an account of how effectively a law is enforced by the police, how intimidated poker players actually feel by the law, and how many of them in fact are willing to run the risk of detection and conviction.

From the juridical perspective, what I am free to do in a given case is not a matter of degree. For any given act or omission, either it is permitted or it is not; I am at liberty (entirely) to do it or I am not at liberty to do it at all. There are, of course, more subtle forms of legal control which employ variable constraints that permit talk of 'degrees' of freedom. If there is a $100 tax on conduct of type A and a $500 tax on type B, I am left by authority, in a quite intelligible sense, more free to do A than to do B. In the case of the criminal law, however, and all other regulations that control conduct by enjoining, permitting, and prohibiting, my freedom to do any act is, from the law's point of view, either entire or non-existent. On the other hand, from the sociological perspective, it is always intelligible to speak of degrees of freedom or unfreedom even of a particular person to do some one given act, and even when that act is unconditionally prohibited by law, if only because the probabilities of being detected and/or convicted vary from offense to offense.[3]

Most of us, of course, do not *feel free* to do acts that are forbidden by rules or authorities that we have accepted, even when there are no effective external hindrances to our doing so and we stand to profit by disobedience. We are constrained from disobedience not by external barriers and threats but by internal inhibitions. Whether the internal constraint is taken to be a restriction of the self's freedom to act depends upon how we model the self, that is, upon which of the elements of the 'total self' we identify most intimately with, upon where in the internal landscape we take ourselves to live. If we are prevented from doing that which, upon reflection, we think is the best thing on the whole to do, by some internal element—an impulse, a craving, a weakened condition, an intense but illicit desire, a neurotic compulsion, or whatever—then the internal inhibitor is treated as an alien force, internal or not: a kind of 'enemy within.' On the other hand, when the inhibitor is some higher-ranked desire and that which is frustrated is a desire of lesser importance albeit greater momentary intensity, we identify with the desire that is higher in our personal hierarchy, and consider ourselves to be the subject rather than the object of constraint. *A fortiori*, when the desire to do that which is forbidden is constrained by conscience, that is, by the 'internalized authority' of the prohibiting rules themselves, we take ourselves to live where our consciences are, and to be repelling the threat to our personal integrity posed by the refractory lower desire which we 'disown' no matter how 'internal' it may be.

A person who had no hierarchical structure of wants, and aims, and ideals, and no clear conception of where it is within him that he really resides, would be a battlefield for all of his constituent elements, tugged this way and that, and fragmented hopelessly. Such a person would fail of autonomy not because he is a mere conformist whose values are all borrowed second-hand, for his wants and ideals and scruples could be perfectly authentic and original in him, but they would fail of autonomy because they lack internal order and structure. This defective condition Durkheim called 'anomie,' a condition which in its extreme form tends to be fatal. It is interesting to note in passing why, on the unitary 'absence of constraint' theory of freedom, it is intelligible to speak of anomie as a kind of unfreedom. Our picture of the undisciplined or anomic man is not that of a well-defined self with a literal or figurative bayonet at its back, or barriers, locked doors, and barred windows on all sides. Rather it employs the image of roads crowded with vehicles in the absence of traffic cops or traffic signals to keep order: desires, impulses, and purposes come and go at all speeds and in all directions, and get nowhere. The undisciplined person, perpetually liable to internal collisions, jams, and revolts, is unfree even though unrestrained either by the outside world or by an internal governor. To vary the image, he is a man free of external shackles, but tied in knots by the strands of his own wants.[4] When he may 'do anything he wants,' his options will overwhelm his capacity to order them in hierarchies of preference; he will therefore become confused, and disoriented, haunted by boredom and frustration, eager once more simply to be told what he must do. To be unfree is to be constrained, and in the absence of an internal traffic cop, and internal traffic rules, desires will constrain each other in jams and collisions. Surely it is more plausible to construe such a state as unfreedom than as an illustration of the dreadfulness of too much freedom.

II Free on balance

A speaker may intend nothing so precise as our schema with the three blanks suggests when he asserts that he or some other person is free; but the second kind of thing he might mean presupposes and builds upon the singular non-comparative judgments discussed above. He may be saying either that he is *generally* free or *relatively* free in the above sense of 'free.' He may intend to convey that he is on the whole free, or at liberty, to do a great many things, or perhaps to do most of the things that are worth doing, or perhaps to do a greater percentage of the worthwhile things than are open to most people; or he might be emphasizing that he is free *from* most of the things that are worth being without in their own right (disease, poverty, etc.) or freer from those things than are the members of some comparison class. 'On balance judgments' of freedom are of necessity vague and impressionistic, and even the comparative judgments that they sometimes incorporate are usually incapable of precise confirmation.

Suppose that John Doe is permitted by well enforced rules to travel only to Chicago, Houston, and Seattle, but may make adverse criticism of nothing he sees in those cities, whereas Richard Roe may go only to Bridgeport, Elizabeth, and Jersey City and may criticize anything he wishes; or suppose that Doe can go anywhere at all but must not criticize, whereas Roe cannot leave home but may say anything he pleases. In reply to the question, 'Which of the two is more free?' it appears that the only sensible answer is that Doe is more free in one respect (physical movement) and Roe in another (expression of opinion). If the questioner persists in asking who is the more free 'on balance' and 'in the last analysis,' we can only interpret him to be asking which of the two respects is more important. If we are then to avoid a vitiating circularity, our standard of 'importance,' I should think, must be something other than 'conducibility to freedom.'

When two or more properties or 'respects' are subject to precise mathematical comparison, there will always be some quantitative element that they have in common. The difficulty in striking resultant totals of 'on balance freedom' derives from the fact that the relation between the various 'areas' in which people are said to be free is not so much like the relation between the height, breadth, and depth of a physical object as it is like the relation between the gasoline economy, styling, and comfort of an automobile.[5] Height times breadth times depth equals volume, a dimension compounded coherently out of the others; but freedom of expression times freedom of movement yields nothing at all comparable. Still, limited comparisons even of incommensurables are possible. If the average American has greater freedom in *every* dimension than his Ruritanian counterpart, it makes sense to say that he has greater freedom on balance; or if they are equally free in some dimensions but the American is more free in all the others, the same judgment follows. More likely, what we mean when we say that one subject is freer on balance than another is that his freedom is greater in the more valuable, important, or significant dimensions, where the 'value' of a dimension is determined by some independent standard.

There seems to follow from this analysis a result of considerable interest. Since 'maximal freedom' (having as much freedom on balance as possible) is a notion that can be made sense of only by the application of independent standards for determining the relative worth or importance of different sorts of interests and areas of activity, it is by itself a merely formal ideal, one that cannot stand on its own feet without the help of other values. One person's freedom can conflict with another's; freedom in one dimension can contrast with unfreedom in another; and the conflicting dimensions cannot meaningfully be combined on one scale. These conflicts and recalcitrances require that we put types of subjects, possible desires, and areas of activity into some order of importance; and this in turn requires supplementing the political ideal of freedom with moral standards of other kinds. The supplementary values, however, are not external to freedom in the manner of such independently conceived rival ideals as justice and welfare, but rather are 'internally supplementary'—a necessary filling-in of the otherwise partially empty idea of 'on balance freedom' itself.

III 'Free' as a legal status word

The third use of the word 'free' does not fit our analytic paradigm, and therefore, can be conceded to be a distinct 'concept of liberty'; but this use, important as it once was, has declined since the fall of feudalism and slavery, and is now almost archaic. The old English word 'free,' like its ancient counterparts, the Greek *'eleutheros'* and the Latin *'liber,'* had as its original meaning, according to C. S. Lewis,[6] simply 'not a slave,' so that to call a man 'free' in this earliest sense was merely to identify his legal status. To be a freeman was to be a full-fledged member of one's political community with all the rights and privileges, usually including various participatory voting rights, that derived from that membership.[7] In societies with two distinct legal statuses—freeman and slave—to call a man 'free' was simply to describe his legal rights and contrast them with those of a slave. (In the extreme limiting case of irrevocable chattel slavery, the slave had no rights at all.) Such judgments were easily verified by examinations of legal documents, branding marks, and the like.

It was a natural and useful extension of this original sense of 'free' to mean 'unconstrained in one's physical movements,' for the freeman was one who could come and go as he pleased. The statuses of slave and freeman, however, were not defined by the presence or absence of *de facto* or *de jure* constraints, but rather by the possession or non-possession of *rights*, which is quite another matter. The slave whose master was benevolent or motivated by *noblesse oblige* might well be free *to* do a great many important things and free *from* most of the conditions whose absences are universally desired for their own sakes. If the benevolent or dutiful master happened also to be rich, the 'on balance freedom' of the slave might even compare favorably with that of most freemen. The permissive master might even leave his slave *at liberty*, within a wide range, to do as he pleased, so that even from a kind of juridical viewpoint, the freedom of the slave might be considerable. There is, however, one crucial difference between the *de jure* liberties of the freeman and those 'permitted' the slave. The freeman enjoys some of his legal liberties as a matter of right: no one else is permitted to nullify or withdraw them. When they are slow to be acknowledged, or where they appear to be withheld, he may lay claim to them and demand them as his due. If others violate them he will properly feel not merely hurt but wronged. Some of his *de jure* liberties are correlated logically with other people's duties of action and forebearance, and even with the state's duties of enforcement and support. They are, in short, *rights*. The liberties permitted the slave, on the other hand, are granted at the mere pleasure of his owner and may also be withdrawn at his mere displeasure. He owes his slave nothing and has no legal duty to 'permit' him any 'liberties' at all. When the owner, then, is benevolent, it is fitting that the slave be grateful, and when permissions are arbitrarily withdrawn, it is expected that the slave might be disappointed or hurt, but not that he be resentful or aggrieved. The slave's liberties, in short, are at best what we now call 'mere privileges.' There is no reason in principle, however, why a slave should not be in many respects 'on balance free,' both from the sociological and juridical points of view, even though his non-possession of *rights* entails an unfree legal status.

IV 'Free' as a status-associated virtue word

By still another easy extension, the word 'free' (and its older Indo-European counterparts as well) became the name not only of a status but also of a set of virtues of character, namely, those taken to be especially becoming to a man of free status. 'Free' in this sense is opposed to 'servile' which was used to refer to those qualities characteristic of slaves, and hence inappropriate in a freeman. A servile person is 'alternately fawning and insolent';[8] a free man, having nothing to fear, is dignified and deliberate, and can look any man in the eye. In asking what freedom truly is, we might be asking for a fuller account of these qualities, and in describing a given man as free, we may be simply ascribing such virtues to him, whatever his legal status might be, or however 'free on balance' we may take him to be.

The linguistic phenomenon exemplified by this extension of the sense of 'free' is that which C. S. Lewis called the 'moralization of status-words':[9]

> Words which originally referred to a person's rank—to legal, social, or economic status and the qualification of birth which have often been attached to these—have a tendency to become words which assign a type of character and behavior. Those implying superior status can become terms of praise; those implying inferior status, terms of disapproval. *Chivalrous, courteous, frank, gentle, generous, liberal,* and *noble* are examples of the first; *ignoble, villain,* and *vulgar,* of the second.

The association of virtues and vices with social classes has probably had some unfortunate effects on the formation of attitudes, but the process that Lewis describes is not without its advantages too. Lewis defends it vigorously against the charge that it reflects the 'inveterate snobbery of the human race,' and at the same time he explains more fully how it has worked:[10]

> A word like nobility begins to take on its social-ethical meaning when it refers not simply to a man's status but to the manners and character which are thought to be appropriate to that status. But the mind cannot long consider those manners and that character without being forced on the reflection that they are sometimes lacking in those who are noble by status and sometimes present in those who are not. Thus from the very first the social-ethical meaning, merely by existing, is bound to separate itself from the status-meaning. Accordingly, from Boethius down, it becomes a commonplace of European literature that the true nobility is within, that *villanie*, not status, makes the villain, that there are 'ungentle gentles' and that 'gentle is as gentle does.' The linguistic phenomenon we are considering is therefore quite as much an escape from, as an assertion of, that pride above and servility below, which in my opinion, should be called snobbery.

How is a philosopher, then, to decide which are the qualities that form the character of a 'free man' in the present sense? Is the philosopher free to select whichever qualities he likes and assign them to a free man's character, thus giving those qualities the benefit of 'freedom's' glitter? Or is he bound strictly to honor the assignments of qualities that have become so traditional that they might plausibly be said even to form part of the meaning of the word 'free' when it refers to a set of virtues? Without opening the technical question of distinguishing between those qualities suggested by a word and those strictly meant by the word, I think we can lay down some rough ground rules. First of all, the philosopher does have some leeway to promote his own favorite qualities. Proposed definitions of 'the free man' are understood by one and all to be attempts to appropriate the phrase for one set of contestable moral conceptions as opposed to others. They mean to be 'persuasive' in Stevenson's sense and 'tactical' in C. S. Lewis's. There is nothing disreputable about this so long as it is frankly acknowledged, and so long as the acknowledgement is not taken to confer a license to avoid the giving of reasons. The best tactical definition, the most persuasive conception, should be the one supported by the best reasons. The character of the free man is not a question forever closed by 'usage.'

But neither is the question wide open. The philosopher, of course, cannot be arbitrary; he must make out a reasonable case that the qualities he favors deserve to be regarded as virtues. Moreover, they cannot be just *any* praiseworthy qualities but only those that are 'appropriate to the status' of freeman (a legal status, incidentally, which is now virtually universal). The key word is 'appropriate.' Part of the description of the freeman's legal status, at least, is clear enough to be beyond cavil. He is, after all, a man who has certain rights, and if he acts *as if* he did not have those rights, he acts inappropriately. Because of common conceptions of the freeman's condition that derive simply from accurate descriptions of his typical circumstances, there have emerged various traditional conceptions of the freeman's 'appropriate' qualities that are relatively fixed in usage, each fastening on an aspect of the freeman's accepted description. While these conceptions are not so fixed as to form part of the very sense of the expression 'free man,' they are sufficiently conventional to require critical examination, at least, before any revisions of outlook are advocated.

As an example of how fluid the game is, consider John Ruskin's celebrated paean to the fly:[11]

> I believe we can nowhere find a better type of a perfectly free creature than in the common house fly. Nor free only, brave; and irreverent to a degree which I think no human republican could by any philosophy exalt himself to. There is no courtesy in him; he does not care whether it is king or clown whom he teases; and in every step of his swift mechanical march, and in every pause of his resolute observation, there is one and the same expression of perfect egotism, perfect independence and self-confidence, and conviction of the world's having been made for flies. Strike at him with your hand; and to him, the mechanical fact and external aspect of the matter is, what to

you it would be, if an acre of red clay, ten feet thick, tore itself up from the ground in one massive field, hovered over you in the air for a second, and came crashing down with an aim. That is the external aspect of it; the inner aspect, to his fly's mind, is of quite natural and unimportant occurrence— one of the momentary conditions of his active life. He steps out of the way of your hand, and alights on the back of it. You cannot terrify him, nor govern him, nor persuade him, nor convince him. He has his own positive opinion on all matters; not an unwise one, usually, for his own ends; and will ask no advice of yours. He has no work to do—no tyrannical instinct to obey. The earthworm has his digging; the bee her gathering and building; the spider her cunning network; the ant her treasury and accounts. All these are comparatively slaves, or people of vulgar business. But your fly, free in the air, free in the chamber—a black incarnation of caprice— wandering, investigating, flitting, flirting, feasting at his will, with rich variety of choice in feast, from the heaped sweets in the grocer's window to those of the butcher's backyard, and from the galled place on your cab-horse's back, to the brown spot in the road, from which, as the hoof disturbs him, he rises with angry republican buzz—what freedom is like his?

There is too much in this remarkable passage to analyze here, and much sly charm that would vanish if subjected to the indignity of analysis. But several points are worth notice. Ruskin's portrayal of the fly is a mixed description, partly an account of the fly's alleged 'on balance freedom to . . . and from . . . ,' partly an account of the fly's 'appropriate traits,' or virtues. These two accounts are not clearly separated and there is much to quarrel with in both; but they are not entirely arbitrary. Amidst many differences, they share a common character with some traditional conceptions of the free man as enabled by his circumstances, or indeed by the human condition itself and his understanding of it, to be self-reliant, self-sufficient, and self-confident. Ruskin slyly carries conventional notions of on-balance freedom to an absurd extreme when he speaks of the 'perfectly free creature' as an 'incarnation of caprice,' free not only of external direction, compulsion, and constraint, but also of inner drives, purposes, life plans, controls, scruples, worries, and 'tyrannical instincts,' a condition that would more closely resemble anomie than autonomy in a human being. Yet Ruskin does draw back from this abyss by ascribing to the fly 'his own ends' and rational means and plans for achieving them. The anthropomorphic ascription to the fly of 'an angry republican buzz' when he is disturbed at his dinner implies a consciousness in the fly of its own rights: servile creatures do not show indignation on their own behalfs, nor even plain anger except in the counterfeit of 'cheekiness,' or in the role of insolent bullies with their peers or other weaklings. There is more genuine pride and self-respect in the fly's angry buzz!

The 'free status' that occasions Ruskin's irony was by his time becoming a general and 'equal' condition, a 'republican status,' and Ruskin has described the traits he thinks appropriate to it not only as free but *as* republican. His 'embodiment of caprice,' he thinks, is naturally cocky, dogmatic, and contemptuous. He takes no orders and no lip from anyone. He has no respect for tradition or for authority. He enjoys his freedom from all of that as a matter of right, not just personal or family rights, but general inalienable rights that he shares with everyone. There are no more masters and slaves, says the liberated republican; now we flies are as much masters as anyone else. The kind of creature who would claim such a life as a matter of right, in a world in which there is no longer a place for authority, says Ruskin, would be 'the perfect egoist.' Ruskin's argumentative purpose is evident: Where the trait in question is clearly not a virtue, he suggests, the condition to which it is 'appropriate' is a poor ideal.

We need not linger over Ruskin's caricature except to describe briefly the traditional ideals of which it is a parody. The common tie is the idea of being one's own man, not having to fear persons of superior power, and having no need to please others as a condition of one's well-being. The man of free legal status and high social and economic position did not enjoy his liberty at the sufferance of any one else. Hence, he could be open and natural, rather than guarded and suspicious, with *every one*. He need not flatter nor cringe before any one. He had an easy and unaffected dignity about him. Perfectly secure in respect both to his sense of worth and his feeling of safety, he need not constantly to be calculating his own advantage and plotting his own advancement. There is nothing small-minded or petty about him. Nor will he be haughty and superior, 'putting on airs,' for he needs not the regular reassurance of others' obeisance and respect. He can get along without it. These are the natural and characteristic virtues (and indeed they *are* virtues) of the man of free status.

In contrast:[12]

The true servile character is cheeky, shrewd, cunning, up to every trick, always with an eye to the main chance, determined 'to look after number one' . . . Absence of disinterestedness, lack of generosity, is the hall-mark of the servile. The typical slave always has an axe to grind.

The character flaws of the slave (or the man of lowly social or economic status under feudalism or capitalism) are in their own way natural to his status, for they are forms of adaptation to a difficult and insecure position. They are not in the same way appropriate to the free man because, his position being easier, he doesn't *need* them. And yet there are other ways for insecure men to adapt: Epictetus would display all the virtues of the free man in confronting, as a mere slave, the terrible tyrant. But then, Epictetus tells us that he has this astonishing virtue only because he is *not* insecure even in the presence of what others take to be great power.

The freeman in the ancient two-status societies had not only his characteristic virtues but also his peculiarly appropriate interests and occupations. The 'liberal arts,' or pursuits appropriate to a man of free and secure status, were 'leisure occupations, things done for their own sakes and not for utility,'[13] not even for money, or for the sake of plaudits and esteem. They include painting, composing, contemplating, and philosophizing. 'Only he who is neither legally enslaved to a master nor economically enslaved by the struggle for subsistence, is likely to have or to have the leisure for using, a piano or a library. That is how one's piano or library is more *liberal*, more characteristic of one's position as a freeman, than one's coal-shovel or one's tools.'[14]

Aristotle, of course, is the philosopher who has made the most of the idea of self-sufficient and intrinsically valuable studies and pursuits, and their unique appropriateness in the life of the man of free status. C. S. Lewis, in a brilliant speculative passage, associates Aristotle's doctrine with Aristotle's circumstances:[15]

> In *Metaphysics* we learn that the organization of the universe resembles that of a household, in which 'no one has so little chance to act at random as the free members. For them everything or almost everything proceeds according to a fixed plan, whereas the slaves and domestic animals contribute little to the common end and act mostly at random.'[16] The attitude of any slave-owning society is and ought to be repellent to us, but it is worth while suppressing that revulsion in order to get the picture as Aristotle saw it. Looking from his study window he sees the hens scratching in the dust, the pigs asleep, the dogs hunting for fleas; the slaves, any of them who are not at that very moment on some appointed task, flirting, quarrelling, cracking nuts, playing dice, or dozing. He, the

157

master, may use them all for the common end, the well-being
of the family. They themselves have no such end, nor any
consistent end, in mind. Whatever in their lives is not
compelled from above is random—dependent on the mood of
the moment. His own life is quite different; a systematized
round of religious, political, scientific, literary and social
activities; its very hours of recreation . . . deliberate, approved
and allowed for; consistent with itself. But what is it in the
structure of the universe that corresponds to this distinction
between Aristotle, self-bound with the discipline of a freeman,
and Aristotle's slaves, negatively free with a servile freedom
between each job and the next? I think there is no doubt of
the answer. . . . In the world, as in the household, the higher
acts to a fixed plan; the lower admits the 'random' element.

Thus the freedom of Ruskin's houseflies is that which Aristotle
'permits' his slaves 'between jobs,' and their virtues and interests,
those Aristotle finds appropriate only to the servile condition.
There is no doubt, I think, which of the two conceptions is the more
persuasive.

V Free as independent, self-governing, autonomous

The final use of the word 'free' that I shall consider has its primary
and probably original[17] application not to individuals but to states
and other institutions. Its inevitable extension to apply to individual
human beings was as part of that elaborate parapolitical metaphor
which since the time of Plato has so colored our conception of the
human mind. To understand its extended use we would be well
advised to consider first its literal application to states, which is a
great deal clearer. When one nation is the colony of another, it is
not said to be free until it gains its independence. Formerly, it was
governed from without; now it is governed from within. Hence,
freedom in this sense, and independence, and self-government all
come to the same thing. Freedom in the sense of independence, as
applied to states, does not at first sight seem to fit the unitary
absence-of-constraint model (though, as we shall see, it can be
made to fit with a little tugging, pulling, and squeezing). The 'free
state' may be an impoverished tyranny with minimal on-balance
freedom for its citizens and also for itself *vis-à-vis* other states and
nature. Self-government might turn out to be more repressive
even than foreign occupation. Yet, for all of that, the state might
still be politically independent, sovereign, and governed from
within, hence free.

Analogously, it is often said that the individual person is 'free' when his ruling part or 'real self' governs, and is subject to no foreign power, either external or internal, to whose authority it has not consented. Now suppose that John Doe wants nothing more than to have all his desires, actual and potential, free of constraints. He wants as many options left open as possible and especially the options that are most important to him. He believes that Richard Roe knows best how to arrange this state of affairs. Hence, he puts himself under Roe's control, obeying as if commanded every piece of advice Roe gives him. The example becomes even more forceful if Doe makes this arrangement irrevocable. Now Doe is no longer self-determined, but he gets rich dividends of satisfaction, having found a more effective way of getting all the particular things he wants or may one day come to want. (Self-direction is *not* one of the particular things he wants, nor is it important to him to keep open the option of one day repossessing it.) He may also want 'breathing space' and 'genuine options,' in which case his benevolent director, Roe, arranges his life with these goals in mind, making key decisions for him always in such a way that his own room to maneuver will be most effectively maximized. Now if this picture is coherent, the situation is analogous to that of the nation which gains freedom from constraint by becoming a colony of a wiser benevolent power. In each case, the subject of freedom can increase its freedom from constraint by relinquishing some of its power to govern itself. Both examples then tend to show that self-government is a different kind of freedom from the absence of constraint.[18]

I think we can continue to speak of self-government as 'freedom,' however, without committing ourselves to the view that it is a kind of freedom unanalyzable in terms of the constraint model. Putatively distinct 'concepts' of freedom frequently turn out to be different estimates of 'the importance of only one part of what is always present in any case of freedom'[19]—the importance of one class of subjects as opposed to another, or of one class of desires or open options as opposed to another, or of one class of missing constraints as opposed to another. The point of calling individual self-direction *freedom*, I think, may be to emphasize the overriding importance of one particular kind of desire or option, namely, that to decide for oneself what one shall do. Even wise and benevolent external direction is a constraint to the desire, actual or possible, to decide for oneself. Hence there is a point in calling the absence of *that* constraint (or the presence of self-direction) freedom.

Of course, almost anything at all can, in a similar way, be made out to be a constraint to *some* desire, actual or possible.[20] Hence the absence of anything-at-all (e.g. cloudy skies) can be identified with 'true' or 'positive' freedom. The point, however, of signaling out the desire to govern oneself for this special status is to acknowledge its supreme and special importance among desires. For those to whom the desire to govern themselves for better or worse is so important that few other desires can yield significant satisfactions so long as it is constrained, there is every reason to pre-empt the word 'freedom' for the absence of constraint to *it*. Nor is this singling out of a supreme desire a purely arbitrary or subjective thing. A powerful case can be made to show that other acknowledged values have self-government as their pre-condition, in particular, that dignity, self-esteem, and responsibility are impossible without it.

I come finally to the problem of applying the political metaphor of self-government to the individual, the question which Peters has so effectively illuminated for us in his discussion of autonomy. In my concluding remarks I can only hope to fill out a little more the picture he has accurately traced, and to anticipate some stubborn philosophical perplexities he had no time to dispel.

The individual self

Just as in the case of 'on balance freedom,' the clear application of the concept of autonomy presupposes an adequate conception of the self that is the subject of freedom: a self that is narrow enough so that we can contrast it with other *internal* elements of the total self over which it is said to rule, but also wide enough to include constitutive elements or properties of its own—basic convictions, allegiances, life plans, ultimate objectives, moral principles, etc. The attributes of the inner-core self that rules the wider self include not only 'Reason,' but materials for Reason to work with, and the latter will be the convictions, ideals, and purposes that are most deeply entrenched in an hierarchical network of similar principles, those which, because of their logically central position in the net-work, are the last to be tampered with when changes of mind or heart must be made. These are the attributes which are often said to 'define the person' or to provide him with his own sense of 'identity.'[21] If we strip our conception of the governing self of all its standards and values, leaving only a bare impersonal Reason imprisoned in its own royal palace, the notion of autonomy becomes empty and incoherent. In order for the word 'free,' in any sense, to have intelligible application, its subject must be an entity with tendencies of its own that can be blocked or fulfilled, 'obeyed' or rebelled against. The human subject of freedom, then, must have some substance, some normative flesh and blood.

There are necessarily two aspects of autonomous self-government.

The governing self must be neither a colony of some external self, or 'foreign power,' nor powerless to enforce its directives to its own interior subjects. If we appropriate William James's usage (modified for our own purposes) and call the 'inner core self' the I and the rest of the comprehensive self over which it rules its Me, then we can put the dual aspect of personal autonomy felicitously: *I am autonomous if I rule me, and no one else rules I.*[22] The absence of dictation from outside the total self is a much desired ideal situation (although *total* absence of external control is not a realistic hope), but since the fulfillment of this ideal of circumstance is largely a matter of luck, it would be odd to consider it also to be a virtue or ideal of character. A man should get credit for his independence of others only to the extent that he doesn't *need* external control (being perfectly in control of himself) and hence, doesn't *allow* it. If it is imposed on him anyway by superior power, that circumstance obviously is no flaw in his character. External control is the sign of a character defect (or should we say 'mental illness'?) only if it is a consequence of a failure of self-government because of the rebellion of ungovernable internal components, or because the inner-core self, lacking cohesion or direction, is incapable of governing.

Authenticity

It is hard to avoid perplexity about the application of that criterion of autonomy that Peters calls 'authenticity.' When *are* we governing ourselves, making or accepting our *own* rules, deciding for genuine not 'artificial' and 'second-hand'[23]) reasons of our *own*? I have always regarded this as a tough personal problem and not merely a theoretical one. Peters, following Piaget, restricts his discussion of authenticity to moral *rules*, but that is only one facet (and I think a relatively easy one) of the problem. Authenticity is a notion that applies also to tastes, opinions, ideals, goals, principles, values, and preferences. We can ask, after all, how we can know when we are choosing in accordance with our *own* preferences or forming our *own* opinions, as opposed to being unknowingly manipulated or self-deceived. When we add these further questions to the problem of authenticity, our personal doubts quicken and philosophical puzzlement deepens. I think these questions are instances of a general problem about knowing one's own *motives* (as opposed to intentions, which are much easier to know): we cannot always know for sure what it is about one object of choice that makes it attractive to us and about another that makes *it* repellent, or what it is about one opinion that 'moves us' to adopt it, and so on. Not uncommonly we are plainly wrong about the basis of appeal to us in some attractive prospect. Sometimes our choices seem over-determined so that it is not evident whether it is the 'good reason' or the prospect of gain that really moves us. When my decisions please others, have I made them because I expected them to please, or for 'genuine' reasons of my own? And when is the desire to please others itself a 'genuine reason' of one's own?

In addition to the general problem of knowing one's own motives, there is the conceptual problem of characterizing the elusive motive of disinterestedness that is the mark of the authentic man. Our standards must be high enough to exclude subtle counterfeits of authenticity, yet not so high as to render authenticity an empty or unrealizable ideal. In particular, we must not demand total transcendence of the culture of one's time and place, for the autonomous Reason even of the authentic man will be at the service of some interests and ways of perceiving the world that are simply 'given' him by the *Zeitgeist* and his own special circumstances. A former colleague of mine, a sensitive and gifted analytical philosopher, once announced to me that after many years of teaching the philosophy of religion he had gradually come to believe in God. My friend had prepared an elaborate and complex rationale for his important new conviction such that I could not doubt the authenticity of his reasonings. Months later he told me that he had joined the local Methodist church. I asked him whether he had done this after a careful examination of the claims to truth of the various Protestant sects against one another, or of Catholicism against Protestantism generally, or of Christianity against the other world religions. Of course, he had not, and my question struck him as merely impertinent. When I asked him what the religious affiliation of his parents and grandparents had been, he answered, of course, Methodist. I took this at the time as strong evidence of inauthenticity, of the acquisition of convictions and commitments in an 'artificial' and 'second-hand' way. But now I'm not so sure. Perhaps my standards of authenticity were pegged unrealistically high. My friend could not even consider becoming (say) a Buddhist or a Roman Catholic. These were, in James's phrase, absolutely dead options to him. After all, if one is a Burmese and finds God one becomes a Buddhist, and if one is Italian or Irish one becomes a Catholic. My friend was not shopping for a different nationality or ethnic identity; his own was too well fixed to be questioned. So he became a Methodist. Was he a 'mere slave' to his time and place in this selection? I think not. We may all be, in some respects, irrevocably the 'products of our culture,' but that is no reason why the self that is such a product cannot be free to govern the self it is.

Contrasts with autonomy

There are a variety of familiar ways of falling short of the ideal of autonomy, a noting of which might be useful for strengthening our grasp of the concept. When the *I* is incapable of governing its *Me*, the result is anomie, a condition which is not control from without, but rather being virtually 'out of control' altogether. Autonomy is also contrasted with forms of passive mindless adjustment (the pejorative term is 'conformity') to the requirements of one's culture. In a book that made a great splash two decades ago,[24] David Riesman and his associates described in detail three 'types of social character,' each one characteristic of human societies at a given stage of their economic and demographic development. In the period of 'tradition-direction' the ideal of autonomy would hardly even occur to anyone. Individuals were 'governed' by rituals and operating procedures worked out by their ancestors. Social and technological change was very slow, so that the dominant character type fits the social conditions well, and such traits as personal ambition, initiative, and flexibility, are not required. Everyone does the same thing without question, if only from fear of being publicly shamed.

Tradition-direction was succeeded in the Western countries by what Riesman called the 'inner-directed' type. The centuries following the decline of feudalism were characterized by 'increased personal mobility ... constant expansion ... vast technological shifts ... exploration, colonization. ...' Needed to meet these challenges was a new type 'who can manage ... without strict and self-evident tradition-direction,' a type with a 'rigid but highly individualized character.'[25] Early in life, a set of 'generalized but nonetheless inescapably destined goals'[26] and standards are implanted in the child, by his parents, their authoritative source internalized, so that they become inescapably his forever more. The inner-directed man thus has within him a kind of 'psychological gyroscope'[27] that keeps him steadily on his course on pain of powerful guilt-feelings, and also permits him to 'receive signals' from authorities who resemble his parents, as well as from his governing internalized ideal.

So much has been written in adulation of our inner-directed forebearers that Riesman is obliged to go to great pains to show how far they too fail to satisfy any reasonable model of autonomy:[28]

First, the gyroscopic mechanism allows the inner-directed person to appear far more independent than he really is: he is no less a conformist to others than the other-directed person, but the voices to which he listens are more distant, of an older generation, their cues internalized in his childhood.

He becomes capable of impersonal relations with people and sometimes incapable of any other kind. This is one of the prices he pays for his relative impermeability to the needs and wishes of his peers, and helps account for his ability, when in pursuit of some end he values, to steel himself against their indifference or hostility.

The social utility of inner-directedness declines, according to Riesman, as industrialization and the population boom run their courses, and an affluent society becomes oriented more toward consumption than production. The other-directed man, character-istic of our own times, is brought up in such a way that he has no inner gyroscope but rather a psychological 'radar-set' extremely sensitive to signals from his own age-group, current fashions, and popular 'media' of communication. In an age when manipulation of persons is a greater economic preoccupation than conquest of the material environment, 'gyroscopic control is no longer sufficiently flexible.'[29] Non-productive consumers form a high proportion of the population and 'they need both the economic opportunity to be prodigal and the character structure that allows it . . . children are made to feel guilty not so much about violation of inner standards as for failure to win social approval.'[30] Extremely sensitive attunement to the wishes of others is implanted early, and the need to be accepted by others becomes the major impetus to thought and action, on pain, not of shame, or guilt, but a 'diffuse anxiety.'

The inauthenticity of the well-adjusted other-directed man is easily shown. If he is plump, he looks better in vertical stripes than in horizontal ones; but if his peers are wearing horizontals this season, so will he, aesthetic considerations be damned. And if inherited temperament inclines him to a life style that is currently out of favor with his peers, he will adopt a different life style instead, even if it ill-fits and ill-becomes his temperament. Even his opinions and 'convictions' he will choose in the way he chooses his clothes for their conformity to the public 'image' he wishes to present for the approval of his peers.

If these are the ways of missing the target, what do they tell us about the target itself? A human being must have a capacity for self-regulation, otherwise he suffers anomie; but if his internal regulator is itself an unregulable gyroscope or radar set, he cannot be autonomous, no matter how happily adjusted (or 'attuned') he is. Yet all of us presumably were given our gyroscopes or radar sets or some combination of the two as children. How then can autonomy be possible for us? Riesman says that autonomous men may be maladjusted to their societies, but that they differ from other dissidents and misfits in that they are capable of conforming if they choose. That is to say, they are 'free to choose whether to conform or not,'[31] and if they choose not, they are not subject to immobilizing guilt or pervasive anxiety. They will conform when and only when there are good reasons for doing so; and they can attend to reason free from the interfering static of 'signals' from other voices. They can control the speed and direction of their gyroscopes, if they have them, or rotate their radar apparatus, or turn it off. The autonomous man will buy his clothes in part to match his purse, his build, and his functions; he will select his life style to match his temperament, and his political attitudes to fit his ideals and interests. He cannot be indifferent to the reactions of others, but he *can* be moved by other considerations too.

If 'other-direction' is becoming the prevalent mode of ensuring conformity in our time, as Riesman maintained, then the autonomous man will have to exercise his autonomy by overcoming or outwitting, somehow, his own deeply implanted radar receptor. One can see today how difficult that problem can be, as youths, eager to be authentic, still keep cultishly attuned to one another. Perhaps the best hope of educators is to utilize the inevitable radar sets, when by-passing them is not possible, by feeding 'rationalistic' signals into the transmission system. Suppose that the schools and the media cooperated in creating images of rationality that would be immediately picked up by the sensitive receivers of the young and made part of their own network of signals, so that the 'in' way of buying commodities, for example, would be to check *Consumer's Union* tests and evaluations, rather than responding to the polished images of the advertising men. Suppose that *that* kind of prudent rationality were taken to be characteristic not of egg-heads and other alien groups merely, but also of what real swingers generally do, so that teenagers would lose standing with their peers for acting out of their assigned judicious roles. The practice of independent deliberative judgment might then begin as a kind of other-directed play acting, but if constantly reinforced by incoming signals from peers (not 'authorities') it could become a fixed and functionally autonomous habit.[32] Perhaps the product of such arrangements would not be perfectly pure autonomy, since the basic motive in people would still be to win the approval of their peers, but it would surely be a closer approximation than most people have ever achieved, and how many of *us* have achieved anything 'purer'?

Rational reflection

I wish my final emphasis to be on the danger of taking autonomy too seriously as a goal of education either in the home or the school. One can do this either by conceiving of autonomy in such an exalted way that its criteria can never be satisfied, or else by promoting the ideal prematurely in a self-defeating way. To reflect rationally, in the manner of an autonomous man, is to apply some already accepted principles in accordance with the rules of rational procedure, to the test of more tentative principles or candidates for principles, or to possible judgments or decisions. Rational reflection thus presupposes some relatively settled convictions to reason from and with. If we take autonomy to require that all principles are to be examined afresh in the light of reason on each occasion for decision, then nothing resembling rational reflection can ever get started.

Ten years after the publication of *The Lonely Crowd* Riesman wrote that autonomy presupposes 'the power of individuals to shape their own characters by their selection among models and experiences'[33]—a power, I might add, that we find more and more college age youths bent on exercising in the current variegated search for 'identity.' My modest point is simply that a person must already possess at least a tentative character before he can hope to *choose* a new one. The other side of that point is that if a child needs to 'learn to be autonomous,' it must be the case that he is not already autonomous when he starts. There can be no magical *ex nihilo* creation of the habit of rational reflection. Some principles, and especially the commitment to reasonableness itself, must be implanted in a child, if he is to have a reasonable opportunity of growing in the proper direction.

The rough equivalent of 'anomie' in the realm of beliefs and ideals is that corruption of the ideal of open-mindedness, where everything is always 'up for grabs,' and every conviction or allegiance is to be examined afresh each time it comes up, as if past confirmations counted for nothing. The 'cognitively anomic' man thus has no firm direction in his reasonings, nothing unquestioned with which to compare and test the questionable. This description begins to resemble Ruskin's picture of 'the embodiment of caprice.' If *that* is what autonomy is, then it is neither an ideal state nor a virtue appropriate to free status, and the comprehensive ideal of *a free man all-told* must be incoherent. But to conceive of autonomy in that way is a mistake which Piaget, Kohlberg, and Peters, with their careful attention to stages in the gradual progression up to autonomy, do not make.

Summary

My aim has been to probe for conceptual linkages between the idea of a free man and the idea of a free society, by considering how the word 'free' has come to apply to both. I have divided the inquiry into five parts corresponding to the five alternative ways of interpreting the sentence 'I am free.' The results are not easy to summarize. The idea of an *absence of constraint* is essential to one pattern of usages, the idea of a *status-right* to another, the idea of *appropriateness to a status* to another, the political metaphor of *self-rule* to another. Much unity can be seen to underlie this diversity if we accept internal and negative factors as constraints, and allow the desire simply to be rid of something for its own sake and the desire to decide for oneself what one will do to be among the possible objects of constraint. Even the idea of general or relative freedom from constraint, however, requires supplementation by normative standards for determining the relative worth of conflicting wants and interests. Indeed, three of the patterns discussed above (on-balance freedom, the virtue of freedom, and autonomy) have been penetrated at several points by standards and values of other kinds: standards of worthiness, fittingness, and reasonableness are of necessity built into them. But that in no way detracts from their coherence or importance. *A free man all-told* will be free on-balance *to* do what is most worth doing and *from* those constraints most worth being without. The characteristic images of on-balance *unfreedom* are the barrier or locked room (external constraint), the bayonet at one's back (compulsion) and the internal traffic jam or hang-up. The free man all-told will also be fortunate enough to be a freeman, but he will show his worthiness of this legal status by his possession of virtues appropriate to it: a secure sense of his own worth, generosity, high-mindedness, disinterestedness, and self-sufficiency. inquiry into five parts corresponding to the five alternative ways of Finally, he will 'govern' himself rather than be directed in all his choices and preferences by unexamined traditions, or signals from an unmodifiable gyroscope or radar-set within him. Most of these components of the composite ideal, it can readily be seen, presuppose for their intelligibility, an acquaintance with social systems to which the word 'free' or its antonyms can also have application.

Notes

1 R. S. Peters, 'Freedom and the Development of the Free Man', p.120.
2 Cf. Isaiah Berlin, *Four Essays on Liberty*, O.U.P., 1969, 'Introduction', p. xliii n.

3 According to Felix Oppenheim, if we know that only 70 per cent of
  the parking violations in a given city are detected and penalized,
  then, given certain other assumptions, we can predict with 70 per
  cent probability that a given overparker will be fined, and this
  entitles us to say (from the sociological perspective, of course!) that
  'drivers in that city are officially unfree to a degree of 0.7 to overpark
  and their freedom to do so is 0.3'—*Dimensions of Freedom*, New York:
  St Martin's Press, 1961, p. 187.

4 To vary the image still again, he is subject to 'hang-ups,' and even
  'hoist with his own petard.'

5 Cf. Oppenheim, *op. cit.*, p. 200.

6 C. S. Lewis, *Studies in Words*, Cambridge University Press, 1961,
  p. 114.

7 In the ancient world, says Lewis, 'Freedom can mean simply
  "citizenship," and when the centurion tells Saint Paul that he had
  paid a lot of money to acquire Roman citizenship (*politeia*), the
  Authorized Version says "At a great price obtained I this freedom"
  . . . This meaning is fossilized in the surviving English use of
  franchise to mean the power of voting, conceived as the essential mark
  of full citizenship.'—*Studies in Words*, p. 125.

8 *Ibid.*, p. 114.

9 *Ibid.*, p. 21.

10 *Ibid.*, p. 22.

11 John Ruskin, *The Queen of the Air*, ch. 3.

12 C. S. Lewis, *op. cit.*, p. 112.

13 *Ibid.*, p. 126.

14 *Loc. cit.*

15 *Op. cit.*, pp. 128–9.

16 Aristotle, *Metaphysics*, 1075b.

17 C. S. Lewis, *op. cit.*, pp. 124–5.

18 Compare Isaiah Berlin, *op. cit.*, p. 130: 'The answer to the question—
   "Who governs me?"—is logically distinct from the question— "How far
   does government interfere with me?" It is in this difference that the
   great contrast between the two concepts of liberty in the end
   consists.'

19 Gerald C. MacCallum, Jr, 'Negative and Positive Freedom',
   Philosophical Review, vol. 76, 1967, p. 318.

20 An unconstrained possible but unactual desire is an 'open option.'

21 What social scientists call the 'problem of identity,' if I understand
   them correctly, is that of selecting out of the class of true descriptions
   of a person (e.g. he is male, young, brown-eyed, poor, American,
   Catholic, a philosopher, a ball player, a liberal, a flutist, a father)
   those that are to be in some way *essential* to his own conception of
   himself, as opposed to those that are trivial, dispensable, and
   accidental; the status as essential, in the normal case, being partly
   chosen by the not-fully-formed young person himself in accordance
   with whatever 'inner-core' principles he already has (or is).

22 This account of autonomy also satisfies John Austin's famous

definition of *sovereignty*. Perhaps the two concepts come to the same thing in their political application. Perhaps the expression 'personal sovereignty,' which we do not use, would be preferable to 'personal autonomy,' which we do use, in that its character as a political metaphor would be less concealed.

23 Peters, *op. cit.*, pp. 123–4.

24 David Riesman, *et al*, *The Lonely Crowd*, New Haven, Yale University Press, 1950. My references will be to the abridged edition (Yale Paperbound, 1961).

25 *Ibid.*, p. 14.

26 *Ibid.*, p. 15.

27 *Ibid.*, p. 16.

28 *Ibid.*, p. 31, p. 56.

29 *Ibid.*, p. 18.

30 *Ibid.*, pp. 19, 21.

31 *Ibid.*, p. 242.

32 In similar ways, in an inner-directed period, parents who are dedicated to autonomy might 'instill' it in their children by means of a psychological gyroscope whose unswerving aim is in the direction of the parental ideal. The voices to which the child would listen would be his parents', but their only message would be: Think for yourself!

33 *Op. cit.*, 'Preface', p. xlviii.

Part 5

Rights and duties in education 10

Frederick A. Olafson

It is widely believed that there is a universal right to education. While one might expect that a right of such evident importance would have been the subject of careful philosophical analysis, this turns out not to be the case at all. The text of the Declaration of Human Rights, which in Article 26 declares that 'everyone has a right to education' does not give any indication of what the basis of the right to education is held to be; and a survey of the philosophical and legal literature dealing with human rights reveals that there have been almost no serious attempts to show just what is implied in the existence of a universal human right to education or what rational justification there can be for the assertion that there is in fact such a right. Appeals to a right to education are, of course, frequent; but they typically serve to express a moral or social claim for which an adequate and perhaps even self-evident rational basis is simply assumed to exist. Self-evidence is, however, as unhelpful a notion in these contexts as it is in most others; and an effort to provide a philosophical analysis of the right to education is long overdue. This paper is a contribution to such an effort which will, I hope, increasingly engage the interest of philosophers.

Perhaps one of the reasons why the right to education has not been subjected to careful analysis is a belief that the existence of such a right can be straightforwardly derived from more general human rights. Thus if it is assumed at the outset that every human being has a right to the 'realization . . . of the economic, social, and cultural rights indispensable for his dignity and the free development of his personality,' as the Declaration puts it in Article 22, then it will not be difficult to derive a right to education as an instrument to the effective realization of these more general human rights. Without wishing to adopt a skeptical attitude toward the latter, I have decided not to adopt this line of argument which for various reasons seems unsatisfactory to me. It very often leaves quite unclear what is the basis of our assumed commitment to the superordinate rights from which the right to education is derived; and it casts no light at all on the special relationships among human beings to which the right to education owes much of its validity, at least as it is com-

173

monly interpreted. This decision to treat the right to education in abstraction from wider human rights does not reflect so much dissent from the conclusions reached by other routes of argument as it does doubts about their cogency; and I am certainly not suggesting that it is possible to make a case for the existence of a right to education outside any wider framework of moral relationships. I do think it is useful, however, to explore the local context of relationships in which claims to a right to education plausibly arise before introducing an appeal to more general moral considerations. In this way, I hope the basis of both the wider and the more specific rights will be made more evident than is the case when the one is presented simply as a subordinate means of implementation for a higher moral principle.

One further preliminary point. To approach the whole matter of making provision for education as a matter of rights and duties, as I will be doing in this paper, is not to deny even by implication that there may be other kinds of reasons that would justify such provision. In other words, a person who did not have a duty to contribute to the education of a certain person or persons might nevertheless have a rational motive for doing so. At the level of collective action these reasons will be those of what we call 'public policy'; and an example of educational provision based on such considerations might be the decision of an underdeveloped country to allocate resources to the training of middle-level technicians in order to assist a program of industrialization. Such a decision might be made simply on the basis of national need; and the trainees might be selected solely on the basis of aptitude without any question of their having a *right* to this education arising. I have chosen to approach the matter from the other side, i.e., from the side of the claims to education which are based on rights which we are morally bound to recognize; but a negative view of public policy arguments for educational provision is in no way implied thereby.

With these understandings, then, I will begin by noting a feature of the right to education about which there should be little disagreement, even in advance of a general analysis of this right, but which is of great importance in determining how to come at such an analysis. This feature has to do with the duties which are correlative with the right to education which it is claimed all human beings have. To say that a person has a right, of whatever kind, is normally to imply that other persons have a duty not to interfere with his exercise of that right. To this rule, the right to education presumably forms no exception; and so, if there is a universal human right to education, there must also be an equally universal and binding duty not to interfere with or frustrate the holders of such rights in the exercise thereof. Sometimes this negative duty of non-interference is the only duty that is correlative with a right like that of property. But in the case of the right to education—and this is the preliminary point I want to make—this can hardly be the case. Obtaining an education is not an activity which an individual can carry on by himself and which, therefore, requires of others only that they not interfere or otherwise put obstacles in the way of that activity. It may, as an individual matures, become progressively an activity which an individual can carry on in at least quite substantial independence of positive support from others; but in the earliest years when an education gets under way, it is just such positive cooperation and support that is required in all but the most unusual cases. It follows that if the right to education is to amount to something more than the right of each child not to be interfered with by others as he educates himself, the duty correlative with the right to education must be a duty to provide positive support in the form of the various relevant resources for the education in question. It also follows that any case we construct with a view to showing that there is a right to education must also be a case showing that some person or persons have a duty to support and assist the education of the persons for whom the right is claimed. It is central to the approach I have adopted to this whole issue that the interdependence of the right to education and of the positive duty to expend resources in support of education be recognized at the outset. I do not, of course, wish to imply thereby that there is anything trivial about the duty of non-interference with another individual's effort to educate himself—a duty which requires, for example, that free access be allowed to sources of information and which is thus closely related to the wider freedoms on which a democratic society depends. But it would be a serious mistake not to distinguish clearly between this kind of freedom from the interference of others and a right to education which requires the positive support and expenditure of resources by others. It may even be the case that the right to education is not most appropriately thought of as a freedom at all, although a good education will certainly respect and protect the freedom of those to whom it is provided.

The right to education with which I will be concerned in this essay is thus a right to which a duty to expend resources in support of education is a counterpart; and much of the subsequent discussion will therefore be concerned as much with that duty as with the right to which it answers. This circumstance in turn both explains and justifies the strategy of argument I have chosen which consists in demonstrating that educational rights and duties are special rights and duties rather than general ones. If a man is to be shown to have a duty to expend substantial resources in support of something, that duty should not be made contingent upon his accepting as a premise some proposition about the desirability of the end which would be furthered by his contribution for he can then— whether in good faith or bad makes little difference—simply decline to endorse that objective. But when it can be shown that a person is already involved in the operation of a co-operative practice of some kind and has presumptively benefited by so doing, then he can no longer simply repudiate the principle on which that practice rests. The weakness of the argument which seeks to deduce a right to education and a corresponding duty from very general moral principles is that there corresponds to the latter very little in the way of operative schemes of co-operation among human beings. While a man may agree that it would be a good thing if everyone were to treat everyone else in the manner called for by the moral principle in question, he can scarcely feel *obliged* to do so. On the other hand, the existence of such hard obligations *can* be shown among the members of more restricted human groups in the co-operative practices of which they are implicated by their own participation; and it is with groups of this kind and specifically the family as the prime locus of cross-generational relationships that I have chosen to begin my examination of rights and duties having to do with education. It may not be fanciful to think of the various contexts of human co-operation as so many concentric circles, the innermost of which—the family—is unquestionably operative while the outermost—mankind—is more ideal than real. In terms of this image, the strategy I have chosen is to begin with the innermost circle in order to determine how extensive a basis for a right to education the relationships discoverable there may afford. To begin in this way with special and as it were local duties is certainly not to pre-judge adversely the possibility of a movement outward to the wider circles of mutuality which the theory of a general right to education treats as already actualized. What I do object to, however, is the practice, which has become common in contemporary ethics, of neglecting all the special relationships in which human beings stand to one another and of treating all moral relationships as though they formed part of a universal scheme of moral co-operation from which our duties can simply be read off. I would argue that the duties so derived are necessarily very weak ones and that it is more realistic to explore the obligations generated by special relationships that unquestionably exist before invoking a much more abstract set of principles which will inevitably lack the 'purchase' on the individual that is assured in the case of duties based on special relationships.

Finally, a question may arise about the meaning that is to be assigned to the word 'education' in the phrase 'the right to education.' The definition of this term has often been the occasion for introducing a list of praiseworthy educational goals; but I want to assign a minimal sense to the term which will, I hope, be uncontroversial and at the same time appropriate to the context of discussion of this paper. An education, in this minimal sense, would simply be the acquiring of certain forms of competence through instruction or other appropriate forms of assistance. By 'competence' I understand trained capacity or the ability to carry on some activity or perform some function more or less on one's own; and it must be understood that the 'activity' may be one that involves overt operations as a surgical technique does; or symbolic operations in the way that reading a French text or solving an algebra problem does; or, as is most often the case, some combination of both. While terms like capacity and ability suggest that education is concerned with 'knowing how' rather than 'knowing that,' the intent of my analysis is not adequately expressed in these terms which tend to imply that there *is* some sort of knowing—'knowing that'—which can be divorced from the ability to 'go on' beyond the recitation of a fact or law to the deployment of such knowledge in some continuing activity, whether at the level of discourse or not. I am assuming that the acquisition of such capabilities of the latter sort is the business of education; and that, at least at the early stages of our education, we need the assistance of other persons who are substantially more advanced than we are in respect to the possession of these capacities, if we are to acquire them successfully ourselves. How such learning can be most successfully assisted—whether through traditional instructional methods or by other means, whether in schools or in other 'learning environments'—is a question which I will not raise in this paper. The only assumption I am making is that all of these methods will require the application of resources of various kinds—time, materials, and money—and will thus have to be supported by someone other than the person receiving the education. I should also add that the negative connotations that for many persons apparently attach to the notion of 'competence' are entirely irrelevant to my use of the term. So far is it from signifying merely a capacity for mechanical or rote performance of a task that at least a minimum ability to improvise and to adapt old routines to novel circumstances would be a necessary condition of possessing almost any form of competence.

Certain distinctive features of the right to education and its correlative duty should now be noted. A right is something that is normally cited or appealed to by the person to whom it belongs in order to justify his claim to non-interference or to the relevant kind of assistance from others, and in certain circumstances, the duty to provide assistance may not in a strict sense become operative until a claim based upon the right has been explicitly made. In the case of a right to education, however, this is not so. The reason is quite simply that those who have a right to education are in the first instance young children who do not know what a right is and who are not capable of claiming what is theirs by right. That claim must, therefore, be made *for them* by other mature persons who may in fact be the persons on whom the duty to provide for their educa-ation devolves. Now this initial inability of the possessors of the right to education to claim that right, and the resultant necessity for others both to make that claim in their name and to satisfy it, may serve as a useful clue to the relationships that hold generally between those who have a right to education and those who have the duty to make provision for their education. That relationship is typically a relationship between persons who belong to different generations; and for purposes of simplification I am going to speak as if only two generations were involved although of course I recognize that things don't arrange themselves quite so neatly in real life. In any case, the relationship between persons belonging to one generation and another is dominated by two facts that are so familiar to all of us that we may fail to realize how profoundly important they are. One of these is the fact that the members of one generation—the younger—come into being as the result of actions performed by members of the other generation—the older one. The other fact is somewhat harder to state in an uncontroversial way—particularly at the present time—but it is, I believe, no less patent when correctly understood. It is the fact that human beings come into the world without the forms of competence of which they stand in need; that they acquire these over a considerable period of time; and that initially the members of different generations are therefore asym-metrically related in respect of the possession of these forms of competence. The right to education and the duty to provide an education seem to me to be capable of being understood only in the context of the special relationship that is defined by these two features of the relationship between generations; and it is therefore appropriate to refer to them as generational rights and generational duties, that is, as rights and duties that accrue to persons by reason of their occupying one position or another in the relationship I have described.

The duties of which I have been speaking are duties to provide something to which every human being is believed to have a right and without which anyone's chances in life would be much reduced.

This is to say that an education is to be provided because having an education is in the interest of the person to whom it is provided. This may seem to be a truism; but I think that it is really a point of great importance and that if it were consistently borne in mind when decisions are made about such things as the way in which the elements of civic culture can be imparted to a young person, it might generate quite significant implications. I do not, of course, mean that instruction can ever be completely adjusted to the requirements of each individual child; and the concept of interest to which I am appealing is one which not only reflects certain assumptions about what human beings generally require, but also assumes that what is in one person's interest will be at least compatible with and certainly not directly harmful to the interest of others. Furthermore, what is in one's interest, in the sense in which I am using this term, may very well not be that in which one is interested. What is in one's interest is rather something in which one has a stake, something on the possession or attainment of which some advantage or benefit to oneself depends. It is important to recognize, moreover, that at the beginning of his education a child cannot normally form any adequate idea of what his long-run life-interest comprises and has not yet reached the stage at which he is capable of making the kind of principled choice on which the design of an instructional program depends. A child simply knows too little about the world and about the various departments of knowledge to which he is to be introduced to be able to decide where to begin, in what order things are best taken up, why one thing is a prerequisite for some other form of study, and a host of other matters that go into the elaboration of any instructional sequence that rests on more than impulse. What one *can* hope for in very young children is a state of general receptivity and curiosity and perhaps a desire to learn about certain kinds of things. These are precious assets for any teacher; but to treat them as though they were comparable to adult choices and as though respect for such incipient forms of academic preference rendered unnecessary any independent judgments by the teacher as to the content and direction of the child's academic work, seems to me to be a species of self-delusion on the part of adults.

In so far as education undertakes to impart any more or less definite form of competence, decisions about the way in which study and instruction are to be organized must rest with those who possess that competence already and are charged with helping others to attain it. In other words, the adult persons who have the duty to provide for the education of the young must not only recognize and respond to a right which the child is scarcely able to claim for himself; but they must also make a number of momentous decisions as to how the interest of the latter is to be interpreted for purposes of instruction. These adults—and I am assuming that both parents and teachers should be involved in such decisions—know or should know what kind of a society the child has been born into, what the duties of citizenship entail and on what kinds of competence the life-chances of a young person are likely to depend. In a relatively stable society, the obligation to make such decisions for others would not be experienced as a painful personal responsibility since in such a society it can be assumed that the future will be very like the past. But when instability becomes the norm in one sphere of life after another, these decisions have to be based on what are often no more than conjectures as to what will best serve the long run interest of those who will have to live in a world in many respects quite different from the world one knows oneself. This duty, if taken seriously, can be very much more onerous than that of paying taxes to support the schools; and it is not surprising that there are those who seek to evade it by extracting curricular guide-lines from the unformed impulses of the children themselves. There are even those who declare that an adult's making any such decision for a child is a kind of criminal aggression against the latter. But if the positions of the adult and the child in relation to the forms of competence to be acquired are really different and if the capacity of the child for decisions that organize work over substantial periods of time is very limited, then it would appear that this element of 'aggression' or asymmetry in educational decision-making is un-eliminable and that the important thing for adults is to recognize it and to accept the responsibility it entails.

The notion of responsibility is central here and needs to be explained. As I conceive it, the members of the senior generation on whom the original determination of educational policy devolves expose themselves by the decisions they make to an eventual judgment by those in whose behalf they act. Stated in different terms, this means that the ultimate definition of the interest of a new generation or its component parts rests with its members; and they will have to judge how appropriate and how useful the educa-tion which others designed for them has in fact proved to be. I do not wish to seem to be implying that that education will be laid down *en bloc* through another's decision. In every sensibly designed educational sequence there will be built-in choice-points at which the student will have the opportunity to make decisions as to the direction some portion of his studies is to take. But the decision as to how much choice he will have will not normally be his; and so even the elements of indeterminacy and freedom it comprises will

Rights and duties in education

depend upon decisions that are made by what I have been calling the senior generation. In any society that is not stagnant it would be surprising if the retrospective judgment of a generation on the education it received did not include some criticisms which would presumably lead to changes in the kind of education that generation then offers to *its* successor generation. On the other hand, total rejection—at least if it amounted to more than a rhetorical flourish—would in a clear sense constitute a failure for the preceding generation, not because its policies would have been invalidated before some impartial tribunal, but because, for whatever reason, their effort to identify and serve the interest of the ascendant generation would have failed.

Some may object that in fact the judgment of a generation on its education is not an independent criterion of its worth since the minds of those who judge will have been formed by the very education they are to judge. Others may draw just the opposite conclusion and argue that it is intolerable that an education be judged by persons who may have failed to assimilate just those standards which alone give their opinion any claim to consideration. But the more reasonable view seems to me to be that these critical estimates are not automatically validated or invalidated by the fact they reflect in one way or another the influence of the education they deal with. While no evaluation of an education would be likely to command much assent if it were not based to some extent on standards that had been learned in the course of the education itself, there is no reason why criticism should not extend to the standards themselves or to certain aspects thereof, provided only that it is not so total as to be self-diremptive. In any period of change the most that can be hoped for by anyone who has a share in the formulation of educational policy is that his judgment will be partially sustained by the generation that follows; and that his way of distinguishing between what is of permanent value and what is evanescent will find enough confirmation to make a measure of continuity between generations possible. This kind of responsibility which requires that the senior generation make judgments in behalf of another generation—judgments which are then ratified or revised in the light of the latter's own conception of its interest— is certainly one that is difficult to bear under the best of circumstances and it is not surprising that many shirk it. But it is an indispensable adjunct to the thesis of asymmetry in respect to certain kinds of competence that underlies the rights and duties I have been discussing. For just as that asymmetry with respect to competence is in principle self-liquidating and gives way to a situation in which teacher and student stand in the same relation to the body of knowledge in question, so the asymmetry in respect of educational decision-making is also self-liquidating and the generation for which decisions were made becomes the generation that makes decisions in behalf of its successor and with the same kind of responsibility which I have been describing.

This point will bear emphasis for if it is not understood, the line of reasoning I have been developing will be even more offensive to contemporary sensibilities than it need be. Thus, against what has been said here it might be argued that we are all—parents and teachers and children—in the position of learners and that there cannot be any hard and fast distinction of superordinate and subordinate roles in respect of any body of knowledge without a distortion of the nature of knowledge itself and an implied denial of the human dignity of those who are placed in the subordinate position of learners. (I pass over the egregious suggestion of Dr Margaret Mead who holds that an asymmetry rather than an equivalence in respect of knowledge does indeed obtain but runs the other way.) There is a deeply antinomian flavor to this objection, appealing as it does to the great human commonalties of ignorance, uncertainty, and error, to the end of washing out the falsely imposing distinctions on which established claims to authority rest. More relevantly, however, the objection expresses an understandable resentment of the way in which these distinctions may in fact be interpreted or at any rate perceived in some schools and universities. We are, of course, all learners; and the status of student or learner is not a kind of *état civil* which is assigned to certain persons for life while that of 'knower' or teacher belongs to others in the same way. These positions are, in the first place, specific to certain forms of competence and probably also to a particular period in a person's life. They are also in principle exchangeable since a person who is a learner at a certain time may come to occupy the position of teacher at another and one who is a teacher of a certain subject will normally be a learner and perhaps a not very apt one in other areas. Moreover, no one is just a teacher or just a learner even within a single field of knowledge; and even though the learning of a teacher and a student go on at quite different levels, there is always the possibility that the former can learn something of real value from the latter. These elements of exchangeability and relativity attaching to the positions of teacher and student need to be kept in mind if the distinctions between them are not to be frozen or absolutized into something like caste distinctions. If that were to happen, one could validly argue that the asymmetry implicit in educational transactions had become inimical to a recognition of the shared *human* dignity and equality of *all* the participants in that transaction.

There will, I am sure, be disagreement as to whether something like this has really happened in our schools and universities or whether the character of relationships that do exist, while not ideal, has been misperceived by many students and sometimes deliberately distorted by others who have an independent motive for doing so. I do not want to venture my own judgment on this issue here, but merely to point out that even if these accusations were true, the remedy would not be to dismantle the institutional structures that express these asymmetries, but to see to it that their true character and their justifiability in the light of the student's own interest are made manifest by the solidity of what the school has to offer and the fairness of its procedures. Finally, it may be well to point out that the most fervid exponents of educational egalitarianism or of reverse asymmetry tend uniformly to disregard just those areas of human concern in which relatively secure distinctions between knowledge and error have been progressively worked out and to show a strong predilection for the swampy and uncharted wastes of 'life-style' and the wisdom of the viscera.

So far I have been discussing the nature of generational rights and duties in respect of education, and it is now time to consider *where* these duties rest. Since the paradigm for all generational relationships is clearly the relationship of a parent to his or her child, it seems reasonable to assume that the moral basis of the right to education and its correlative duty can be most readily exhibited in the context of that relationship. Parents are precisely those persons who, by having sexual intercourse with one another, cause another human being to be conceived and, in the normal course of events, to be born. This is, moreover, a fact about what they do that is known to them; and their responsibility for the consequences of their act is in an important sense dependent upon that knowledge. It is said that there have been primitive peoples who did not understand the relationship between intercourse and procreation in terms of direct causation and for them, if this report is correct, parenthood would presumably not be a matter of individual moral responsibility in the way it tends to be for us. Indeed, this moral character of parenthood has been sharply accentuated in our time by the increasing availability of effective devices by means of which it is possible to separate intercourse from the likelihood of conception as never before in human history. The effect of this change is to make any act of intercourse without the use of contraceptives very much more of a conscious acceptance of the likelihood that as a result of one's act another human being will be born. But it is also known that that new human being will be in a helpless condition and that its survival will be absolutely dependent upon its being cared for by others over a long period of time. Clearly if any one has a duty to provide the care that is required by the infant, it must in the first instance be the parents themselves, since they could scarcely claim that any one else had a duty to care for this child if they themselves were to neglect it. If morality requires that we recognize some duty on our part to alleviate the suffering and contribute to the well being of persons to whom we stand in no special relationship at all, how much stronger must that claim be in the case of persons whom we ourselves have caused to exist. For here the right of the infant to care and indeed to love from his parents derives not just from the fact that he has needs which he cannot satisfy and which they can; but also from the circumstance that they are responsible for the fact that these needs exist as they are responsible for the fact that the child exists. If in these circumstances parents were to repudiate their duty to their child and thus the child's right to their care, it is unclear how they could defend their conduct against the charge of radical incompatibility with the most elementary requirements of morality or even of consistency.

Here certainly it is not possible to avoid invoking in some form the general principle of morality against a hypothetical parent who might simply refuse to honor the claim his child has upon him. If such a person really regarded the effect of his actions upon others as of no consequence except in so far as it could be reckoned in terms of some difference it would make to his own eventual satisfactions, there would be nothing one could say to him about the rights of his child that would have any compelling force. But if the general principle of morality has to be invoked for the purpose of showing such parents that their action is absolutely irreconcilable with its minimal requirements, it is still being invoked only within the very narrow context of a certain special relationship and not, so to speak, at full strength as a universal duty of benevolence. Scaled down to the limits of the relationship of parent to child, what the principle of morality requires of parents is that they care for the human being whom they have brought into existence; and if there are few parents who fail entirely in this duty, we know that among those who do there are many who recognize few, if any, duties to persons who stand outside this special relationship. Those who *do* repudiate their duty to their children, are appropriately called 'unnatural parents'; and generally the human, as distinct from the biological, concept of parenthood seems to involve as one of its essential elements just this acceptance of the moral implications of one's own actions. Here, in any case, we reach the moral bed-rock on which our duties to our children and thus, by derivation, their right to education must finally rest. I am thus arguing that a recognition of a right to care on the part of the child one has brought into the world and of a correlative duty to provide that care is inseparable from the relationship of parent to child unless that concept is deliberately and artificially isolated from all contexts of morality and justification.

Now I want to argue that the child's right to education rests on the same basis as does the wider right to care and nurture which I have been discussing. The goal of such care is to bring the child to the point where it will be able to care for itself and generally to lead a life of its own; and to this end the acquisition by the child of certain basic forms of competence is as necessary as it is that its health be cared for or that it learn the elementary procedures of social cooperation. Until quite recently the level of what may be called basic cognitive competence that was required in most societies was very low and it was possible for a child to reach that level without very much, if anything, in the way of formal instruction. In most industrialized and urban societies, however, that level is now considerably higher and the penalties incurred by those who do not attain it are considerably greater than they were in the past. It is, of course, not easy to say just how this level of minimum competence should be defined; but I am going to assume that these difficulties are not such as to make us give up altogether the notion of such a minimum competence, that is to say, of a point at which a child has a reasonable chance of being able to function in a more or less adequate way in the several spheres of life. What I am claiming is that every parent has a special duty to assist his children, by whatever means are judged appropriate and in a manner consistent with the other duties he may have, to achieve at least that level of competence. This is, it should be emphasized, a special duty in the sense that it is owed to a particular individual and owed to him by reason of a special relationship to him to which one's own actions have given rise. In these respects, the duty to provide for the education of one's children is like the duty to repay one's creditors or to keep a promise.

Now on the interpretation of the generational duty concerned with education which I have offered so far, all that I am entitled to claim is that such a duty holds distributively, i.e., that each parent in the senior generation has this duty to *his* child or children and that each member of the junior generation has this right *vis-à-vis his* parents. While the statement in the Universal Declaration of Human Rights says nothing about the duties that are correlative with the right to education which everyone is said to have, it seems safe to assume that the duty of each parent to his child does not exhaust the underlying import of that document. For while the argument I have proposed would insure that each child would—if we disregard the case of orphans—have a right to education, there would be persons in the senior generation—the non-parents—who would have no duty to support anyone's education if such duties are derived only in accordance with the argument as outlined so far. It is a fact, however, that generational duties are not always or even normally construed in this narrow, distributive way. At least we often speak in such a way as to suggest that there are duties owed by one generation to another that are collective in the sense of being owed by all the members of one generation in their capacity as members of that generation to all the members of the following and succeeding generations. I take it that the duty not to despoil the environment and plunder its resources is such a collective duty; and this duty may be only a specification of a more general generational duty to save and perhaps to accumulate a surplus as well. Is there such a collective duty of all the members of one generation to all the members of another in respect of education?

This question which I take to be the fundamental one that arises out of any serious consideration of the right to education is not in any sense an artificial one or one that we resolve readily in practice even though it may give us trouble at the level of theory. Not only do we normally take our duty to contribute to the education of our own children a great deal more seriously than we do any duty we may recognize to other children; but it is by no means uncommon to hear people deny in principle that there is any such universal duty to contribute to the education of children other than one's own. In the interest of simplifying the issue somewhat I am going to assume that the *duty* to support the education of all children is to be interpreted as meaning *all* the children within some political unit to which we ourselves belong, whether it be a municipality, a state or the country as a whole, provided only that that unit is constructed in such a way as to include both parents and non-parents and, in addition, persons with quite different levels of resources available for supporting the education of their children. If there should prove to be a wider duty to contribute to the education of all children in all the political units in the world, that fact would presumably emerge as the result of an argument that builds on whatever conclusions we are able to reach with respect to duties to all children within some limited political unit.

The conclusions reached so far in effect specify a primitive system of educational provision in which each parent separately assures the education of his children. In the simplest version of this system, the parent would meet his duty to his child by acting himself as the latter's teacher. In a slightly more complex arrangement, he could employ someone else as the teacher of his child. There are obvious disadvantages connected with both of these arrangements and the logical next step is for a number of parents to engage the services of a teacher or teachers who will then instruct all their children. Normally this step will lead to the creation of a school as a corporate body of teachers; but such a school would remain an entirely private entity, supported solely by the contributions of the parents of the children who attend. Not only would non-parents be under no obligation to assist the education provided in such schools; but all persons who do not currently have children in the school would be equally free from any such duty. In such a system as this, there would undoubtedly be children who would receive no education, either because their parents were dead or because they were unwilling to meet their obligation to their children by paying for their education. There would also be children who would receive very much less education or a very much poorer education than others because their parents had fewer resources available for educational purposes. The question, therefore, arises again as to whether there may not be a collective duty to support the education of children, whether or not they are one's own. This is an issue similar to the one that arises in respect of medical care for which each family has traditionally provided what it could for itself—usually very little—out of its own resources since a general obligation to contribute to any universal system of providing medical care for all is even now not fully recognized in practice. In the case of education, the corresponding issue is whether all persons have a moral duty to contribute to the support of a universal and public system of education, whether they have children who might use it or not. This question must, of course, be separated from the question as to whether the schools thus supported should be maintained and administered by public authorities or whether funds should be made available to parents for use in a school of their choice.

I wish to propose several lines of argument which support the conclusion that there *is* a collective generational duty to contribute to the education of the young. Clearly, this issue of the duty of non-parents to support the education of other people's children arises in pressing form only when some children are in fact receiving no education at all or a significantly inferior one under the circumstances postulated in my primitive educational model; and, as I have noted, one reason for the former situation might be sheer unwillingness of a child's parents to spend money on its education. Now in the latter case, even in a society characterized by unlimited free enterprise and private purchase in the field of education, it would seem entirely legitimate for the public authorities to intervene in behalf of the child whose parent is not providing an education to it by requiring that the parent send it to some school and bear the expense of doing so. Such a legal requirement would serve in part the same purpose as our present compulsory school attendance laws which were often designed to protect the interests of the child against the parent who is uninterested in education and wants to have his child gainfully employed at an early age. In such a case, the legal requirement of school attendance would simply be a recognition and enforcement of the child's moral right to an education which its parents had neglected; and this collective action of society in the child's behalf would leave the burden of supporting that education with the individual parent. Consequently this kind of intervention which merely prevents a default on the part of a parent in his duty to *his* child effects no decisive breach in the system of educational provision which I have been considering so far; and it requires correspondingly limited attention. The more serious case and the one to which the arguments I will propose are addressed occurs not by reason of the unwillingness of the parent but rather by reason of a lack of means such that with the best will in the world he simply cannot pay for the education which would be commensurate with the duty he owes his child. Is it then the duty of others and among them non-parents to contribute to the education of the child which the latter's parents cannot adequately finance?

One way to demonstrate the invalidity of the position which limits the duty to support education to intra-familial relationships is to show that such a limitation is incompatible with other relationships which transcend the confines of particular families—relationships which are not those of parent to child but which are nevertheless of such a nature as to carry with them a duty of assistance that might extend to the area of education should the need arise. The obvious candidate for such a relationship is the bond of common citizenship in some political society. Every child is a fellow-citizen-to-be of the adult members of the society into which he is born; and in that capacity he will come to have certain rights and duties which are those of all citizens. In a democratic society these will include the right to vote, the right to engage in political activity that seeks to influence the direction of public policy and to protect his own interest, the right to hold office if elected and so on; and as a citizen he will also have certain obligations like those of jury duty and military service. Furthermore, the attainment of at least a certain minimum level of education is a necessary condition for the exercise of these rights and the discharge of these duties; and these rights would be illusory and the duties they entail unfair if the requisite level of education were not assured. It follows that the whole body of citizens who assign these rights and duties to one another have a duty to make such a level of educational attainment possible for all. The logic of this argument is the same as that of the argument which passes from the fact that everyone has the right to a trial by jury of his peers to the conclusion that everyone has an entailed right to legal assistance, and if he cannot pay for that assistance himself, a right to public support for the legal aid he requires. Similarly, everyone has the right to participate in the political process and since he cannot do so effectively or intelligently unless he has at least a minimum education, he has a right to that education and if his parents cannot provide it for him, his fellow citizens have a duty to do so. Each child has a right to their assistance should the need arise since without this right the wider political and civic rights which others *are* pledged to secure to one another lose their meaning and their value.

The argument I have just presented resembles the kind of argument which I set aside at the beginning of this paper—the kind that derives the right to education from a more general right. The difference is that the more general right to which I have appealed is a political right rather than a directly moral one; and it is a political right which is recognized, though not necessarily given effect, in a great many societies. Since it is thus imbedded in the theory of democratic institutions of government to which citizens appeal as the most general basis for their civic relationships, it is somewhat harder to ignore or repudiate without producing glaring inconsistencies in the overall rationale of civic life to which we are committed in practice. Of course, a really radical defense of the distributive interpretation of duties in respect of education will not be deterred by such considerations as these; and it will challenge whatever elements of the democratic theory may seem to be in conflict with it. To meet this kind of rebuttal another kind of argument is available which shows that there is a *prima facie* inconsistency—in this case not between one's democratic political principles and a disclaimer of responsibility for the education of other people's children—but between the latter and the acceptance of certain benefits that are unacknowledged in the kind of argument that supports that disclaimer.

These benefits are of two types: those that accrue to the individual by reason of the education his fellow-citizens receive and those that accrue through support that has been given by others in behalf of his own education. With respect to the former it scarcely needs to be pointed out that all of us benefit in countless ways from the fact that our fellow citizens have achieved at least a minimum level of education and that we can therefore be expected to pay something for those advantages. In the case of employers who utilize the trained capacities of their employees—capacities that were at least partially developed through schooling at public expense—the demand that some payment be made for their use of such skills seems particularly appropriate, but in weaker form the same kind of argument might have much wider application. Thus, for many persons, support of the education of others is in the nature of a partial compensation of the public for its outlays in developing a capacity from the use of which one has benefited. If each family were required to defray the whole cost of the education of its children out of its own resources, then the cost to the employer, and eventually to others as well, of the skills formed through this increased personal investment in education would rise correspondingly. It is, therefore, not unfair if such a person, though himself childless, is required to contribute to the education of children of other people. Nor is it the employer alone who benefits from the fact that other people's children are educated since all of us, with and without children, benefit from a higher general level of education through improvements in technology and administrative efficiency, the availability of cultural advantages, a decrease in crime and in countless other ways. While it would be hard to attach a money value to these benefits, their existence is sufficiently clear to show that in fact our personal economies comprise a great many 'external savings' thanks to the education other people's children receive. If a refusal to contribute to that education were to be consistently carried through, then, as I have already remarked, a charge should logically be imposed for such unacknowledged benefits and it is not likely that it would be lower than our present tax bills for education.

This brings me to the second type of argument which turns on the fact that no one or almost no one can truthfully claim that he or his parents have met the full cost of his own education. Quite obviously, anyone who has attended a public school or university has been supported in large part by tax monies which are contributed by many persons who do not have children or do not have children in school. Even in private universities where the costs to the individual students or rather to their parents are much higher, it is estimated that tuition charges cover only about one-half of the cost of a student's education. The rest is made up out of the income from the university's endowment which has accumulated through private benefactions. The point I am making is that a person could justifiably refuse to contribute to the education of children other than his own only if he could show that no one other than his parents had contributed to his own education. To accept that support is to place oneself under *prima facie* obligation to make a similar contribution oneself, not just to the education of one's own children but to that of all the children in the relevant community. It is as though the money given to the support of the education of all children were in the nature of a loan from one generation to another, a loan which is to be repaid by the generation which receives it but repaid not to the generation that makes the loan but to the former's successor generation in the form of aid to *its* education. This distinctive kind of restitution is what I mean by a collective generational duty. It may be that it can be shown to have an adequate basis in a general duty of benevolence or in a recognition of each human being as an end in himself; but I have tried to show that it is also generated in the form of an obligation entailed by certain acts and acceptances of ours. This derivation of course leaves open the possibility that someone may try to avoid the duty of supporting anyone else's education by avoiding these acceptances, i.e., by accepting no external support for his own education. Whether such a quixotic and implausible undertaking could really succeed is very doubtful, not only because of financial limitations but because every education, however private, utilizes what one might call the fixed cultural capital which has been accumulated by the labor of countless past generations and from which everyone who obtains an education benefits in ways which even the most sophisticated cost-accounting procedures can hardly encompass. To argue that because no one except one's parents has paid for one's education one stands outside this relationship of indebtedness to an immemorial human effort that is essentially collective and anonymous and not organized on family lines is really absurd and cannot possibly justify an exemption from the burden of contributing to that effort through aiding the education of the ascendant generation. Finally, it does not seem to me to make any difference that the motives people have for extending this kind of cross-generational support may be variegated and not entirely disinterested or even that it is often given reluctantly and under protest. As long as it is in fact given and used for the support of education and as long as it is accepted and utilized by those for whom it is intended, the kind of duty I have described will be generated.

It seems to me that with this second type of argument the basis for our conception of the right to education has been broadened in an important way which in terms of my simile of concentric circles might be compared to a movement from a narrower to a wider circle. In place of the special relationship of a child to its parents we now have the special relationship of the members of one generation to another within which the contributions of particular adults are not made exclusively to the education of their children. In this relationship the obligation of the succeeding generation is to make as substantial a contribution to the education of its own children as its predecessor made to its own education; and while it may be possible and desirable for it to do more than was done for it, I do not think that we would normally say that there was a strict duty to do so. To move outward in this way from intra-familial relationships to a relationship of one generation to another does not, of course, by itself bring into being a universal human community within which support for education is recognized as an obligation which every adult owes to every child. For that the limits of particular political communities would have to be transcended so that my obligation to assist the education of a child in Ceylon would, if need arose, be on a par with my obligation to my own child and to other children in the community in which I live. Nevertheless, the widening that has been effected in our obligation to contribute to the education of children other than our own is a major one and it may be adequate to meet most of the objections by which an unwillingness so to contribute normally seeks to justify itself.

While my account of the generational rights and duties and their bearing on the right to education is now complete, there are two further questions which may be raised in connection with this general topic to which some attention should be given. One has to do with the scope of the right to education: to *how much* education does everyone have a right? The other is the question whether the education to which everyone has a right is to be defined in terms of outcomes or opportunities, 'outputs' or 'inputs'?

Earlier in this paper I invoked the admittedly vague notion of a minimum or basic level of education to which everyone has a right; and this rather clearly suggested that beyond that level one would either pursue one's education at one's own expense or that one's education may be publicly supported for reasons that are different from those that were valid and adequate up to that point. This is in fact the view that I do wish to defend although I will not be able to do much to clarify the notion of a minimum education. It need not of course be exactly the same for everyone and it would not necessarily coincide with any of the educational termini—the end of grade school or of high school—which have been widely recognized in our society. If well conceived, a basic education would enable the student to acquire the competencies I have described to a degree that will permit him to use them effectively and to go on learning by himself in at least some areas. It would also afford an adequate opportunity to the student to discover his own interests and to demonstrate his degree of aptitude for various forms of continuing study. As regards the criteria to be used in selecting persons for the various forms of publicly and privately subsidized further study, these should be social need and individual ability rather than any universal human right to indefinitely prolonged public support in the pursuit of one's studies. I would certainly agree that in one sense every human being has a right to seek to attain the highest level of education of which he is capable; but I interpret this to mean that no one should stand in the way of anyone's effort to achieve that goal and not as implying the existence of any kind of public duty to subsidize his further studies. What this means is that a man may have the desire and perhaps even the ability to pursue a particular career and yet not have a right to the public support that would enable him to do so because a case for such an employment of public resources cannot be made. Alternately, it means that a person might have a desire to study for a certain kind of career for which there is a compelling social need and yet be justly denied that further education on the grounds that he does not have the requisite level of ability. We all know that such judgments of social need can be shortsighted and that assessments of individual ability are by no means always accurate. When we believe that we have been denied support for our educational projects because one or another of these estimates was faulty, we may well claim that we have a *right* to the education that is being denied. But it would be something else—and in my opinion quite unjustified—to pass from this limited assertion of a right that is recognized to be dependent on criteria of merit and need to a wider claim that such a right exists independently of such criteria or that the latter are so unreliable as to be unworkable. In a general way most systems of publicly supported education appear to recognize the prior claims of merit and social need over a universal right to education at some point in the educational sequence, usually in the middle or late teens at the completion of secondary school work. There has naturally been a great deal of dissatisfaction with the decisions that are made at that time as to who shall go on to do what. In the United States we seem to be in the process of postponing the point at which criteria are switched until later with the result that our model of basic education is now beginning to include a college education. There are advantages to such an arrangement but there are disadvantages, too, both for the individual and for the colleges, in the kind of prolongation of adolescence that such postponement entails. Even in as rich a society as ours the time inevitably comes when one must discriminate among the many hopes and ambitions for further education and do so on the basis of criteria other than those of the initial right to education which we all share.

I turn now to the question about the terms in which the right to education is to be defined; and by way of introducing it I may point out that my discussion of educational rights and duties has been pretty much in the style of classical liberalism. I have been arguing that opportunities for publicly supported education are to be offered to all on an equitable basis up to a certain level; and whether people make proper use of these opportunities is, by implication, their responsibility. But it is well known that even when these opportunities are offered, our ability to take advantage of them varies widely in a way that reflects the decisive importance of such influences as socio-economic status, the quality of family life, the medical and nutritional care a child receives and so on. The outcomes of education—the relative success or failure of differently situated children to achieve the goals of education— vary in a way that testifies to these influences; and many draw the conclusion that the right to education, if it is to be at all meaningful, requires that all of these factors that influence educational outcomes be substantially equalized. Only then, it is argued, will the opportunity for education be really equal for all and the universal right to education, a reality. From this view it is only a step to the conclusion that a right to education based on the formal openness and availability of educational opportunity has little value and that the right to education must henceforth be construed as a right to equal educational outcomes, especially as between members of differently circumstanced racial and economic groups. It is this reinterpretation of the notion of a right to education which I want to appraise briefly.

No one, I suppose, can seriously dissent from the view that a formal right loses much of its value when the conditions which are required for exercising it effectively are not present. It is also apparent that the conditions for the successful exercise of the right to education cannot be confined to the strictly educational 'input' in the form of facilities, materials, quality of teaching staff, etc., but includes a very wide range of social and psychological factors. In respect of both these intra-educational and extra-educational conditions, deepseated inequalities persist throughout our society; and even when the former are corrected, the impact of the latter upon the life of even the most scrupulously egalitarian schools persists. The case for the elimination or mitigation of both these forms of inequality is very strong; and it probably does not make much difference if we interpret the conditions for the effective implementation of the right to education as including substantially equal extra-educational as well as intra-educational conditions or if we interpret them instead as including strictly only the latter and treat the former as relating to a wider social right to equality on which the right to education is finally dependent for its effectiveness. In either case, there will be *prima facie* evidence of inequality whenever the outcomes of schooling vary systematically in a manner that correlates with the intra- and extra-educational advantages which children in various assignable groups within the total population enjoy. If these inequalities are of such a nature as to be remediable through forms of intervention that do not themselves involve an even graver violation of human rights, then it seems clear that the right to education requires that action be taken to equalize the conditions in the schools and in the society under which children receive their schooling.

It is important, however, to understand that this does not entail that everyone has a right to equal educational outcomes. It is always possible that different individuals for whatever reasons may make different use of substantially equal initial conditions for schooling and while these differences will often reflect negative attitudes toward education which might themselves be affected through certain forms of social intervention, they are nevertheless likely to persist in one form or another, partly because we don't know how to change them and partly because we feel that changing them would require intolerable violations of the freedom and privacy of individuals. If so, and if an obsession with equal outcomes does not lead us to disregard these inhibitions, then we will still have to retain the liberal conception of the right to education as an opportunity to which all are entitled but which some may not use effectively, even when initial conditions of equality have been substantially realized. The alternative to that liberal interpretation of the right to education would be a view that holds that education is not an opportunity which, finally, individual persons must decide to utilize or neglect but an enterprise of social engineering which, in order to assure the overriding social goal of equal educational outcomes, may intervene in any manner that seems to further this goal. We should take care that our present wholly proper concern with educational outcomes serves its legitimate purpose of casting light on the intra- and extra-educational conditions that affect these outcomes and that the knowledge so gained is not used in such a way as to eliminate the opportunity-character of the right to education and the freedom—perverse though its use may often seem—which it implies.

Olafson on the right to education

I I

A. I. Melden

Granted on all hands that education is desirable but supposing, further, that persons are entitled or have a right to it, what sort of a right is it? Is it a human right, as the Universal Declaration of Human Rights would have it,[1] or is it no more a human right than certain rights specified elsewhere in that same document, e.g., the right to periodic holidays with pay,[2] or the right to the protection of one's material interests resulting from one's scientific achievements, literary compositions, or artistic productions?[3] Surely the violation of these latter rights, important as it may be that persons have and enjoy them, is hardly that attack upon the status of the person with its actual or threatened destruction of his moral dignity, which traditionally has been taken as the distinctive hallmark of the violation of human or natural rights. Is, then, the right to an education on all fours with the special right to holidays with pay that workers here and now have by virtue of contractual agreements into which they or their representatives have entered, or by statutes or whatever devices it may be that such a right is secured—devices in the absence of which the claim that an employee in some factory ought to have a periodic vacation with pay, justifiable as it may be in terms of its contribution to his welfare, his increased productivity and the resulting increase in the firm's profits, could hardly include a right or an entitlement. Professor Olafson thinks that the right to education is, in this respect, different. He concedes that a consideration of public policy might well afford good reasons for providing the members of our society with the sorts of education that would enable them to contribute in various ways to the common good, but he contends that, quite apart from these reasons, there is another consideration that provides us with good warrant for making education available to them, namely, the fact that they are entitled to it. If he is correct the point he makes is of a degree of importance that is obscured by those who rest content with the declaration that a right is a good reason for getting or receiving that to which they have the right, as if nothing further needs to be said by way of elucidation.

For (a) we need to be reminded that having a right provides the person who has it a measure of authority that he has with respect to others, an authority quite different in character from that of the good or the worth-while character of the outcome of any action. A worker who is not entitled to a vacation with pay may plead for one on the ground that it would benefit all concerned, but the force of this argument would be made immensely more powerful if he were to couple with it a reference to the fact that he was entitled to it. But there is not only the authority that he has as the possessor of the right, but (b) the accountability of others to him in any course of action they take that interferes with or restricts its exercise. If A has a right, by virtue of that moral fact alone, is one to whom others are from interfering with A's exercise of his right, or, positively, to act in ways that meet the obligation he has to A, then B's failure, of commission or omission as the case may be, requires that in some way appropriate to the circumstances of the case, he make amends and secure his moral peace with A either by restitution, explanation or, if need be, even by securing A's forgiveness. The possessor of the right, by virtue of that moral fact alone, is one to whom others are thus accountable. 'Why did you (did you not) . . . ?' may invite the retort 'I am not accountable to you' when what is at issue is merely the question of whether it would or would not have been preferable to act in some other way. But the busy-bodying that warrants this rebuff is quite out of place in the case of one whose right has been violated; in cases of this sort, the retort evidences moral blindness and/or a compounding of the moral offence. And (c) it is peculiarly incumbent upon the possessor of a right to respond, not as a passive spectator and moral critic, to those who may be unable, unwilling, or, who merely fail through neglect or inadvertence to accord him his right, but, depending upon circumstances and the nature of the right, to ignore, waive, relinquish, excuse, forgive, or, if need be, to lay on morally upon the offending party. Here it is incumbent upon the possessor of the right to decide, out of the resources provided by his own sense of the facts in the case and his moral understanding of the relevant issues, to respond in ways in which he, as the person with a right, is both peculiarly privileged and responsible.

Given that there is a right to education, certain of the above features will not apply; for of course neither the very young nor even adolescents are able, although hopefully they will be when their moral education is completed and they become mature and fully responsible adults, to exhibit the degree of understanding and responsibility outlined above (although even in this case one who has been denied an education may, in later years, declare, not metaphorically and rhetorically, but literally and properly, not

197

only that he had been unfortunate but that his right had been violated). But far from showing that they are without the right to education, this demonstrates that the notion of a right, while it must be understood in terms of the full-blooded ways in which a right operates in the transactions between fully responsible and accountable agents, still applies when in varying respects and in different degrees the features present in the full-blooded cases are diminished in scope and degree or even altogether absent. To take only one instance, the notion of claiming one's right is obviously involved in our understanding of how rights provide reasons for doing and hence of what it is to have a right; but the supposition that a right is not a right unless it is actually claimed or that the individual who possesses it must be able, in some strong sense of that term, to make a claim on his own behalf—even that a claim has been or can be made on his behalf—is mistakenly to elevate one feature of our notion of a right into a necessary condition of its application. Hence unless I misunderstand his intent which may well be to remind us of some very special sorts of rights, I would disagree with Olafson's remarks (on p. 178) that in certain cases— admittedly not in the present instance of the right to education— the reciprocal obligation 'may not in a strict sense become operative until a claim based upon the right has been explicitly made.' An infant has rights, but it would be preposterous to demand that it register its claims. And a slave has rights even though he may be unable or, because of his contentment with his lot and his failure to understand how much better off he might be if he were to live freely and act responsibly on his own behalf, unwilling to stand up and with Frederick Douglass declare, as he did during the abolitionist movement in America, that 'the man who has *suffered the wrong* is the man to *demand redress*, that he who has *endured the cruel pangs of slavery* is the man to advocate Liberty . . . that we must be our own representatives and advocates, not exclusively, but peculiarly—not distinct from, but in connection with our white friends.'[4]

But from whom may the person who is deprived of his rights, or whose rights are violated, demand redress? In the case of the Southern slave, the guilt was shared by, but by no means was it restricted to, those who were actively engaged in the cruel and inhuman treatment of slaves. For had the guilt been so confined it would have been difficult to understand the full force of the resentment against slavery. The redress needed was a redress to be exacted from, because of the guilt shared by, all who had viewed with complacency, indifference, or had acquiesced in the existence of, the practice of slavery itself. For so to live with, let alone profit from, slavery was to be morally indifferent to that treatment of human beings that deprives them of their very integrity as persons. The rights violated by slavery have as their correlative obligation the obligation imposed upon every person to treat any human being as a moral agent who in principle is capable, out of the resources of his own understanding, of knowing how to conduct himself with others, and able, in the particular circumstances of his life, to act freely and responsibly in the conduct of his affairs. To acquiesce in or to remain indifferent to the dehumanization of the slave by which he is thus read out of the moral community of which, as human beings, all of us are members is itself a moral wrong of a very high order. To undo and to redress the moral damage thus inflicted upon the slave is what Douglass rightly demanded, and by thus touching the morally sensitive nerves of those who wittingly or unwittingly had given moral offense to the slaves he helped arouse the effort to redeem them as human beings.

Professor Olafson deliberately avoids any attempt to make good the claim that all persons have a right to education on the basis of any human rights that they may have. He does not deny that education might be held necessary to the achievement of human rights, but he finds any such attempt unsatisfactory in part because of the underlying unclarity with respect to the character of these rights, and in part because 'it casts no light at all on the special relationships among human beings to which the right to education owes much of its validity' (p. 173). His strategy, therefore, is to attempt to found this right upon special relations between persons or groups of persons. And in order to do this he focuses attention upon what he takes to be the distinctive obligation that is the correlate of that right, namely, the obligation not only not to interfere with those engaged in the process of securing an education; but, positively, to provide the assistance and support of whatever form that the education to which persons are entitled requires.

Unfortunately Olafson does not always adhere consistently to this line of attack. While he tells us that the right to education that the young have, along with the obligation on the part of adults to supply the necessary support, is intelligible only in terms of the special relation that holds between the members of these distinct generations, he also maintains that the education is to be provided the young 'because having an education is in the interests of the person to whom it is provided,' where by 'being in one's interest' he explicitly intends 'something on the possession or attainment of which some advantage or benefit to oneself depends' (p. 179). Unfortunately he does not appear to recognize that the latter requirement introduces a consideration that is independent of the rights of children and independent, therefore, of the duty

o

correlative with that right that parents have to their children. Now it may be true that education is advantageous or beneficial to those who receive it, although the misologists to whom Kant once referred in the *Foundations of the Metaphysic of Morals* were neither the first nor the last to question this bit of optimism. But it is hardly enough, assuming that education is in this sense in the interest of those who receive it, to argue that the child has a right to it. It would in this same sense be in the interest of an obviously needy stranger were I to give him a ten dollar bill; but it is hardly plausible to maintain that the fact that he needs it provides him with a right to it and imposes on me an obligation to him that I can meet by giving it to him.

More to the point is the generational relationship cited by Professor Olafson which holds between parent and child. His thought here is that the sexual intercourse of the parents, eventuating as it does in the birth of the child, provides a moral basis for the child's right to an education. Certainly no creature is more needy than the newborn infant; it is, as we know, completely dependent for its survival upon the care it receives from others. And if the needs of others ever call for our efforts for their satisfaction, then the needs of newborn infants impose very strong requirements upon us. But what is at issue here is not that we ought to make efforts to assist in the survival and development of the infant, but that the needs, either together with or because of the sexual act performed by that pair of adults that eventuated in its birth, suffice to provide a moral basis for the right that it has to the care it requires for its survival and, given the kind of life that human beings lead, to the education it requires in order to share in that life.

Here I must record my misgivings. My pet cats, a male and a female, are in heat and I put them together in the same cage knowing full well what is about to take place. I am not surprised, therefore, by the outcome. In due course kittens are born, darling little creatures wriggling about in search of their mother's milk. Certainly, in the event that the mother dies, I ought to care for them not only, as Hume once put it, out of a sense of the gentle usage we owe any inferior creature, but also because I did after all put those cats together. Not I, but they, engaged in the sexual act, but that act was as much in the cards as anything could possibly be, given what quite deliberately I did in fact do. But I doubt that we need in this case to invoke the rights of kittens in order to argue that I ought to care for them. For it is very problematic, given that so much of the conceptual framework of rights must be stripped off in this case, that talk about the rights of kittens is in order. I helped bring them into existence and I would be *particularly* unfeeling if I were now to toss them into the garbage can. But cruelty to animals that is rendered particularly heartless because of our contribution to their suffering is not a quite unproblematic violation of their rights, tempted as we may be by superficial resemblance to assimilate our talk of how we ought to behave towards our pets with our talk of the obligations we have towards our children.

The question is whether that parental relation to the child which Olafson takes to be the basis of the moral obligation to the infant—correlatively of its rights to the sort of education it requires—is to be identified with that sexual relation in which parents stand to the child. Olafson does concede that ignorance of this relation in quite primitive societies could have this effect, that 'parenthood would presumably not be a matter of individual moral responsibility in the way it tends to be for us' (p. 183). Hence Olafson would seem to concede that the sexual act in itself does *not* create the obligation if there is ignorance of the connection between such acts and the births of infants. But then how does the knowledge of the connection make that much difference? It is when I perform the sexual act I think to myself, 'You know what's going to happen in nine months' time.' But suppose no such thought crossed my mind as my passion takes hold of me—I think . . . What thoughts indeed do people think on these occasions? And whatever it is that I do think, by what magic does my thinking at the time or the knowledge available to me about sex and other matters make a difference to the responsibilities I have both to the compliant woman and to the helpless infant that comes into being later on?

Suppose in fact that the newly born infant came into my life not through any sexual act of mine but as a result of being left at my door by some unknown woman unable or unwilling to care for it. Would that weaken or destroy the responsibility I have when I proceed to take it in and care for it as I would an infant that was 'of my own flesh and blood'? Whether by unknown accidental causes or by the design of adoption agencies, these eventualities do occur. Shall we deny that in such cases as these the child has rights and, correlatively, that those into whose lives the child has been brought have obligations to it?

At the risk of raising the hackles of those who are turned off by the terminology, what is missing in the account Olafson gives us is any reference to the language game in which parents are involved with each other and with their children, when they anticipate their birth, prepare for them, and after they are brought into the world, care for them and increasingly bring them into the circle of family life—this being the context within which, primarily and peculiarly, the notion of the rights of children and the obligations of parents

A. I. Melden

have a place. Or, in more usual terms, it appears to me that the parental relation must be construed in terms of the ways in which parents live and conduct themselves with their children, and not merely if at all with the mere sexual act, the causal relation between it and the birth of the infant along with the knowledge of this causal fact.

But whatever the nature and basis of the requirement that parents provide their children with an education, the right, if it is one, of the young to an education, cannot be confined to the limited circle of family life. Professor Olafson attempts, therefore, to establish that any child of any generation has a right not merely *vis-à-vis* his own parents but against all of the members of the group into which he is born. Nor does he wish to rest his defense of this thesis on our shared commitment to the ideals of a democratic society, a commitment that carries in its wake the requirement that those who participate in its political function and who, in one way or another help determine the course of public policy, must achieve a certain level of education. Instead, he argues on a quite different ground, namely, that having benefited from our own education that we received through the support received from the generation preceding ours, it is incumbent upon us to make restitution by contributing in a similar way to the support of the education of that generation that succeeds ours. There is, therefore, an obligation that all of the members of each generation have to all of the members of the generation that succeeds and a right to education that all of the members of any given generation have *vis-à-vis* all of the members of the generation that precedes it.

I must confess that I do not understand this at all. It is alleged that it would be inconsistent for members of generation B to accept the benefits given them by members of generation A, without according similar benefits to the succeeding generation C. Inconsistency here, surely, cannot be logical inconsistency. It appears to be no more than a following suit. But why should we repeat the same pattern with respect to a new generation? One answer seems to be (cf. p. 191) that in helping generation B, generation A has made a 'loan' to B, which is repaid by B when it assists generation C. This, we are told, is restitution. But this talk of 'loans' and 'restitutions' is peculiar to say the least. For the 'loan' is never repaid, on the account we are given, since the repayment so-called is made, not to those who have made the 'loan,' but the members of a third party, the next generation who seem to have had no part at all in the original transaction. So, too, with the 'restitution.' The point is that if I repay a loan, I make restitution, and I make it to the person who has made the loan. And given the repayment, that closes the matter. But here the alleged repayment or restitution turns out to be an unending series of passings of the buck. But why should the buck be thus passed? Is it because the members of generation C have a right to this so-called restitution or repayment? But that is the very point to be established and nothing so far has been offered to support that conclusion.

The problem can be brought into quite sharp focus by considering the play of obligations and rights on the account that we are given. Since generation A supports the education of generation B, B is under an obligation to A. The reciprocal or correlative of this obligation is the right of A with respect to B, Now B, we are told, must make restitution; presumably this means that it meets its obligation. But it meets its obligation by benefiting a third party: generation C. But how is this possible unless, embodied in the right that A has is the idea A's right will be honored or respected if B benefits C? And this sometimes happens when I contract with or promise X that I will provide certain benefits to Y in whom X has some particular interest. But have the members of generation B promised or contracted with the members of generation A to do for the members of generation C what the latter have done for the former? Surely not. But even if they had, that would not establish that the members of generation C, in addition to being beneficiaries, had any right in the matter. Something has gone wrong in the account given of the reciprocity of rights and duties or obligations.

Or is it that we need to inject a consideration of fairness? It would be unfair if members of generation B, having received the support needed for their education from the members of generation A, failed to provide these same benefits to members of generation C. But does this establish the claim that the members of generation C have a right to the support necessary for their education? It is not at all clear that it does. For unfairness in this instance comes down to this, that there is *no reason* for excluding members of generation C from receiving the sorts of benefits that members of generation B have received from members of generation A. And this hardly shows that members of generation C, if thus excluded, would receive the sort of moral damage that consists in the violation of their right. For consider the following example. I have an abundant supply of lollipops, enough to go round to all of the members of a group of urchins clamoring for them. But I hand them out only to those whose surnames begin with one of the first thirteen letters of the alphabet. I am arbitrary and in this way unfair to the Smiths and the Thomsons. But the complaint made by these urchins against whom I have discriminated, is hardly the complaint that their right to lollipops was being violated. They had no such right.

Nor can Olafson's line of argument deal with the case of persons who, quite unlike those of us who have benefited from the support of others in our own society, have been far less fortunate in their society and who are now called upon to make the sacrifices necessary for the support of the education of their young. Consider, for example, the outcast and neglected Indians living on a reservation, who, having been brought into some contact with white civilization so-called, are made aware of the importance for their children of an education that they themselves did not receive. They are now asked to let them go to schools, even at the expense of the limited food supply to which these children contribute, or, more severely yet, to provide the support necessary to establish schools for their children. If this is done in the name of the right that these children have to an education, the contention that they have such a right cannot be dealt with in the terms specified by Olafson, for the alleged right is a right to an education that their parents did not receive and it is a right, if indeed it is one, that can be accorded them by their parents not by 'restitution' or 'repayment' of a 'loan.' Or does Olafson think that because no such considerations apply, they have no right to education, notwithstanding the rhetoric of the Declaration of Human Rights and however desirable it may be that, in such cases, institutions be established and support be given, in order that these children may obtain the kind of education that will enable them to fare better than their parents, by enabling them to profit from dealings with a technologically more advanced society?

My own preference in this whole question of whether and how children have a right to education proceeds along quite different lines. There are, after all, human rights, the rights of persons to live with dignity and integrity in the pursuit of their own well-being, in their efforts to flourish with others in their various forms of social interaction. But as the neglected absolute idealists of a much earlier period remarked, these rights are abstract rights if they are not brought down to earth in the particular circumstances of human life. They become doubly defective when thus abstracted from the conditions that must determine their mode of application. For, given this diremption, small wonder the complaint, echoed by Olafson himself when he considers but eschews any appeal to human rights, that all this talk of human rights is 'vague' or 'obscure.' But, as he himself argues, it is necessary in any discussion of education relevant to our concerns to deal with it in the given setting of our technologically if not culturally advanced society; so too must we in our talk of a right to education. All persons have a right to education; but who are the persons—Bushmen and Britons, ancient Romans and modern urban dwellers? If, without attention to the specific nature of different sorts of cases or to their varied circumstances, we attempt to specify what any human being whatsoever should have, whether as a matter of the education he needs or of any thing to which he is entitled, any account we offer must necessarily be so abstract as to invite the charge of vagueness. But, further, of what value are human rights—and this is a complaint that has been made by men of practical affairs—when nothing is done to the social order in order that persons may enjoy those rights that human beings are alleged to have, namely, the rights to life, liberty and the pursuit of happiness? Are we to require that human beings, who are bereft of any of those advantages that education can provide them, somehow and in some way go about their affairs in conditions of abject squalor, complete political impotence and cultural impoverishment, with a dignity and a demeanor unrelieved by any Chaplinesque humor, because of the bitterness and dullness that pervade their lives? Talk about human rights is idle talk indeed, when nothing is done to engage or connect it with the actual conditions of human life, by establishing, on the moral grounds that human rights themselves are at stake, just those special rights—legal, political, educational, etc.—that are needed if persons are to secure the things to which they, as human beings, are entitled. This is the point and the force of the legal measures taken in recent years, imperiled as they may be by even more recent political events, of a variety of civic and legislative measures as well as judicial rulings in matters of schooling for minority groups, employment practices, housing, etc.

Is there a right to education? Importantly although logically truistic, but not mentioned by Olafson, is the most fundamental right to education—the right to a moral education that any child has, failing the achievement of which there is the failure to achieve moral agency itself. Do children have the right to an education designed to provide them with an understanding of their cultural and political heritage along with those skills necessary for their effective participation in the society into which they are born? Surely they ought to receive such education. But do they have a right to such an education? What is at stake here is far too important to be left to the good-will and generosity of human beings. It is for this reason that we, in our own day and age, have enacted just those measures and made just those arrangements by which these benefits may be secured for our children as a matter to which they are entitled. And it is well that they do have, not only the benefit but the right, because only in this way is there much hope that these benefits themselves will be transmitted to succeeding generations.

We do not, therefore, need to view the right to the sort of education we deem necessary for our children as a human right, or to deduce it from such rights, in order to understand how human rights themselves operate in the justification of our giving our children the right to an education or in granting them the education they need. Neither should we debase the moral coinage that is our talk about the right to such an education, by construing it as an equivalent but only rhetorically more moving kind of talk about the beneficial results that education provides those who receive it.

Notes

1 Adopted by the General Assembly of the United Nations in 1948.
2 Cf. Article 26.
3 Cf. Article 24.
4 The quotation appears in L. Bennett, *Before the Mayflower: A history of the Negro in America 1619–1966*, revised edition, Chicago, Johnson, 1966, p. 149.

Part 6

Philosophies-of and the curriculum

12

Israel Scheffler

The recent rapprochement between philosophy and education creates new opportunities but also new problems: how, fundamentally, to bring philosophical thought to bear significantly on educational practice? Many of us have for a long time been critical of the old gulf between general philosophy and philosophy of education; we have also attacked the inspirational role of the latter in teacher training and its presentation in stale typological categories that could only seem artificial in the context of the general development of our subject. Yet the old way must be conceded to have had its advantages. Though cut off from the philosophical mainstream, it was at least acknowledged on all sides as having a legitimate place in teacher training. Though oversimplified and often naive in conception, it at least addressed issues recognizable to the practitioner. Though frequently artificial in structure and treatment, it at least provided a recognizable traditional framework for course development by those assigned to teach it.

What have we, the critics, proposed to put in its place? We have urged a desegregation process, a closer connection between general and educational philosophy, in the interests of an enrichment of the former and a sounder and more sophisticated development of the latter. These motivations were and, I believe, continue to be, worthwhile. They provide challenging options for beneficial intellectual innovation in a variety of directions. Yet the very diversity of possibilities has created a diffuseness of purpose, a hesitancy or ambivalence as to the roads to be taken. The departure from tradition has exacted the usual penalty of unsettled directions, amorphous and confused strivings, threatening freedom. Moreover, in bringing educational philosophy nearer the condition of general philosophy, the desegregation process has produced a new remoteness, by comparison with the older tradition. Attention has, naturally, tended to focus increasingly on issues of general interest, and the largely analytical cast of contemporary philosophy has, moreover, invited an increasingly detailed and theoretical development of issues in place of a largely practical orientation. With the best will in the world, educational philosophers have been drawn into the delights of the maze, and the road back has seemed harder and harder to find. Without a clear channel of address to questions of the practitioner, the role of educational philosophy in teacher training has become more obscure.

No one supposes, to be sure, that the philosopher's task is practical engineering or applied science. And it should certainly be insisted that the quest for philosophical insight is generally long and circuitous, ranging far beyond local arrangements and predicaments. Yet the *linkage* of philosophical and practical concerns must nevertheless be maintained; the *continuity* of theoretical understanding and the questions of practice must still be affirmed. Even the critics aimed, after all, at a desegregation of fields, and desegregation is not achieved by swallowing one field whole. The challenge is to create a genuine communication between the methods and ideas of current philosophical work and the concerns and categories of learning and schooling. The aim is, to be sure, philosophical understanding, at the *level* achievable in contemporary inquiry generally, but the *object* of such understanding remains the educational process.

Nor should it be supposed that the current difficulties of rapprochement that we have been describing could somehow have been avoided by a formula, that their very existence therefore testifies to human error or blindness. On the contrary, it seems to me that such a rapprochement between fields is a genuinely open affair, in which the range of potentialities cannot possibly be foreseen and in which a period of exploration and experimentation is rather to be anticipated. The old barriers were, after all, limiting—they channeled intellectual effort into a relatively small set of fixed directions. Like social segregation, they provided a structured system hampering the fullest communication between separated segments. Elimination of such hampering conditions does not, in itself, provide new and richer channels; it merely sets the stage for their discovery or invention. Such discovery and invention are not automatic products of some magical routine. They depend upon exploration of objective possibilities in an experimental frame of mind. There is risk in such experimentation and there are no guaranteed successes. But there is also no turning back to the false security of limited perspectives. The opportunities need to be tried, the many pathways explored, in a pluralistic and scientific spirit. If there is current unsettlement, there is also the promise of new ideas and new understanding to be gained. To bring the rich heritage and contemporary sophistication of philosophy into significant relation with the multiple concerns of education represents a high challenge to creative effort.

It is my conviction that no single program ought to dominate in such effort. There are many things that need doing. Continuity is not the same thing as uniformity. It is perfectly compatible with a pluralism of programs and aims; what it requires is only that there be connecting paths available for those who would travel from theory to practice and back again. These paths may themselves be diverse; there are footpaths and highways, difficult mountain passes, sea-lanes and jet routes. Nor is the construction of a given path the work of one man or program. Work in cultivating an isolated area may become significant through the forging by others of a remote, though vital, link. The last completed link makes the chain, but its significance depends on the availability of all the others. In the linking of philosophy and education there are numerous directions to be explored, promising routes, for example, between moral philosophy and studies of character development, between epistemology and cognitive psychology, between social philosophy and the setting of educational aims, to name but three. In outlining the specific attractions of philosophies-of in the remainder of my paper, I would thus by no means be understood as denying the claims of other possibilities. Rather, my aim is to develop the indications of promise that seem to me to point in one given direction, in the hope that this direction at least will receive some attention. For though many routes are possible, a mere contemplation of their several potentialities will in itself make no new pathways. My suggestion is that we have, at least here, a worthwhile place for constructive work—work that promises, moreover, to link philosophy with educational practice in a concrete and articulate manner.

I was first led to this suggestion several years ago, through teaching certain introductory courses in philosophy of education to prospective teachers, and perhaps I may therefore be pardoned for calling upon my personal experience to explain the appeal of the idea. The central themes of these courses were taken from epistemology, and touched on such topics as knowledge, belief, evidence, truth, understanding, and explanation. In elaborating these themes in lecture and discussion, an effort was made to relate them to educational notions such as learning, teaching, and curriculum organization, and illustrations were drawn from different teaching areas. Nevertheless, it seemed to me that something more was needed to tie the main thread of the course work to particular regions of teaching with which the students would be individually concerned upon graduation. For this purpose, each student was therefore requested to acquaint himself with the philosophical literature bearing on the foundations of his own teaching subject, and was further asked to write a paper relating such literature to selected aspects of teaching. To facilitate this assignment, students were given bibliographies listing recent philosophical works bearing on the several teaching areas, e.g., books treating of philosophy of mathematics, philosophy of history, philosophy of science, philosophy of language, philosophy of art, etc. It was suggested to students that they might use the assignment as an opportunity to deepen or broaden their grasp of their subjects, and they were encouraged to integrate philosophical with any other materials they deemed relevant, in the writing of their papers.

To my great surprise, I found that the typical student had been simply unaware of the existence of a serious philosophical literature relating to his teaching subject; if, in a rare instance, a student *had* known of such a literature, he had practically in no case himself investigated it. Moreover, although the assignment seemed generally to be undertaken with some trepidation, many students soon reported their delight at finding a new and fundamental source of insight into materials with which they would presently be working as teachers. Repeated trial over the years has led me to judge the assignment a definite success: it has again and again elicited papers worth reading, in which students reasonably well-trained in their teaching subjects were, for the first time, challenged to reflect deeply on the foundations of these subjects, and to relate their reflections to the task of teaching. The prior training and the imminent prospect of teaching both provided concreteness and focus to the philosophical materials; conversely, these materials were immediately seen to have point in the framing of general conceptions and selective principles required in teaching. And the initial purpose of the assignment was, moreover, also fulfilled: the general epistemological themes of the course were themselves heightened and intellectually activated by linkage with the concerns of a particular teaching subject.

I have above referred to general conceptions and selective principles required in teaching, and this is perhaps the central point in seeing the potential contribution of philosophies-of to teacher training. To appreciate the point, we may first examine the particular example of philosophy of science, and notice its complex relations with scientific practice. The time is now long past in which philosophers could pretend to a vantage point of superior certitude than is offered by the sciences themselves. They no longer construe themselves as legislating, from such a vantage point, to the scientific practitioner or as taking sides in scientific controversies, at least in their professional capacity. Their philosophical work, in so far as it is addressed to science, takes its initial departure from scientific practice itself, striving to describe and codify it, and to understand and criticize it from a general epistemological standpoint that is, however, shared by scientists as well. Philosophy of science thus springs from scientific practice, but its descriptive and explanatory effort, like all second-order reflection on practice, has the potentiality of closing the circle, of feeding back into practice and altering it. That it springs from practice does not prevent it from exercising a critical and reformative function; that it exercises such a function does not, on the other hand, mean that it is an indispensable starting point for practice. One can, and regularly does, acquire competence within a field of scientific inquiry without preliminary grounding in philosophy of science. Even the strongest proponents of the value of the latter field of study would not, I believe, wish to argue that every scientist requires prior sophistication in this field in order to do his own job ideally well. It is enough that the field itself exists and is cultivated in such a way that communication with practice is possible.

Contrast this situation now with that of the teaching of science. The teacher of science is, of course, also a practitioner, but his practice is of a critically different sort from that of the scientist himself. He needs to have a conception of the field of science as a whole, of its aims, methods, and standards; he needs to have principles for selecting materials and experiences suitable for inducting novices into the field, and he needs to be able to communicate both with novices and with scientific sophisticates. Whereas the particular scientific investigator need have no overall conception of science but requires only sophistication in his special subject-matter, the science teacher's subject-matter embraces scientific thought itself; his professional purpose, that is to say, can be articulated only in terms of some inclusive conception of scientific activity which it is his object to foster. Whereas the scientific researcher need not at all concern himself with the process of training others for research, the science teacher needs to reflect on the proper selection and organization of scientific materials for educational purposes, and so to presuppose a general perspective on those materials. Whereas, finally, the scientific worker requires only sophistication in the special jargon of his intellectual colleagues, the teacher requires something more—the ability to step out of the inner circle of specialists and to make their jargon intelligible to novices aspiring to sophistication. The teacher requires, in other words, a general conceptual grasp of science and a capacity to formulate and explain its workings to the outsider. But the scope of this requirement is, I suggest, virtually indistinguishable from that of the philosophy of science. No matter what additional resources the teacher may draw on, he needs at least to assume the standpoint of philosophy in performing his work.

The philosophy of science is thus, it appears, related to two forms of practice, that of scientific investigation and that of science teaching. But these forms of practice are themselves diverse in level. If philosophy of science is a second-order reflective approach to scientific inquiry, science teaching itself incorporates such a second-order reflective approach as well. The science teacher needs to do other things than reflect on science, to be sure, but whatever he does is likely to be qualified by his second-order reflections on the field of science. Unlike the researcher, he cannot isolate himself within the protective walls of some scientific speciality; he functions willy-nilly as a philosopher in critical aspects of his role. And his training is, correspondingly, likely to profit from the special contributions that philosophy of science offers.

Analogous considerations apply, I believe, to the other teaching subjects as well; for example, to mathematics, to history, to art, to literature, and so forth. This, it seems to me, is the reason why students found the assignment earlier described so pertinent to their work. Their reaction, if it can indeed be generalized, suggests that prevalent conceptions of teacher training are curiously restricted. For these conceptions typically emphasize three features: subject-matter competence, practice teaching, and the psychology and methodology of teaching. Since subject-matter competence is, moreover, interpreted as relating exclusively to the first-order proficiency of the practitioner, no attention is given to the need for a second-order, or philosophical, perspective on the subject-matter in question. And since, as I have argued, such a perspective is demanded by the teaching role in any event, the result is that it is gained haphazardly and inefficiently by each teacher, without guidance and without awareness of alternatives. Lacking a systematic and critical introduction of philosophical considerations, dogmatic and incoherent philosophical attitudes are enabled to grow and to proliferate.

It is perhaps worthwhile at this point to attempt a more specific characterization of the contributions that philosophies-of might be expected to make. I have already suggested that the educator, like the philosopher, seeks a general account of those fields represented by teaching subjects, that he requires some reflective grasp of the 'forms of thought' they might be said to embody. To speak of 'forms of thought' is of course a simplification, for what is in question relates not only to inference but also to categorization, perception, evaluation, decision, attitude, and expectation, as crystallized in historical traditions of a variety of sorts. The simplification nevertheless serves to illuminate a critical point, for forms may be embodied as well as articulated. And the successive embodiment of forms of thought, which constitutes their perpetuation, does not itself require an articulate grasp of their general features. To acquire the traditional mental habits of the scientist, that is to say, requires only that one learn how to deal scientifically with some range of problems, and to treat critically of the materials bearing upon them. The philosopher, on the other hand, takes these very mental habits as his object, rather than the scientific problems to which they are, or may be, applied. His task, in short, is to articulate and analyze the forms themselves, and to try to understand their point. He wants to achieve such comprehensive analytical understanding not for some ulterior practical motive, but for its own sake, although he does not, of course, deny that understanding may affect practice.

The educator, by contrast with the philosopher, is concerned with the deliberate processes through which forms of thought may be handed on; he strives not only to understand these processes but to institute or facilitate them, so that the mental habits in question may in fact be properly acquired. Although an articulate grasp of these habits is *not* required for their acquisition, it *is* involved in the task of understanding and facilitating such acquisition. To make his own objectives intelligible, the educator needs to be able to analyze and describe those habits which it is his purpose to hand on to the next generation. An articulate grasp of such habits does not, in general, itself figure as part of the content he transmits to students; it does not therefore follow that it is of no use to the educator. A parent's sophisticated understanding of sexuality is of the utmost usefulness in helping him to discuss the issue with his children, though he would generally be ill-advised simply to recount such understanding to them.

If the philosophy-of a given subject is, thus, directed toward the analysis and understanding of the form of thought embodied by the subject, it is of potential use to the educator in clarifying his own objectives. The educator is not, to be sure, necessarily concerned with such understanding for its own sake—he needs it in order to facilitate the acquisition of the mental habits in question. Certainly, for this larger practical goal, he needs more than simply a clarity of objectives. Equally, however, no amount of educational experimentation or psychological information can substitute for such clarity of objectives.

In so far as the analytical understanding of a form of thought is the task of the philosophy-of that form, it has, then, a contribution to make to education. But such contribution does not exhaust its role. Understanding merges with criticism and evaluation, with issues of justification and appraisal. The philosophy of science, for example, is traditionally concerned not only to define inductive methods, but to evaluate their epistemological warrant, not only to describe forms of probabilistic inference, but to inquire into their justification. Analogously, questions of aesthetic value, of mathematical certainty, of the reliability of historical reasoning, of the function of literature, all relate closely to the question of defining correlated forms and fall within the philosophies-of those forms.

For the educator, surely, such questions are inescapable. He cannot define his role simply as it is given by received traditions; he must be prepared to justify his perpetuation or alteration of them as a consequence of his efforts. This means that the process of clarifying his objectives has a critical and normative aspect to it. He needs, of course, to strive for a clear grasp of the form of thought embodied in the tradition to which he is heir. But in taking on the responsibility of educational transmission, he assumes the obligation of evaluating whatever it is in that tradition he elects to perpetuate. At the risk of oversimplification, we may say that he requires not only a descriptive but a critical clarification of the forms of thought represented by his subject. It goes without saying that philosophies-of do not provide the educator with firmly established views of justification; on the contrary, they present him rather with an array of controversial positions. But this array, although it does not fix his direction, liberates him from the dogmatisms of ignorance, gives him a realistic apprehension of alternatives, and outlines relevant considerations that have been elaborated in the history of the problem.

The analytical understanding and critical appraisal of the form of thought which the educator takes as his objective provide him with some help in curriculum formation. With a general notion of the form in question, he has some idea of exemplifications in concrete materials to be employed in teaching. To complete his task, he certainly needs to call upon elements outside philosophy; he needs independent acquaintance with materials, and information or hypotheses as to the educational effectiveness of various selections and sequences. But the latter alone are also, in themselves, insufficient. For he is concerned to hand on materials, not just as materials, but as embodiments or exemplifications of form, that is to say, of method, style, aim, approach, and standards. Having a general view of the latter, and an independent knowledge of received materials, he can strive to select, shape, and order exemplifications so as to satisfy the further demands of educational efficiency and comprehensiveness.

In the very process of shaping, philosophies-of make a further contribution, which may be illustrated by the philosophy of science once more. For it is clearly a mistake to suppose that the latter field is limited to general accounts of scientific method, or of inductive reasoning, etc. On the contrary, it embraces also the analytical description of historical cases or systematic branches of scientific endeavor in such a way as to bring out their methodological or inferential characteristics. Such analytical description typically proceeds in two phases: first, a refined articulation of the content of the historical inquiry or branch of science in question, and second, a systematic account of the elements of the articulation and their relations, designed primarily to exhibit their methodological or epistemological linkages. Philosophy of science is thus capable of aiding the educator not only in formulating a general conception of scientific method, but also in processing scientific materials so as to display them as embodiments of that method.

Philosophers have traditionally undertaken a further task of significance to education: the tracing of connections between specialized exemplifications of forms of thought and common-sense conceptions. They have, that is to say, been concerned to interpret, translate, or explicate the content of such exemplifications in terms that are intelligible to the non-specialist. To make science generally understandable, they have, for example, tried not only to specify the forms of reasoning implicit in scientific argumentation, but also to translate or reduce particular scientific concepts and theories to those familiar or at least accessible to common sense. Assuming the common-sense or outsider's point of view as a basis, they have attempted to explain the specialized or insider's conceptions in terms of it. Although their construals of common sense have varied radically, the function fulfilled by their efforts is nevertheless, I believe, of great significance from an educational point of view. For the educator is constantly in the position, not only of representing and advancing specialized exemplifications of thought, but also of explaining and interpreting such exemplifications to the outsider, that is, the novice. In this translational or explanatory role, he has in the philosopher an experienced ally.

To summarize, I have outlined four main efforts through which philosophies-of might contribute to education: (1) the analytical description of forms of thought represented by teaching subjects, (2) the evaluation and criticism of such forms of thought, (3) the analysis of specific materials so as to systematize and exhibit them as exemplifications of forms of thought, and (4) the interpretation of particular exemplifications in terms accessible to the novice.

My suggestion has been that philosophies-of constitute a desirable additional input in teacher preparation, beyond subject-matter competence, practice in teaching, and educational methodology. Nor do I wish to suggest, by any means, that the matter concerns simply the organization of teacher training. On the contrary, if the contributions of philosophies-of for teacher training are to be made practically available, thought needs to be given to the general process of relating such philosophies to education, and I believe that this effort may provide an important focus for educational philosophy. A rich body of materials relative to each teaching subject lies ready for such effort, structured in such a way as to make it naturally amenable to educational interests, and inviting philosophical analysis pointed toward teaching practice.

Yet, I by no means wish to suggest that educational philosophy should be wholly confined to the direction I have outlined. There is certainly, in my view, a role for more general conceptions, even from the point of view of a special interest in teacher training. To mention one consideration, the contributions of philosophies-of that are outlined above are altogether internal: they relate, for any given philosophy-of, to the particular teaching area which is its object. But the educator's scope cannot in general be thus confined, even in the case of the teacher whose teaching responsibility is limited to one given subject. For even he must concern himself also with external relations: how, for example, if he is a science teacher, does his subject relate to mathematics or to the arts, or to literature? How is it linked to technology? What are its bearings on human values and the enlightenment of human perception and choice? Analogous questions arise for each teaching subject and they require an attempt to deal with relational issues which outstrip the scope of any particular philosophy-of. Here is the continuing significance of general philosophy—of epistemology, logic, ethics, and aesthetics, for example.

Consider, finally, the fact that teaching subjects cannot be taken without question as exclusive and fixed points of the educational process. The educator needs to consider the possibility of new classifications and interrelations among the subjects not only for educational but also for general intellectual purposes. He must, further, devote his attention to aspects of human development that are too elusive or too central to be encompassed within the framework of subjects: for example, the growth of character and the refinement of the emotions. He ought, moreover, to reflect on schooling as an institution, its organization within society, and its consequences for the career of values. Philosophies-of represent, I believe, a very promising focus for educational philosophy, both with respect to its theoretical development and its potential applications to teacher training. But this focus should not preclude an insistent and continuing recognition of the significance of general studies, both philosophical and other.

On educational relevance and irrelevance

13

Kingsley Price

In these days, everyone talks about education; and the consequent clamor of tongues is devoted, frequently, to the relevance and, even more frequently, to the irrelevance of some part or aspect of the subject. 'The study of James Baldwin and Eldridge Cleaver is relevant, and the study of Homer and Shakespeare is irrelevant'; 'the student's construction of his own examinations is relevant, and the teacher's construction of examinations is irrelevant'; 'the student's participation in policy decisions is relevant, and his exclusion from such decisions is irrelevant'—these remarks typify a large part of the discourse of student reformer, journalist, politician, philosopher, and many another in that numerous band of persons newly designated by nature, if not by reflection, judgment, and experience, as thoroughgoing experts on education. In their remarks, the terms, 'relevance' and 'irrelevance,' together with their cognates, are used to put forward the legitimacy of new pictures of education, and to remove legitimacy from those older pictures their users would replace.

But these terms, although familiar in some contexts, are strange in that of education. Their use, in the latter *milieu*, has not been much explained; and as a consequence, we cannot rule out the possibility of spurious agreement or disagreement because of confusion as to what it is to which our terms refer, and which their employment praises and condemns. It is well to consider, then, what the concepts, 'relevance' and 'irrelevance,' come to when applied to education.

I

One employment of 'relevance' and 'irrelevance' and their cognate terms will not be treated here. Often, they serve only to express their users' approval and disapproval of some part or aspect of education although, no doubt, 'irrelevance' is used in this way more frequently than its positive counterpart. The context shows this merely expressive use; and since, when it occurs, it is quite clear, it need not occupy our attention in this essay. But there is a more complex employment of our concepts which deserves careful inspection, and to which we shall turn at once.

II

The first point to notice is that the terms, 'relevant' and 'irrelevant,' can be applied properly, no matter what the context, only in a situation that contains two or more items. If there were only one item in a situation, it would not be significant to say of it that it is relevant or that it is irrelevant. For if a thing is said to be relevant or irrelevant, it is always appropriate to ask: 'relevant to what,' and 'irrelevant to what.' But if there were just one item in a situation, it would be unintelligible to ask of it either of these questions. There would be nothing to which it could be relevant or irrelevant. So that if any one thing is to be relevant or irrelevant, there must be at least two—one that may be relevant or irrelevant, and another to which it may be so.

III

Since they carry concepts of relation, there is no logical difficulty in applying the terms, 'relevant' and 'irrelevant,' to the same item. 'To the left' is also a concept of relation; and one and the same item can be both to the left and not to the left—to the left of one thing and not to the left of another. So, one and the same item can be both relevant and irrelevant. A single bit of evidence, for example, can be relevant to one proposition and irrelevant to another.

In this respect, the terms, 'relevant' and 'irrelevant,' are unlike the terms, 'red' and 'not-red.' These terms cannot apply to the same item[1] without generating the nonsense of contradiction. A single item may not be both red and not-red, but it may be both relevant and irrelevant.

But while it is possible that our different terms may apply to one and the same item, it is not possible that they should apply to it with respect to one and the same plurality of items. One single thing cannot be both to the left of another and not to the left of that same other, and one single bit of evidence cannot be both relevant and irrelevant to the same proposition. If 'relevant' and 'irrelevant' are opposed terms, they must be taken as applying to the same item in conjunction with another item, also the same. The ascription of relevance to the study of Baldwin and Cleaver is opposed to that of irrelevance only if both terms are applied to the study in relation to one and the same other item.

Moreover, to describe an item as relevant, and to say no more, is to make an incomplete assertion; and to deny such an assertion is to make an incomplete denial. One who asserts that Jones is to the left of something, but does not say what that something is, does not assert quite nothing; but does assert what he should be able to fill in; and one who denies the assertion about Jones will be denying nothing precise until the assertion is completed. It is certain that Jones is to the left of something; so that the denial of that assertion will surely have no point until those who make the denial discover what it is that Jones is to the left of. In the same way, to assert that the study of Baldwin and Cleaver is relevant, without saying to what it is so, is to make an incomplete assertion; and to assert that it is irrelevant—to deny its relevance—is to assert an emptiness until the filling in is accomplished. Since 'relevance' and 'irrelevance' are relational concepts, the complete assertion that any item possesses either is a reference to some other item as well, and their opposition consists in the assertion and denial that one and the same relation holds between one and the same pair of items. It is with this opposition of the complete assertion of relevance and irrelevance that we shall be concerned.

IV

The terms, 'relevant' and 'irrelevant,' in the discussion of education, apply only to educational practices. The study of subjects may be described as relevant or irrelevant; the method of teaching them, as relevant or irrelevant; and the administration of their teaching, as relevant or irrelevant. But the practices of celebrating the Mass in the vernacular, of voting in primary elections, and of fines for overparking cannot be described as educationally relevant or irrelevant, however much they may be characterized as relevant or irrelevant religiously, politically, and juridically. In order that a thing should be relevant or irrelevant in the discussion of education, it is requisite not merely that it bear or fail to bear a certain relation to some other item, but that it be, itself, an educational practice— a practice of curriculum, of method, or of administration of instruction. The practices of the Congress, however much they influence education, are neither relevant nor irrelevant educationally speaking.

But the item to which an educational practice is relevant or irrelevant is not, in this way, educational in character. The relevance or irrelevance of the practice of studying Homer and Shakespeare does not involve a relation to studying Hesiod and Marlowe, to the method of teaching poetry by requiring its memorization, to taking attendance, or to any other educational practice. One educational practice, of course, may have important relations to another. One may make another easy or difficult, one may presuppose or be presupposed by another, etc. But the relevance or irrelevance of an educational practice, unlike these other relations, is a relation between it and something else not itself an educational practice.

To describe an educational practice as relevant, thus, is to assert that it bears a certain relation to something else, not an educational practice; and to describe an educational practice as irrelevant, where the use of the term is opposed to that of 'educationally relevant,' is to assert that it does not bear that relation to that same item. To apply the term, 'relevant,' to the study of Baldwin and Cleaver is to attribute to it a certain relation to some event—the clarification, for example, of interracial problems; and to apply the term, 'irrelevant,' to it is to deny to it that same relation to that same clarification.

Let us call the relevance and the irrelevance of educational practices 'educational relevance' and 'educational irrelevance,' respectively; and let us now try to discover what the circumstances are whose presence makes a practice educationally relevant, and whose absence makes it educationally irrelevant.

V

Educational relevance is not logical relevance. The latter concept applies only to propositions. 'All men are mortal, and Socrates is one' is logically relevant to 'Socrates is mortal'; 'the students, Smith, Jones, and Robinson believe everything I say' is logically relevant to 'all students believe everything I say.' In these cases, what is logically relevant are items that are true or false, probable or improbable, and their logical relevance consists in the fact that their truth or probability determines the truth or probability of other propositions—of those propositions we may conclude from them. Similarly, logical irrelevance is a relation between propositions. 'All men are mortal, and Socrates is one' is logically irrelevant to 'Socrates is Greek'; and 'the students, Smith, Jones, and Robinson believe everything I say' is logically irrelevant to 'all students believe only what is true.' A proposition is logically irrelevant to another if its truth or probability does not determine that of that other.

The items that are educationally relevant or irrelevant are educational practices, not propositions. The reading of poetry and novels, the constructing of examinations, and the making of policy decisions, as such, are events or happenings; and they cannot be, as such, true or false, probable or improbable. Consequently, they cannot determine, logically, the truth or probability of propositions. And the educational relevance or irrelevance that we may attribute to those practices cannot be logical relevance or irrelevance.

VI

Now, it might be held that although educational relevance may not be constituted by logical determination, it does consist, none the less, in determination of another kind. Jones's sitting in a draft determines, given certain circumstances, that he should come down with a cold; and his sitting in a draft does not determine, given any circumstances, that he should grow to six feet in height. Cases of the first sort are cases of causal determination; those of the second, of causal non-determination. If one event determines another in this way, it is causally relevant to it; if it does not determine another in this way, it is causally irrelevant to it.

It might be supposed that educational relevance is the causal relevance an educational practice has for some event, and that its educational irrelevance is its causal irrelevance to that same event. So, it might seem plausible to hold that the educational relevance of studying Baldwin and Cleaver is its conduciveness to the clarification of interracial problems, while the educational irrelevance of studying them is its failure to bring about that effect; that the relevance of student construction of examinations is its conduciveness to student self-discipline, while its irrelevance is its failure to yield that discipline; and that the relevance of student participation in policy decisions is its contribution to the social responsibility of those who participate, while its irrelevance is its failure to contribute to that responsibility. These assertions suggest that educational relevance is the conduciveness of some educational practice to some event, and that educational irrelevance is the absence of conduciveness[2] of that practice to that event.

One single consideration, however, shows that educational relevance and irrelevance cannot consist in causal relevance and irrelevance. People might agree that a certain educational practice is conducive to a certain event, and yet disagree as to its educational relevance. One person might hold, for example, that the student's participation in policy decisions tends to bring about his social responsibility and assert that it is educationally relevant; while another might agree that it tends to bring about that responsibility, but hold that it is educationally irrelevant. The first might support his view by asserting that the social responsibility of students is desirable; the second, by asserting that the social responsibility of students is not desirable. The possibility of these two positions shows that to describe a practice as educationally relevant or irrelevant is not simply to describe it as possessing or failing to possess conduciveness to some event. Educational relevance is not the same thing as causal relevance, and educational irrelevance is not the same thing as causal irrelevance.

VII

If we may not conceive educational relevance and irrelevance in terms of the presence and absence of conduciveness, may we conceive of it in terms that are closely similar—in those of the relation of means to end? Let us look into this relation a little further.

If two things are related as means to end, one (the means) helps to bring the other into existence. Bodily exercise is a means to health; and it could not be so unless it were its cause, at least in some measure. But the end is not merely what the means helps to bring into existence. Bodily exercise is conducive to health; but health, as such, is only a physiological condition, not an end. In order to be an end, it must be more than a physiological condition; it must be desired by someone. The person who desires the end must be the person who employs the means to it. Bodily exercise is not a means to health unless the person exercising is the person who desires health. Jones's exercise may be a cause of his health; but if the latter is desired by his commanding officer, and not by Jones himself, his exercise is not a means to, but only the cause of his health. We may add that a means is always an activity. Not the body, but the activity of exercising the body, is a means to health. Wherever there is a relation of means to end, there is an activity that is conducive to something else, the latter is the object of someone's desire, and the person who desires it is the person who engages in the activity.[3]

We should notice that the denial of the proposition, 'This is a means to that,' holds true under any one of five conditions. If 'this' is not a means to 'that,' then it may be that, first, 'this' is not conducive to 'that,' even though the actor desires 'that.' If bodily exercise is not conducive to health, it is not a means to it even though the actor desires it. Second, if 'that' is indifferent to the person who does 'this,' then 'this' is not a means to 'that,' even though it is conducive to 'that.' If health is a matter of indifference to the person exercising, his bodily exercise is not a means to it even though his exercise produces health. Third, if 'that' is indifferent to the person doing 'this,' and if 'this' is not conducive to 'that,' then 'this' is not a means to 'that.' For one whose health is indifferent to him and whose exercise does not produce it, exercise is not a means to health. Fourth, if 'that' is an object of aversion to the person who does 'this,' then 'this' is not a means to 'that,' even though again, it produces 'that.' If health is repugnant to Jones, then his bodily exercise is not a means to it, however much it may be conducive to it. Fifth, if 'that' is an object of aversion to the person who does 'this' and if 'this' is not conducive to 'that,' then 'this' is not a means to 'that.' If one hates health, and if his exercise does not produce it, his exercise is not a means to health.

Does the educational relevance of a practice consist in its being the means to some end? At first sight, the answer seems to be in the affirmative. The study of Baldwin and Cleaver is conducive to the clarification of interracial problems, and those who study these authors do, often, desire that clarification. Moreover, it easily appears that those who would assert that the study of these authors is irrelevant would assert one or more of the five ways of denying that the study is a means to the clarification of interracial problems. They would assert, either, that the study of our authors is not conducive to that clarification; that although conducive to it the clarification is indifferent for those who study; that the clarification is indifferent, and the study is not conducive to it; that those who study our authors are averse to the clarification, although their study is conducive to it; or that they are averse to the clarification and that the study of our authors is not conducive to it.

None the less, educational relevance and irrelevance cannot be conceived in terms of the means-end relation; for people might agree that an educational practice is a means to a certain end, but disagree as to its educational relevance. Students from the inner-city, for example, might agree that their study of Homer and Shakespeare is a means to their insight into the universal human spirit. In their agreement, they all might hold that their study gives them the insight, and that they desire to possess the latter. Still, they might disagree as to the relevance of the practice. Some might describe it as educationally relevant, pointing out that in troubled times, a perspective that embraces all humanity ought to be developed and cherished. Others might describe the practice as educationally irrelevant; but their assertion of its irrelevance need not consist in any of the propositions that constitute denials of the means-end relation between the practice and the insight. They might hold, in fact, that the study does not fail to bring about the insight; they might hold, in fact, that the insight is not averse or indifferent to them; they might hold, in fact, that the insight presents itself to them in the liveliest colors of desire. They might agree with those who assert its relevance that the study of Homer and Shakespeare is conducive to something they desire, but they might insist that it is irrelevant. They might assert that insight into the universal human spirit, however much desired, is not what educational practices ought to be directed toward in the present

225

juncture of events. Their assertion that the study of Homer and Shakespeare is irrelevant is not the denial that it is a means to a certain end; and the assertion that that study is relevant is, therefore, not the assertion that it is a means to that same end. Consequently, we cannot construe educational relevance and irrelevance by reference to the relation of means to end.

VIII

Still, educational relevance is not altogether unlike the means-end relation. The study of Baldwin and Cleaver could not be relevant to the clarification of interracial problems if it were not, to some degree, conducive to it. And just as a means must help to bring its end into existence, so also, a practice that is educationally relevant must help to bring into existence that to which it is thus relevant.

But while an end must be desired by someone, no desire need color the state of affairs brought into existence by a relevant educational practice. The essential trait of such a state of affairs is that it ought to exist. If the study of Baldwin and Cleaver is relevant, the clarification it fosters ought to exist quite independently of the fact of its being desired or not desired.

In order that educational relevance should attach to an educational practice, at least two things must be true:[4] first, that the practice is conducive to some state of affairs, and, secondly, that the state of affairs thus influenced ought to exist. To attribute educational relevance to a practice is to assert that it is conducive to a state of affairs that ought to exist. And to attribute educational irrelevance to a practice is, at least, to deny that it is relevant. Let us examine the ways in which an assertion of educational relevance may be denied in order to discover the nature of educational irrelevance.

First, one may deny that an educational practice is relevant by asserting that it is not conducive to a state of affairs that ought to exist. The denial that the study of Baldwin and Cleaver is relevant to the clarification of interracial problems may be the assertion that it does not help to bring about that clarification.

But one may also deny the relevance of an educational practice by asserting that it is conducive to a state of affairs whose existence is not obligatory. There are actually two possibilities here, however; for there are two ways in which the existence of a state of affairs may be not obligatory. It may be a state of affairs that ought not to exist; war is not obligatory in this first way. Or it may be a state of affairs that neither ought, nor ought not to exist—one that is morally neutral; the wearing of long hair by men is not obligatory in this other way.

Now, second, the denial of the educational relevance of a practice may be the assertion that although the practice is conducive to a state of affairs, the existence of that state is morally neutral. Studying the story of Samson may lead to the wearing of long hair; but if the latter state of affairs neither ought nor ought not to exist, if its existence is morally neutral, the study of Samson's career is not, so far, educationally relevant.

Third, one may deny the educational relevance of a practice by asserting not merely that the state of affairs involved is morally neutral, but that the practice is not even conducive to it. Thus, one who holds that studying the biography of Samson is not relevant might insist that not only is wearing long hair morally neutral; but that, in these days of Freudian enlightenment of the young, studying the story does not even lead to the style.

Fourth, the denial of the educational relevance of a practice may consist in the assertion that the practice is conducive to a state of affairs that ought not to exist. If clarification of interracial problems ought not to exist, then any educational practice that leads to it must not be relevant. It is possible to imagine that such clarification ought not to exist. Some people might hold that it is better to enjoy the cool gloom of confusion about the races than to suffer the bright radiance of understanding. Such a person would deny relevance to the study of Baldwin and Cleaver by asserting that what it is conducive to ought not to exist.

Fifth, to deny the educational relevance of a practice may be to assert both that the practice is not conducive to a certain state of affairs and that that state of affairs ought not to exist. Thus, one who denies the relevance of studying Baldwin and Cleaver might assert both that the clarification it is alleged to bring about ought not to exist and that, in fact, the practice does not bring about the clarification.

Of these five ways[5] in which a practice may be not relevant, the first and fourth clearly deserve the description, 'educational irrelevance.' That the study of Greek literature, of medieval Japanese poetry, of unappliable mathematical systems is not conducive to what ought to exist is surely what is meant by many of those who decry these studies as irrelevant, and who reiterate their view by use of other terms like 'useless.' Surely, also, an educational practice is irrelevant if it is conducive to what ought not to exist. The allegation that the study of economics, the teacher's construction of examinations, the student's exclusion from policy decisions are irrelevant is surely the allegation that they are conducive to what ought not to exist—that they perpetuate the established structure of power.

But the second, third, and fifth ways of denying educational relevance to a practice are not ways of attributing irrelevance to it. The study of Samson, ordinarily, would not be called 'irrelevant' because it is conducive to the wearing of long hair if that hair style is regarded as morally neutral. It would be described, more likely, as 'optional,' 'harmless,' or something of the sort. And if an educational practice is not conducive to a morally neutral state of affairs, or is not conducive to some state of affairs that ought not to exist, it is quite clear that it does not deserve the description, 'irrelevant.' If the study of Samson is not conducive to wearing long hair and if that style is morally neutral, then one who has these things in mind would describe the study as pointless or idle; just as one who believes that the study of Baldwin and Cleaver does not bring about a clarification that ought not to occur would describe the study, holding these things in mind, as without purpose or meaning. Since these three ways of denying relevance to an educational practice do not attribute irrelevance to it, let us say that they attribute non-relevance.

The concept, 'educational relevance,' contains two parts. One is the relation of 'conduciveness to' between an educational practice and some other state of affairs; the other is the obligation to exist carried by that state of affairs. It is a concept whose character results from a mixture of the concept of the relation, 'conduciveness to,' and that of moral value. The concept, 'educational irrelevance,' is applied to an educational practice in either of two cases: either where the educational practice is not conducive to what ought to exist, or where it is conducive to what ought not to exist. Because of the vast difference between not being conducive to what ought to exist or being conducive to what ought not to exist, on one hand, and being conducive to what is morally neutral or not being conducive to what is morally neutral or not being conducive to what ought not to exist, on the other, these latter ways of not being educationally relevant may better be described not as educationally irrelevant, but as educationally non-relevant.

IX

One other feature of the concepts, 'educational relevance' and 'educational irrelevance,' should be noticed, namely, their degree. Any educational practice may be highly, moderately, or slightly relevant or irrelevant; and there are many degrees that fall between. What makes for degrees of educational relevance and irrelevance?

The degree of relevance that an educational practice has is a function of the degree to which it is conducive to something, and the degree to which that something ought to exist. One event may be more or less conducive to another. The study of Baldwin and Cleaver may be more or less conducive to the clarification of racial problems than is the study of *The Merchant of Venice* or of Christianity. But the morality of the existence of a thing is also a matter of degree. Universal peace ought to exist more, for example, than should universal bodily beauty.

So, the relevance of an educational practice possesses a degree that varies with the degree to which it is conducive to the event that makes it relevant, and with the degree to which that event ought to exist. With respect to the clarification of interracial problems, the study of Baldwin and Cleaver may be highly relevant; it may be highly conducive to that clarification. With respect to the same clarification, the study of American history may be less relevant; for the vivid presentation of problems may be more influential in bringing about the understanding of them than is a dispassionate and scientific account. And the study of our authors may also be highly relevant because a clear apprehension of the nature of interracial problems carries an urgent obligation with it. That study is more relevant than is the study of *Black Beauty*; for while kindness to horses ought to exist—and may be brought about by the study of that story, its obligation to exist is of a lower degree than that of a clear understanding of interracial problems. Thus, one can see that the relevance of an educational practice is very high if it is very conducive to a state of affairs whose existence is obligatory to a high degree, and that its degree of relevance falls off as does either the degree of its conduciveness or the degree of the obligation to exist possessed by the state of affairs to which it leads.

There is no degree of irrelevance of the first kind—of irrelevance constituted by the fact that an educational practice is not conducive to what ought to exist. If the study of Homer and Shakespeare is irrelevant, in this way, to the clarification of interracial problems, it is absolutely so. Possessed of no conduciveness to the clarification, it cannot be more or less irrelevant. And the degree of irrelevance of the second kind—of irrelevance as influence upon what ought not to exist—varies with the degree of conduciveness of the educational practice concerned, and the degree to which what is influenced ought not to exist. It is important, then, to notice that there are degrees to which things ought not to exist. War ought not to exist, for example, more than artificial manners ought not to exist. Now, the degree of irrelevance of the second kind possessed by an educational practice is determined both by the degree of the conduciveness that it possesses for something else, and by the degree to which that other event ought not to exist. The study of *Mein Kampf* by the very young is irrelevant to a degree determined by the degree to which it fosters warfare, and by the degree to which warfare ought not to exist— a degree of irrelevance that will vary with variations in the degrees of each component. And the study of Oscar Wilde is irrelevant to a degree determined by the degree to which it inclines toward artificial manners, and by the degree to which artificial manners ought not to exist. If the studies of Hitler and Oscar Wilde are equally conducive to the consequences mentioned, the study of *Mein Kampf* is more irrelevant than that of Oscar Wilde since warfare ought not to exist more than artificial manners ought not to.[6]

The relevance of an educational practice of curriculum, of method, or of administration is its conduciveness to some state of affairs that ought to exist; the opposed irrelevance of that educational practice is either its failure to be conducive to the state of affairs that ought to exist, or its conduciveness to that state of affairs where, in fact, that state of affairs ought not to exist. The degree of relevance of an educational practice is a function of the degree to which it is conducive to what ought to exist, and of the degree of obligatoriness possessed by what ought to exist.

The irrelevance of an educational practice that possesses no conduciveness to a state of affairs that ought to exist is absolute, i.e., possesses no degrees; but the irrelevance of an educational practice that consists in its conduciveness to what ought not to exist possesses a degree that depends upon the degree of conduciveness of the practice and the degree to which the state of affairs ought not to exist.

Notes

1 With the usual qualifications: at the same time, etc.
2 In this essay, I deliberately refrain from any phrase more precise than 'conduciveness to.' A discussion with a different purpose would need to make rather fine distinctions within the notion.
3 This paragraph is not presented as a definition for the phrase, 'means-end.' Rather, it is a statement of some of the conditions necessary for a relation's being one of means to end.
4 They are necessary conditions for a thing's being educationally relevant. I do not consider the question whether they exhaust the necessary conditions, nor the question of sufficient conditions.
5 The reader will notice a parallelism of structure between the five ways of denying that one thing is a means to another and the five ways of denying that an educational practice is relevant to something. The parallelism is generated by the similarity between what is desired, what is indifferent, and what is averse, on one hand, and what ought to exist, what is morally neutral, and what ought not to exist, on the

other; and by the fact that the relation of 'conduciveness to' is involved in both cases. It is perhaps the confusion of this parallelism with an identity that tempts one to suppose that educational relevance and irrelevance may be conceived in terms of the presence and absence of the means-end relation between an educational practice and something else.

6 I do not consider here the way in which the degree of relevance varies with differing degrees of its components—differing degrees of conduciveness and of obligatoriness; nor do I consider the way in which the degree of irrelevance is determined by differing degrees of its components—of conduciveness and of obligatoriness not to exist.

Analytic philosophy of education at the crossroads

14

Abraham Edel

On the American scene, there was a sharp change in the philosophy of education that was manifest at least by the late 1950s. It consisted in a shift from what was to a great extent either a Deweyan-centered outlook (whether in acceptance or attack) or an outlook identified in terms of one or another large-scale philosophical system, to a new-broom analytical model. In part it was tied to some effort of rapprochement between academic and educational philosophy, bringing to the latter the mood that was in the ascendant in the former.

The sort of analytic philosophy that proved attractive was not the formalistic positivist type, but the British ordinary-language type. After all, education did not and does not operate with refined or high-powered symbolic systems; it is still itself an ordinary-language activity. Yet the turn to analytic philosophy of education of this type[1] was in one sense surprising at that time. For it was after World War II, the world was in ferment, colonialism was breaking down, Africa and Asia were emerging into the modern world, a massive upsurge was imminent of the oppressed and the dis-advantaged everywhere including the United States, and the demand was in sight for the extension of educational opportunity as well as for some share in political power. Traditional institutions in all areas of life were questioned, if not actually already crumbling. One might have expected to find in American educational phil-osophy at least an echo of the demands for social reconstruction as an educational obligation that had been loudly advanced by philosophers of education in the depression decade of the 1930s. A revolutionary educational philosophy might have seemed much more plausible than a cool analytic one. But perhaps the fuller social picture itself makes the intellectual outcome understandable. America was in the throes of a revived capitalist ideology, corres-ponding to its dominance after World War II. There were calls for the restoration of the status quo in the global cold war. Neo-conservative ideologies in an atmosphere of McCarthyite repression made a virtue of obscurantism and equated intellectualism with near-subversion. Dominant educational groups had themselves called for gearing American education to the objectives of the cold war. Although with the Russian launching of Sputnik I, the up-grading of the intellect was demanded as a crash program for American education, this meant chiefly producing scientists and engineers. Perhaps the demand for neutral analysis was itself as revolutionary a step as the philosophical intellect could venture under these conditions! It may be recalled that in academic philosophy, political and social philosophy were at very low ebb; the brightest spirits went into the logic of the social sciences instead.

Now it is generally evident that the analytic approach has in the past fifteen years turned into a 'school,' with all the philosophical disadvantages of hardening lines of division, attack and counter-attack familiar in the conflict (as contrasted with the dialogue) of philosophical schools. This would be less significant if the attacks on the analytic philosophy were just rearguard actions by older entrenched philosophical tendencies, or by philosophical romantic importations. In fact, however, they come increasingly, in the philosophy of education, from the younger people who are con-cerned with the problems of actual teaching in a period of intense social transformation, and who see little relevant guidance coming from philosophy of education in its analytic shape. I was particularly struck by these complaints and the polarization they involved, at a recent conference on 'New Directions in Philosophy of Education' held April–May 1970 at the Ontario Institute for Studies in Educa-tion.[2] One of the younger critics put it this way: 'I come from the trenches of teaching to the Pentagon of Philosophy, and am dis-mayed to find the generals playing chess.'

Now of course philosophers of education are not generals, and they have no inclination to give orders to teachers; indeed, value-neutrality is a major tenet in the analytic creed. But the discontent expressed in the metaphorical quip is not so easily thrust aside. For even practitioners in analytic educational philosophy have begun to raise the question whether it is adequately fulfilling its promise. In this sense, what is currently called analytic philosophy of education may be thought of as standing at the crossroads. What is at issue is precisely its potential in the philosophical contribution to educa-tion. The aim of the present paper is to diagnose the situation and to suggest what is required to enhance its contribution.

I The theoretical diagnosis

A central difficulty in analytic philosophy of education seems to me to reflect a soft spot in the analytic theory generally—how to judge what is a correct or adequate analysis. Insofar as the analysis is linguistic

Q*

analysis, one would expect it to issue either in an empirical-linguistic outcome or in a phenomenological resolution—in both of which the decision of adequacy would be a factual issue—or in some pragmatic-evaluative judgment determined by the purposes of the specific inquiry. Instead, we find a costly hesitation. In part, as early participants in the British analytic movement will say, the question did not arise. They had wandered into new pastures and were too busy culling the uses; there were enough to go around and if anyone stopped short, he could usually be brought to continue by a counter-instance. Where would it end? It might never end.

But this was a symptom. The basic diagnosis lies deeper. Analytic method was given a certain cast by the dogmas it inherited from logical positivism. There was the sharp separation of philosophical analysis from empirical inquiry, the sharp separation of the analytic from the normative, and the sharp separation of the analytic from genetic-causal accounts. (Left on its own in this way, analysis was robbed of all vital criteria for decision; hence the symptom fixed on above.) Now all these sharp separations were essential to positivism. And they made a certain sense, for positivist analysis was concerned with building large formal systems. System-building can go on by itself in some degrees, without asking what factual structure it might apply to, or what purposes it might further, or what socio-cultural forces begot it. Analysis here can call its own tune without being brought to account till it is finished. The risk it runs is having a beautifully elaborate formal system that serves no purpose after it is built! But ordinary language analysis cannot defer payment in this way. It is analyzing linguistic uses that are thoroughly embedded in particular contexts. It has to face promptly non-formal conditions which are material in character, and the context when fully explored is inherently purposive—not only in the general purposes of language, but in the specific goings-on that give meaning to the uses. It is not surprising that the more J. L. Austin explored the uses of words, the more he was led to abandon the great dichotomies—to see illocutionary elements in the idea of truth and to reject the broad fact-value dichotomy.[3] Indeed, all the dogmas would have been rejected in analytic philosophy if the notion of context had been taken with full seriousness and if linguistic change had been as well-tilled a field as linguistic pattern.

If such a diagnosis is correct, the remedy would seem to lie in a fuller integration of the empirical, the normative, and the contextual (especially the socio-cultural) *within* the analytic method. This is the major point of the present analysis. I shall try to show by selected case study from analytic philosophy of education that there is a growing loss of faith in analysis as a separate self-sufficient process, but that a remedy is being sought only by *adding* empirical, genetic, or normative elements. The key to an adequate remedy lies in the demonstration that these are not elements to be added to a separately performed analysis but play an internal part in the analytic products themselves. Hence integration, not just addition, is the cure.

II The unhappy analytic consciousness

The first step in presenting my thesis is to see the form taken by the loss of faith in the powers of the analytic method. I have not carried out a study of the field from this point of view, and am relying largely on impressions which others may not share. Let me take, as a good example of what I have in mind, a recent paper by Professor Jonas F. Soltis of Teachers College, Columbia University, himself an avowed analytic philosopher of education, entitled 'Analysis and Anomalies in Philosophy of Education.'[4] Professor Soltis sets his account in the framework of Thomas Kuhn's theory of scientific revolution.[5] Soltis traces the rise of the analytic paradigm in educational philosophy, how it displaces or sweeps into oblivion traditional questions and approaches, how it achieves dominance, and then how it develops its own anomalies. He explores two such anomalies. One is internal to the analytic paradigm itself 'in that careful, cumulative, and persistent use of analytic techniques to clarify the concept of learning has brought with it disturbing results which run counter to the expectations of those who believe in the power of the paradigm to make clear, precise, and distinct "fuzzy" categories.' The second anomaly is external: 'previous educational questions concerning values and social issues persist as major philosophical problems in education, but seem to be resistant to the strategies of analysis.'

Whether these anomalies—or the situation as a whole—fits Kuhn's pattern is not my present concern. The second anomaly seems to amount simply to the fact that having expunged values from analysis as such—'One can ask for clarification of the idea of equality of opportunity, but he cannot ask if the schools *should* provide for equality of opportunity'—it remains frightfully difficult to prevent them from creeping in sideways. Soltis illustrates from R. S. Peters's varying attempts to locate the *worthwhile* within the analysis of 'education.' Soltis takes Peters in effect to be asking and answering general ethical questions which the analytic paradigm would disallow. This question—whether 'worthwhile' should be included or omitted from the analysis of 'education'—seems to me to raise problems chiefly for the reason I indicated at the outset, that there is no well-defined procedure for deciding which of competing analyses is more adequate. I shall look at Peters's treatment more explicitly later.

The first anomaly is the more formidable one. It concerns the distinction into types of learning that was the outcome of analytic grappling which began with Ryle's distinction between *knowing that* and *knowing how*. Voicing no dissatisfaction with the analytic job that developed the distinction and turned it from kinds of knowing to kinds of learning, Soltis offers it as a matter of fairly general consensus that there are at least four types: learning *that*, which is propositional; learning *how to*, which furnishes procedures or skills; learning *to*, whose outcome is dispositions, propensities or tendencies; and states of attainment via learning, such as appreciation and understanding. (One can, he illustrates, learn a poem but fail to appreciate it.) I should like to stress that Soltis's dissatisfaction arises not from the analysis but from the state of affairs we are left with when the analysis is finished. I need not go into his several reasons for dissatisfaction; more important is why he regards the outcome as an anomaly. The anomaly is that analytic procedures intended to produce distinctions end up with distinctions that do not distinguish. He illustrates with the way in which the very conditions of propositional knowledge involve procedures (*how* to pattern data to constitute a proof), and attainments (appreciation or understanding). He reinforces this with reference to Scheffler's detailed analysis in *Conditions of Knowledge*.

I have given this brief sketch of Professor Soltis's points to show the character of the unhappy analytic consciousness. As an analyst in the philosophy of education, Soltis simply wonders whether his methods have done jobs that get anywhere. He conjectures that what may be needed is 'to try to find more acceptable answers or different ways to ask the questions. . . .' He toys with an appeal to a philosophical-empirical study of genetic epistemology for the first anomaly, and a kind of hybrid 'analytic-pragmatic' paradigm for the second. In short, he wants to stop shutting out the empirical and the evaluative in the name of a 'normal' paradigm of analysis.

If Soltis's account is at all typical of the dissatisfactions with the analytic method among analysts, then there is obviously a reaching out for what the method has kept beyond bounds. But it is not a thoroughgoing reconstruction of the method—simply an adding of the empirical and the evaluative to the analytical. I have suggested in the proposed remedy that this is not enough. I think I can suggest the line of integration needed if we go over the ground in the examples Soltis has given, and ask how the analyses themselves took place. I focus first on the distinction between kinds of knowledge.

III The strange career of 'knowing that' and 'knowing how': a closer look

The relation between analysis and philosophy of education in the examples given illustrates the one-way sovereign stance: educational philosophy is the handmaiden of philosophy; philosophy furnishes the analytic products; philosophy of education digs them up, brings them to teaching and structures learning and teaching. But what do these analytic products represent? As they come from ordinary language, they represent collective and accumulated ordinary experience. There is here the assumption that learning and teaching fall into the ordinary middle-sized domain. They are not like physics, which has had to dip to the micro-domain and fashion its own language; or mathematics which, as Ryle said of formal logic, had to drill ordinary words to behave in strange ways. Now there is much to be said for this whole approach. At best it might presuppose a view parallel to the effort in one stage of positivism (e.g., Neurath) to give physical-object sentences a primacy (over other forms like sense-data, for example) as the protocol sentences of science; and to turn micro-constructs into instruments of macro-description. This would show the continuity of science and ordinary experience.

But education, after all, represents a large domain of experience in its own right. Can we impose on it the framework of our ordinary language categories? Even if they fit because it is a domain of ordinary experience, why should they be derived from analysis of ordinary uses elsewhere, rather than from its own experience? And why cannot its own experience be used to correct and revise run-of-the-mill ordinary language, precisely because education too is happening in the common ordinary life? Analytic philosophy and analytic philosophy of education have scarcely begun to explore the assumptions inherent in their partnership.

The division into types of learning we have looked at above, as an analytic product, started in Gilbert Ryle's well-known separation of *knowing-how* from *knowing-that*, in his *The Concept of Mind*.[6] Ryle was primarily attacking the intellectualistic language as set in the dualist philosophy—the intellectualist legend that doing something is first to do a bit of theory and then to do a bit of practice (p. 29). Actually, it seems to me, Ryle was waging a battle in a series of strategically superb stages. One step is to distinguish knowing how from knowing that—in short to rescue practice from the intellectualist grip. Paradoxically, this may enshrine the separation in types of knowledge, itself a residual dualism. The next step is to give primacy to the practical: efficient practice precedes the theory of it (p. 30), and even the competence to apply theory must be present first (p. 31). Understanding too is a part of knowing how—the knowledge it requires is simply some degree of competence in performances of that kind (p. 54). When doing has thus been safely ensconced in primacy and has had most of the book to show its capacities, the final attack on the enemy is launched (chapter IX, 'The Intellect'). This interesting chapter is in effect a massive reduction of theorizing to the activity of teaching: 'Having a theory involves being able to deliver lessons or refresher-lessons in it' (p. 286). Unfortunately some teaching is like spectator sport rather than participant athletics. Ryle says: 'Had arithmetic and chess been brought into the curriculum before geometry and formal logic, theorizing work might have been likened to the execution of calculations and gambits instead of to the struggle for a bench from which the blackboard can be clearly seen. We might have formed the habit of talking of inference in the vocabulary of the football field instead of in that of the grandstand, and we should have thought of the rules of logic rather as licenses to make inferences than as licenses to concur in them' (p. 306).

Now there is a great deal in all of this that is of interest to education. It reminds one of the case method in legal education. It is suggestive of the questions long debated in educational theory about the best ways of learning specific subject-matters—whether by relation to practical activities and cultural interests, or in a pure symbolic manipulation. It suggests also the psychological-educational inquiries into rote-learning and insight learning. It suggests, again, the issues in the history of science teaching—how far success is achieved, and at what stages of schooling, by exposition of formulae and systems of laws, by student participation in experiments, by retracing the history of science in careful studies of problems and the way they were solved. No doubt, it will suggest many other educational problems as well. But the last thing I think it should have suggested is the distinction of knowing into a set of types certified by ordinary language and amplified by appeal to linguistic counter-instances.

Even when this became the setting of the problem in analytic philosophy of education, and progress was made, it seems to me to have come from letting the lessons of educational experience break in—even if only surreptitiously—upon the analytic process. Let me illustrate this briefly from one of the very able articles that made a contribution to the development of the topic of modes of knowing—Professor Jane Martin's 'On the Reduction of "Knowing That" to "Knowing How".'[7]

Martin, after expounding Ryle's basic distinction, considers an attempt by Hartland-Swann to reduce 'knowing that' to 'knowing how.' This, she says, rests on regarding 'know' as a dispositional term; thus to 'know that' is to 'know how' to answer questions about the material involved. Martin objects that even if such a reduction is carried out, the newly expanded category of 'knowing how' requires a distinction within itself based on the fact that two very different sorts of dispositions are involved. Suppose, she says, Jones witnessed the murder of Y. Jones accordingly knows that X murdered Y and knows how to answer the question 'Who murdered Y?' But such a capacity is essentially different from Jones knowing how to swim or to speak French. Martin suggests a feature to explain this 'intuitively obvious' essential difference. It is that the one set of capacities had to be learned *through practice;* learning to answer the question about the murder did not require practice.

Martin offers considerable discussion of alleged counter-instances and ends with a distinction of several types of 'knowing how.' One implies that the capacity has been learned through practice, and a second does not. My interest is not in the types, but in questioning why she introduced the distinction between what is learned by practice and what is not, as intuitively essential. There are, after all, so many distinctions that might compete for essentiality between knowing how to answer questions and knowing how to swim. For example, one involves talking, the other does not; but this may be ruled out because she coupled 'knowing French' with swimming. Why isn't the division made between acts that involve communication and acts that one can do alone? Thus knowing French goes with knowing how to answer questions, as against swimming. I need not labor the point, nor raise difficulties about the fact that the child learns to answer questions by practice in human communication, though he need not practice each answer; nor again that he can learn one activity without practice if he knows another activity (e.g., to run a motor boat if he can drive a car). Surely what is happening is that it is intuitively essential to Martin the educator to consider the difference between what requires practice and what does not because that is a vital lesson from the experience of learning and teaching. Here Martin the analyst profits from Martin the educator and the analytic products are steered precisely along those distinctions that are important to educational experience. Martin is less applying analytic distinctions than setting them up to be useful to what the lessons of educational experience have shown to be important.[8] And I am inclined to think that this is precisely the way in which analytic products come about. There must always be some purposive context that calls the tune.

Let me give another example of the way in which Professor

Martin's sensitive combination of her double role is philosophically profitable. In a paper on 'Basic Actions and Education,'[9] she examines the controversy over the idea of a basic action in the currently fashionable theory of action. She starts out to see how the theory that has been built up about basic actions may help the theory of learning, and she reckons with the analytic works of Vesey and Melden and Danto on this question. But gradually Martin the educator begins to call the tune. The distinction between doings to which a person attends and devotes effort and those doings to which he does not attend and does not direct effort—that is, the educationally relevant distinction—takes over. Not only is the idea of a basic action relativized (or rather, contextualized), but the normative question for education is raised, 'whether we want whatever it is that a person is learning how to do to be learned as a basic action or not.' In the progress of the investigation from this point of view she has been led to question the analytic distinction of bodily movements and actions, to find a halfway house in some phenomena and to wonder whether the whole framework is not shaky.

Note the implications of such a study. It calls for a two-way interaction of educational problems and experience and analytic process and products. It does show the operation of the educational purpose in the type of analytic product that emerges. But it does not simply make action theory dance to the educational tune. For action theory is a meeting place of other interests as well—legal and moral, for example—and so the analyst in considering action should be listening to many tunes, and his products, when tried out in any *one* field, in effect are bringing models from other fields. The analytic philosopher could be the integrator of wide areas of human thought and effort, if he kept open his sensitivity to them instead of isolating his craft in a misguided conception of analytic autonomy. (He might also be the inventor of new models and new distinctions to be tried out in specific areas.)

Now what would a full-scale investigation of the distinction between knowing that and knowing how involve? Let me suggest a few lines of inquiry for the philosopher of education, concerning (i) the socio-historical stage of development of education as an institution, (ii) the underlying psychology of human action as it affects educational theory, and (iii) the kind of linguistic-philosophic inquiry that may be relevant.

(i) To what extent has the distinction of knowing that and knowing how been written large in the development of educational institutions? I think, for example, of the difference between academic and vocational high schools—say, in New York in the 1930s. One was directed to the kind of learning that got one college entrance, the other to having skills that might get one a job. This is surely knowing that and knowing how, roughened and magnified. Of course one could point out that many of those in colleges ended up in professional work (engineering, teaching, etc.) that gave one a know-how; and the vocational schools thoroughly impoverished the preparation of their pupils in knowing how, because they had dilapidated old-fashioned machinery discarded from manufacturing. In any case there were no jobs in the 1930s, till we moved from a depression economy to a war economy that needed skills. I leave it to the philosophers of education—especially those who may have had teaching experience in these schools—to expound the evils that the separation gave rise to. Impressionistically, I recall the repeated demands and arguments for a comprehensive high school on the ground that the separation impoverished both. Similarly, I recall the writings in vocational psychology that worked hard to show how intelligence enters into skilled labor and urged intellectually-minded students not to scorn those areas as against the then over-crowded professions. Maybe the distinction between knowing that and knowing how draws the line at the wrong point. It might be drawn instead between enlightened action (professional and skilled labor) and unenlightened action. (But this might be socially temporary, for unskilled labor is being automated anyhow.) Think of how much Marx inveighed against the massive social dichotomy of brain and brawn as an exploitative set-up.

The fact is that the more complex production becomes the more the integration proceeds. I recall in the early 1940s, when the Board of Regents of New York State proposed a set of Institutes for post-high school education which would combine technical and liberal education in something like what is now the partially technical community college, opinion in the labor movement was at first very suspicious of the proposal. There were fears that on the one hand it might bring a free flow of non-unionized cheap labor into the market (memories of depression and unemployment were still strong) and on the other hand that it was short-changing the workers who wanted an education. In Rylean language they might have said: if you want to know that, go to liberal arts college; if you want to know how, join the union as an apprentice. To meet the situation a gathering of top labor leaders was addressed by the State Commissioner of Education. I recall the skilful way in which he explained how the growth of complexity and the rapidity of technical change was making a basic education in science more and more necessary for actual work—down to the care and running of a diesel engine. In a way, it was parallel to the situation that had prompted Robert

Hutchins, as dean of the Yale Law School in the earlier 1930s, to demand basic education in the law school: the New Deal was sweeping away old laws so rapidly that a law student who studied in the old way would graduate with a knowledge no longer relevant to the laws on the books. But whereas Hutchins advocated a basic education in terms of a classical conception of mind and man, the break-down of the liberal-vocational distinction called for an integration in which in the long run the dichotomy of enlightened and unenlightened action would become the central one. That such movements have advanced in the contemporary world is evident in the increased role of basic research in relation to productive effort. In the long run, it is the whole dichotomy of theory and practice that is being brought under scrutiny.

All this, you may be tempted to say, is interesting reminiscence. But has it anything more than the association of ideas to do with Ryle's distinction? I think it has. It suggests that Ryle's dichotomy, like all dichotomies, is attuned to particular phenomena that give it relevance, whereas in an extended view its severe limitations may become evident. It holds for a limited domain of ordinary activity in which there is sufficient actual (that is, practical) separation of thinking and doing to keep the distinction relatively useful. Look at Ryle's examples of know-how: we ride bicycles and play chess and talk French. We do not operate control-stations at London airport or break codes or build translation-machines. If the distinction of knowing-that and knowing-how remains in the more complex situation, it is only the survival of the distinction between planning and carrying out plans, or it is an invocation of the 'intuitive' element in synthesis or diagnosis or skill. I am not proposing to reduce action to thought as Plotinus reduced production to reason, so that even the creation of the world was an overflow of reason! I am rather suggesting that what has been called knowing-how is a very gross phenomenon, perhaps insufficiently understood, which will not support very precise categorical distinctions. I would not dream of denying that there is some distinction in some contexts, just as I would not obliterate the difference between studying the nature of love and falling in love.

In short, the examination of the institutional embodiments of comparable dichotomies, in their social context and historical relations, suggests that the Rylean distinction holds only within the limited domain in which an apprenticeship system is possible. As a distinction of types of knowledge it is parasitical on the distinction between abstract form and existent instance, planning and carrying out plans, studying and feeling, and a number of others. The educators should then start at the other end and study where apprenticeship learning is possible—not merely the plumber's apprentice, but also the politician's apprentice and the doctor's internship. To make the dichotomy an initial hardened distinction analytically certifiable and coercive on education may be just as much an ideology as Michael Oakeshott's attack on reason in politics in his conservative defense of an aristocracy brought up to rule.[10]

Please note that I am not assuming I have the answer to this type of inquiry into the institutional–historical dimensions of the dichotomy. The inquiry has still to be carried out.

(ii) A second line of inquiry would look to the underlying psychology of human action. I can indicate this briefly by reference. Ryle's distinction is involved, as we saw, in rejecting a dualistic theory of mind. But may it not, in spite of itself, enshrine a dualistic cut between the sensory-cognitive and the motor? At least a very famous reconstruction of the reflex arc concept long ago[11] suggested that the separation of stimulus and response, or of stimulus, central process, and response, retained the older dualisms that were ostensibly rejected. If, as Dewey argued, the stimulus at any point already is different in the light of the previous response which has changed its meaning, and the present response is an effort of reconstruction in the co-ordination of the total situation, can the dichotomy be much larger than between habit smoothly functioning and habit that involves reflection? It is interesting to note that in his *Human Nature and Conduct*,[12] precisely after he attacked the isolated ethereal view of knowledge and even went so far as to say 'concrete habits do all the perceiving, recognizing, imagining, recalling, judging, conceiving and reasoning that is done,' he rejected *knowing how* as knowledge. We may, he said, be said to know how by means of our habits; but this is knowledge only by courtesy. 'Or, if we choose to call it knowledge—and no one has the right to issue an ukase to the contrary—then other things also called knowledge, knowledge *of* and *about* things, knowledge *that* things are thus and so, knowledge that involves reflection and conscious appreciation, remains of a different sort, unaccounted for and undescribed.' And significantly, in presenting the account of the difference—that the more efficient a habit is the more unconsciously it operates, while 'a hitch in its workings occasions emotion and provokes thought'— he returned to the central picture of the basic thesis of the old article on the reflex arc.[13] I cannot pursue this further here, but it suggests that no dichotomy of the Rylean type be admitted as more than a rough ordinary relative distinction—that is, be made the basis of educational theory—unless it makes clear its psychology of the sensori-motor relations.

(iii) It is also clear that the linguistic inquiry involved in this analysis is too limited, in at least several respects.

(a) Its range of expressions involving 'know' that can generate proposed distinctions is too narrow. I need not recapitulate the further distinctions that have developed, as indicated in Soltis's paper discussed above. There are wholly different paths. Aristotle distinguished between knowing-that and knowing-why. His 'that' was differently cut, in that it was limited to the isolated fact as against the explanatory reason. Philosophy of science has developed the whole notion of the relative distinction between description and explanation, or between a descriptive account and a systematic account. This is, of course, highly relevant to educational ideas of explaining and understanding. Again, the difference between 'knowing John' and 'knowing about John' or 'knowing the job' and 'knowing about the job' might support the sort of distinction Russell made at one time between *knowledge by acquaintance* and *knowledge by description*,[14] in which the former involved immediacy of presentation. But it might also support a quite different distinction such as William James made[15] between *knowledge of acquaintance* and *knowledge-about*, in which the extent of the knowledge is contrasted (mere acquaintance *v.* the inner nature of the things). James added that one cannot impart acquaintance with things as one can knowledge about them. But fundamentally he was thinking of the contrast of the relatively simple thought with the articulate and explicit. It is interesting to note the contemporary reversal in ordinary use. To be acquainted with something is almost 'really' to know it, while to know about it may be just what we got from hearsay (or book reviews instead of reading the book). But perhaps the significant differences may lie in what is known. Thus there are tremendous differences between 'knowing John' and 'knowing arithmetic' or 'knowing the town,' in none of which any preposition or conjunctive adverb intervenes. While a Bergson might elaborate a distinction between *outer* and *inner* knowledge (scientific *v.* metaphysical),[16] a Martin Buber would make the cut between persons and things—*thou-knowledge* and *it-knowledge*.[17] And what educator in these days of alienation and bureaucratic manipulation would dare deny the significance of this distinction for educational work!

(b) The linguistic inquiry has not focused sharply enough on whether the cutting line is drawn through 'know' (by distinguishing meanings) or through the difference of preposition and conjunctive adverb or through the type of object. It has thus not been sufficiently aware of the relativity of cuts and the options involved. Thus in the biblical formulation, when David knows Bathsheba and when he knows the strength of his enemies, it is the different sense of 'know' that bears the burden of distinction (carnal, informational or experiential). When we know how, how to, of, about, where, etc., the line of difference is drawn by the preposition or conjunctive adverb attached to the 'know.' When the object takes over the work of distinction, it cannot be a wholly linguistic inquiry. We must have in mind some set of object-types. An interesting example is to be found in R. S. Peters's recent suggestion[18] that the knowledge of what is good is different from either 'knowing how' or 'knowing that' since, as Socrates and Plato argued, it is intimately connected with caring about something (p. 8). If we develop this suggestion, it would seem that to 'know the fact,' 'know the job,' and 'know the good,' would be distinguished by category-words such as FACT, TASK, VALUE. Perhaps to 'know what's up' or 'know what's going on' might add EXPLANATION.

(c) A third shortcoming would be insufficient attention to perspective. Most of the types of knowledge are looked at as attained states of a person. Educationally, they are thus either what the teacher has and is offering to the pupil, or they are what the pupil has when learning is complete. The transition from types of knowledge to types of learning is thus not an automatic one, and the types of learning as a process may be quite different from the types of end-products in learning. Types of learning may furnish some of the ideals for the end-product. But in some cases the end may supervene on very different procedures. Learning may depend in part on the tone of voice of the teacher or the demanding or accepting atmosphere of the classroom, neither of which is reflected in the product. Nor is it possible to regard every feature in learning as itself embodying a further end to be learned. For while there is what Gregory Bateson has called 'deutero-learning'—the child learns in the same situation permissiveness as well as reading— whether permissiveness is to be subsequently redressed is a separate question. The process may be rationalized in the way in which a reading-readiness program concentrates on the separate skills and conditions that when put together will be requisite for reading. But rationalization may not be wholly complete, and means and ends not always congruent.

In general, knowledge is the teacher perspective—he has it. Learning is the underdog view. A shift in emphasis from teaching to learning today is a social shift, quite comparable to the pressure for participation in politics. (It is suggestive, too, that responsibility for the pupil's not learning seems to be shifting from the pupil to the teacher.) J. S. Mill said in his essay 'On Genius'[19] that the end of education is not to teach but to fit the mind for learning under its own consciousness and observation; that we have occasion for these powers under varying circumstances for which no routine or rule of thumb can possibly make provision. For educational purposes the linguistic analysis might better be directed to the uses of 'learn'; and in the educational situation directly, not by new hardened distinctions between 'learning with,' 'learning from,' 'learning by'! The approach from learning would certainly take better account of the situation in higher education where the teacher Socratizes, or where a discussion is begun in a field in which a teacher does not know the outcome, but is bringing analytical skill and educational experience to a seminar in which all, himself included, may learn.

IV How then does one decide which analysis is correct? How Peters II corrects Peters I

I have tried to show the genuine complexity involved in the analysis of 'knowing that' and 'knowing how' and to suggest the way in which empirical and scientific considerations and historical stages of social life and human and educational purposes play an integral part in the very process of analysis. They are not simply added at the end. I would now like to return to the soft spot in analytic method mentioned as the central symptom at the outset, and see how an analysis may be judged for its adequacy. For this purpose I focus on Professor Peters's recent rich paper on 'Education and the Educated Man'[20] in which he revises his previous analysis of 'education.' I want to discern the way in which the revision takes place and why the resulting analysis is regarded as more adequate than the earlier. I should point out that I am not concerned with psychological or other causes in Peters—his shift is not like the old appeal from Philip drunk to Philip sober—but to the content of his analysis. And I choose it because Peters's general position seems here to be like Soltis's above—ready to go beyond analysis after the analysis is finished, but not apparently ready to admit that the beyond operates within the analysis.

Peters's earlier analysis of 'education' as developed in *Ethics and Education*[21] included: (1) the transmission of worthwhile activities to those who become committed to them, (2) some knowledge and understanding and cognitive perspective which is not inert, and (3) the exclusion of some procedures as lacking willingness and voluntariness on the part of the learner. This conception was criticized by some as being normative and laying down values of knowledge as against passivity. But in the familiar analytic fashion it could be said that the values were packed away in linguistic uses of 'education.' The analyst need not advocate them any more than in, say, the analysis of the meaning of 'law and order' in familiar current use he need approve of the streak of violence he will find embedded there.

In the paper now under consideration Peters is troubled by counter-examples, especially by the use of 'education' for societies (his example is Spartan education) where the second condition of the three is not satisfied. He considers proposals to make the value condition (1) the sole one; thus any society could fill in its values for its educational system. And, on the other hand, he considers making the cognitive condition (2) the only one. He decides against both, and offers instead the distinction between 'education' and 'the educated man.' His older definition, in effect, had viewed education as the family of processes which contribute to the outcome of an educated man. By breaking the contention between the processes and the outcome he is able to accommodate the deviant uses of 'education.' It also helps resolve arguments concerning the first definition that had centered on Peters's contention that we could not speak of the 'aims' of education; since education was initiation into worthwhile activities, it already had all the aims it needed. Now, with the separation of concepts, one could speak of aims with respect to education, but not with respect to the educated man.

This is a very bare outline. The full analysis involves constant resort to uses, to what would simplify and what would complicate the picture of uses, to counter-uses and objections. Now the question I want to consider in greater detail is what makes Peters's revised analysis better than his original analysis. What does he himself have to say, whether directly or in asides, on the question?

The chief passage treating of this is on pp. 12 and 13. Peters tells us that in his previous analysis he had always assumed the connection between 'education' and the development of an educated man. (Even where other people did not have this more differentiated conceptual structure, it was important to make the distinction.)

> But perhaps I did not appreciate how widespread the older use of 'education' is in which there is no such tight connection between various processes of bringing up and rearing and the development of an educated man. It may well be that many people still use the word 'education' to cover not only any process of instruction, training, etc. that goes on in schools but also less formalized child-rearing practices such as toilet-training, getting children to be clean and tidy, and to speak with a nice accent.

Actually, considerable historical examination of changing usage is associated with this confession. There has been an etymological digression in which we were told that the Latin 'educare' was once used for rearing plants and animals as well as children; and the English word in the seventeenth century covered animals, birds, and, in the nineteenth century, silk-worms. The use of 'education' for 'Spartan education' in which there is training without close connection with knowledge and understanding is put into such a category. In addition, there was a precursor ideal to the present educated man in the pre-nineteenth century notion of the cultivated person, who was the product of elaborate training and instruction. It was only with the coming of industrialism and the greater importance of knowledge and the development of schools that the association of knowledge with instruction became close. 'So close has this association become that it is now possible for some people, who do not value anything to do with books or theory, to say that they do not value education' (p. 13).

In short, Peters's old definition represented the outcome of an historical trend not quite completed, and breaking the connection between 'education' and 'the educated man' helps to focus on the relation of the different elements and to understand the surviving uses that were puzzling.

I do not see why, to ensure the greater clarification, it is necessary to carry out a redefinition. The break in connection could be seen by showing that the earlier definition had such-and-such separate components related in such-and-such a way, presupposing such-and-such empirical connections; the historical–genetic reflections and reflections on people's values that enter the process could then be put into an explanatory preamble. Thus in the familiar example of the way in which 'conducting electricity' gets put into the definition of 'copper,' it is seen how copper was identified and defined before we knew anything about electricity and how the growth of the empirical connection and the increase of theory leads from turning what was an empirical generalization into a material leading principle, and formally when the theory becomes extensive and the feature involved significant enough, into part of the definition. In Peters's account the burden of clarification is borne by his historical-genetic-valuational account of the ways in which and grounds on which the usage changed. To put the results of such an account into the re-analysis and change the definition thus reflects some ground of decision on Peters's part, and it is this that I am trying to locate. It is not easy, so I shall probe in a few different ways.

First, though he seems to think of his second definition as more adequate than the first, he is not claiming, in the older analytic style, to be giving the 'correct use.' It is, in the distinction Ryle made between 'use' and 'usage,'[22] rather the usage that is involved—the actual incidence of employment of the term.

Secondly, Peters seems to feel he has to accommodate all the counter-examples, but not in a uniform way. There are analogical uses, secondary uses, by-paths, and so on. Some uses, significantly, have died out. Now in such accommodation there is considerable constructive activity on the part of the analyst. A use that is analogous or secondary is so only relative to a definitional use accepted as primary. If we reversed their roles the other would be secondary. Peters's struggles with 'Spartan education' illustrate this. Drop the knowledge condition for 'education' and the secondary use becomes an instance of the primary use. In fact, this stubborn example plays a large part in Peters's separation of education and the educated man. But if there is a constructive activity on the part of the analyst, there is some meta-analytical decision involved.

Thirdly, the resort to historical explanation of counter-examples is not itself decisive of what will be done with the outcome. For example, there is the counter-example to including a value condition in 'education' that lies in many people's regarding being educated as a bad state (p. 9); people, they say, are better off without it. Peters identifies them as simple, hard-headed, practical men (p. 10). Presumably they are the relics of an earlier form of life suspicious of contemporary civilization. Their judgment that education is bad is a moral judgment directed on the values embedded in the definition. If the definition had no embedded values or left a value-variable to be filled in by each group-use, then they could not say that education is bad, they could only say that education is misdirected in contemporary society or has to be tolerated for some of its instrumental effects. Having seen all this surely does not foreclose Peters's options. He could still have gone either way—to keep his old definition or to shift, as he does, to his new account. Neither would rob the simple practical men of their right of value criticism. They would have to express it in one case as a condemnation of education; in the other as a condemnation of modern life. If anything, the latter would be clearer—and that is a consequence of sticking to Peters's first definition. So there are gains and losses in clarity whichever way we go. Why rob Peters to pay Paul? Simply give an explanatory preamble and choose your path on *conscious and significant grounds*.

What then are significant grounds? Peters seems to be abandoning, as I suggested earlier, his old definition (let me call it E_1) which represents the outcome of an historical trend which has not quite been reached, for a definition (E_2) of two terms which leaves an empirical relation between their material content. So far as I can tell from the considerations I have given, it is because E_2 better reflects the current state of usage. But if his historical analysis is correct, this current state is not likely to last. The forces of industrialism, the importance of knowledge, the use of formal schooling, are likely to become more effective. Some indeterminate time from now, an analyst with the same perspective as Peters in his revision may come to Peters's old definition as his answer! The present counter-examples may die and be neglected by him as Peters thrusts aside 'education' for training of animals (p. 13). If a present analytic answer represents an intellectual investment, doesn't the analyst want to be secured at least about the stability of the linguistic situation? Suppose it is likely to change in a decade? In a year? In a week? Tomorrow? Does it make no difference to him? Actually it does. In his rating of counter-uses, he may sift dying uses which are no longer vital, analogous uses that were once on an older outlook thought continuous, and so on. Having used historical grounds for explaining minor corrections in present use, he might as well expand his historical judgments as a basis for distinguishing more significant from less significant uses. And having seen this integral role of historical factors in the fashioning of his analytical product he might as well recognize the purposive and valuational components that operate both in history and in their own right in the analytic process.

Along these lines, Peters's first definition may be reconstrued as follows: Begin with a preamble, giving the kind of historical information Peters invokes in the paper about industrialism and the growing stress on knowledge. Estimate the extent and strength of the trends and analyze the vital conflicts as they affect the lives of men; for example, the forces of corporatism that make them passive organization men and the pressure of problems that require active participation and inventiveness. Add the kinds of ethical considerations Peters holds to about worthwhile activities, as explicit ethical views. Add the picture of the current state of linguistic usage and the historical and value roots, and whatever coalescences and fissions are taking place. Then, propose the definition as expressive of historical-valuational-linguistic grounds, showing how far it represents trends or resistance to trends, possible solution to problems, and so on. Why not then tie together, as Peters's former definition did, worthwhileness and knowledge and creative activity in one bundle, setting a goal for our social and educational development in the conditions of the contemporary world, genuinely fitting at our present stage of knowledge and social development? How timorous by comparison is a definition attuned to the condemnations of relics of an earlier society, or permissions to speak of 'Spartan education' in an anthropologically neutral way, which anthropologists don't need from philosophers anyhow to carry on their profession! Whatever clarity there is in the second definition about corrections could have been achieved in a richer type of analysis of the first definition.

I hope in this appeal from Peters II to Peters I, I shall not have both Peters set against me. Let me by way of caution add a linguistic ground for my position. If we examine fully the contexts in which 'education' is employed in the modern world, I think it becomes clear that it is often a policy-setting word, or an institution-shaping word. In this respect it is like 'freedom' or 'morality.' Even terms like 'science' or 'family' carry this aspect, though in subtler shades. To include or exclude grandparents in the definition of 'the family' is to take a stand on the institutional shaping, and to make obligations either an inner matter or an outside matter in a fashion quite parallel to what Peters has argued about education. So too the terms 'education' and 'educational activities' function in discourse that determines policy in the schools. Think of the long history of controversy over extension of the curriculum in the United States, in which additions were popularly branded as not education but simply 'fads and frills.' For in the system in which the concepts are involved—I need scarcely remind philosophers, at this stage, that concepts do not stand alone—if an activity is not educational, it does not belong in the schools. You can expect a teacher to keep class records because it is part of the educational job, but you cannot expect him or her to sweep the floor and tend the stove, as in the old one-room school house; that is custodial labor. Soon, too, keeping records may be certified as 'clerical' and come under another jurisdiction. With the growing use of paraprofessionals, we may expect more rather than fewer distinctions. Major questions of policy are likely to be settled under the definition of 'educational activity,' as major questions of the American way of life have been settled under the analysis of 'due process.' To take one example, Peters in his *Ethics and Education* points out that the question may significantly be raised whether teaching belongs in a university. In the United States, the more likely question arising is whether research belongs in the college. Both require for their understanding long historical–valuational explanation. But the solution is rather likely to take the form of what educational contribution the faculty's engaging in research makes in the college—as against having separate research institutes. If we recognize the policy-determining and institution-shaping function of discourse about 'education' and 'educational activity,' it becomes necessary to track down the components that shape the outcome and the values embedded therein.

An afterthought: This should not be construed as an appeal for a persuasive use of analysis. I have no objection to this being frankly done in its own terms. For example, I might urge the old use of 'education' to cover plants, on the ground that it might suggest a good botany class in the early elementary school, in which children could be teacher-apprentices, and the plants be pupils (perhaps on a Buberite approach). But to see my argument in this light is to misunderstand and misrepresent it. Peters in adding a reflection on the limitation and point of analysis paraphrases Wittgenstein: 'conceptual analysis leaves everything as it is.' That is, the ethical and social decisions are separate and come after the analysis is completed. I have been arguing that they are integral to the analysis at the points of choice throughout, together with the empirical, scientific, and historical considerations.

V Concluding notes

I have tried to show the following. There is dissatisfaction in the philosophy of education with the current form of the analytic approach. Some of the analysts are themselves unhappy, professors as well as students. The source of the trouble lies in a weakness, in current analytic method itself, which purports to exclude empirical, valuational and socio-historical components. These cannot be added successfully after the analysis is over—this yields an unsatisfactory half-way house. Such components play a role in the analysis itself, surreptitious if not recognized; they determine in part the shape of analytic products. If you ask what analysis looks like when this is recognized and these components integrated, I am tempted by the way Richard Robinson, in his book, *Definition*,[23] characterized one type as 'any process, whether verbal or otherwise, by which any individual, whether God or angel or man or beast, brings any individual, whether himself or another, to know the meaning of any elementary symbol. . . .' Let me say then that analysis is any way which God or angel or man or beast can devise to make clearer the conceptual instruments one is using and the processes of using them in specific materials, and to dig out the presuppositions in the questions asked, and the problems and purposes involved, so as to be able to refine and improve them in the light of the stage reached by mankind in its total development of life and society.

I do not mean in such a definition to disparage linguistic sophistication, but rather to put language in its human relations. When words are dynamite, it is because of what human beings and milieu are like at the time. When Peters says casually (p. 10) that a non-value use of 'education' would be treating it, 'as indeed it is sometimes called, the "knowledge industry",' I cannot help remembering the explosion set off in California by Clark Kerr's reference to the 'knowledge industry' in his *The Uses of the University*.[24] To the Berkeley students the comparison of knowledge production today to the railroad industry in the nineteenth century and its role in American development, meant accepting the purposes of the establishment and the alienation of students!

If there is doubt and controversy about 'education' today, it is because the concept of education, like most traditional concepts, is itself cracking. Uses are altering and new concepts are in the making because human history and institutions and social life and values are at a point of extremely rapid change and are likely to issue in great creation or great destruction. If philosophical analysis is to be helpful to education today, it must be the sort that is responsive to the problems of education in this rapidly changing world, that will realize the constructive task of fashioning intellectual instruments for dealing with these problems. It cannot limit itself to current uses and even to current problems within education, for the relations of this institutional complex to the whole of the social milieu are being transformed. Education as we have known it as an institution may be breaking up and being realigned in myriad ways. It is no longer clear that *any* domain will keep the shape and isolated problems and isolated concepts that it has had. A constructive philosophical analysis will not sit passively by waiting for something to consolidate either institutional or linguistic form to be retrospectively dissected. Both the owl of Minerva and whatever glottal deities there may be have work to do before the dusk. Philosophy of education today has to use whatever resources it can muster to clarify and cope with the way in which the major problems of men today are impinging on the present state of educational policies, programs, and institutions. Formidable as this task sounds, it can be quite concrete and quite philosophical even though the philosopher will not usually be able to go it alone. But the fact is that in no field of policy or practice today can any professional go it alone without distorting the results.

Such a philosophical analysis in education which involves co-operation with empirical and scientific studies, with historical analysis of development, and with systematic analysis of trends and possibilities, may indeed seem overwhelming. But what other path is possible for a philosophy that can respect its work and win the respect of its students? It may withdraw from the field, of course, finding it too complex, as Plato withdrew from physics, finding nature too Heraclitean—and then proceeded to fashion physical myths! It may, instead, content itself with constructing general schemata, indicating in detail the kinds of blanks that will be filled by empirical knowledge, and the kind by value-determinations. This at least will have the virtue of noting what is needed, instead of making a virtue of ignoring it. But if it gives up both retreat and the hope of all-comprehensive schemes, it may find a host of problems in the actual contexts of today's education which the philosopher can tackle in cooperation with other professionals—the scientists, the historians, the experienced educators—without pretending to more than his philosophical skills.

Such problems may take different shape. One is, for example, the problem of *consistency*, surely a philosophical specialty. Every educational establishment has programs set in objectives and traditional ways of running itself. There are always, and especially in a complex changing society, inconsistencies between different objectives, different programs and policies, different ways of running the school, and among those several categories as well. There are, for example, contradictions between democratic objectives and bureaucratic modes of organization, as well as authoritarian discipline; between equalitarian aspirations and textbook materials and teacher attitudes to disadvantaged and minority groups; between co-operative objectives and competitive methods; and so on. The general search for consistency of educational functioning is certainly an area in which analytical and logical skills should enable the philosopher of education to initiate and explore, even if he will need sociological and psychological support in tracing the unintended consequences of policies, programs and procedures.

Another area of problems concerns the 'external' relations of education to the rest of society. Current demands for community control and current charges from the student left that the universities are instruments of the establishment show vividly the pressing need for an understanding of educational institutions in light of a total analysis of the society rather than simply in terms of a limited set of traditional objectives as the 'essence' of education. Philosophy has worked a great deal on the logic of the relation of parts and wholes, philosophy of history and society on the concept of institutions and the relation of goals, rules and practices to underlying social aims, conflicts and conditions. Both phenomenological and analytical skills are needed to recast our very way of looking at the schools in order to see them in the diversity of perspectives that constitute the contemporary community and to prepare the ground for vital normative judgments that reflect the total historical situation of our age.

Another type of philosophical skill is to discern the reach of a principle over diverse subject-matter. When it becomes a pressing necessity in the contemporary world that an objective be given a central place in education, such philosophical aptitudes have a special responsibility. Thus it is agreed that the schools should play an important part in education for peace. The perfunctory educational tendency would be to add a peace-course or at best even a peace-department. A philosophical analysis would be required to see the reach of peace education throughout the whole curriculum— what elements in teaching of geography, language, history, economics and so on, what attitudes in teaching and administration, what traditional modes of thought and feeling, and presuppositions about human nature, had built-in war and violence proclivities. The philosophical analyst cannot alone answer either the descriptive or the normative questions but he is sophisticated enough to realize that the answers depend to a marked degree on the kinds of questions asked and the scope of the issues attended to. What I have said about education for peace here holds in an even more complicated way for recent controversies over the place of Black, Puerto Rican, Mexican-American, or in general third-world studies. I have not seen—though I may have missed—serious contributions to the *analysis* of such issues in the philosophy of education.

In general, with so much of education today ripe for major reconstruction, philosophy is in the best position to raise the questions concretely—though not always to give the answers—about hardened categories and modes of organization of studies on all levels of the schools. I have suggested above that discussions of types of knowledge may be a pale reflection of such problems and issues. To bring such discussion into relation with the underlying problems is not to dismiss it but to call for its fuller consideration directly and consciously. To take an example of shifting categories from higher education, think of the experiments over the last few decades in combined courses: unified social science courses, contemporary civilization courses, humanities courses, and so on. In these there have been theoretical justifications in terms of inherent unity, simplicity and convenience, least-common-denominator acquaintance, etc. Given all the work that philosophy has done on the division of knowledge into fields and the relative character of the joints in the fabric of knowledge, and how different schemes of the sciences and fields of knowledge have been hardened into schemes of levels of reality, it seems incredible that philosophy of education has not pressed for reform, at least imparting the lesson of contextual relevance to basic categories and divisions in the structuring of education.

Obviously the listing of philosophical tasks could go on endlessly. I conclude with a comment on the notion of *relevance*, so frequently invoked by students today in educational controversy. Too often, it seems to me, it is analytically disparaged as a vague slogan term, and the philosophical analysis is directed to proving its ambiguity. That it is contextually differentiated is clear enough. Sometimes it indicates instrumental importance, sometimes the general sense of 'meaningful' in which the older philosophers debated whether life had a meaning, sometimes it refers to pertinence in solving basic social problems. But it also most of the time refers to pertinence in *understanding* what is going on in a full philosophical sense. I cannot see how the philosophy of education could fail to find both the use and misuse of the notion to be other than the symptom of a growing questioning in education and the occasion for encouraging critical discussion and cultivating insight. An analytical philosophy of education could take hold of this situation in the comprehensive questioning of all life and its organization in that same spirit in which philosophy generally and perennially praises its origins in the Socratic quest.

Notes

1 In this paper I am dealing primarily with the one type of analysis because it is predominant in contemporary philosophy of education. There is, of course, a great deal of analytic work to which my diagnosis may apply only in part.

2 It was the picture of the state of the field emerging in this conference that stimulated the reflections of this paper.

3 J. L. Austin, *How to Do Things with Words*, J. O. Urmson (ed.), New York, O.U.P., 1965, Lecture XI, esp. pp. 141f. Cf. his remarks on the true/false fetish and the value/fact fetish, p. 150.

4 Professor Soltis's paper was presented to the Conference on 'New Directions in Philosophy of Education,' held at the Ontario Institute for Studies in Education (OISE), 30 April—2 May 1970.

5 Thomas S. Kuhn, *The Structure of Scientific Revolutions*, University of Chicago Press, 1962.

6 Gilbert Ryle, *The Concept of Mind*, Hutchinson, 1949.

7 Jane Roland Martin, 'On the Reduction of "Knowing That" to "Knowing How" ', in *Language and Concepts in Education*, B. O. Smith and R. H. Ennis (eds), Chicago, Rand McNally, 1961, pp. 59–71. This paper was included by the editors as an example of educationally relevant analysis that exhibits a kinship to the work of Oxford analysts.

8 Professor Martin may not realize the extent of this penetration of educational experience into the analytic work. In the last part of the paper, she examines implications for teaching and learning on the assumption that 'One test for the utility of our classification lies in its relevance to education,' as if it had been independently established.

9 Presented at the OISE Conference; see note 4.

10 Michael Oakeshott, 'Rationalism in Politics', in *Rationalism in Politics and Other Essays*, New York, Basic Books, 1962.

11 John Dewey, 'The Reflex Arc Concept in Psychology', *The Psychological Review*, July 1896, pp. 357–70. Reprinted in *John Dewey: Philosophy, Psychology and Social Practice*, S. Ratner (ed.), New York, Capricorn Books, 1963.

12 John Dewey, *Human Nature and Conduct*, New York, The Modern Library, 1930, pp. 177–8.

13 *Ibid.*, pp. 179–80.

14 Bertrand Russell, 'Knowledge by Acquaintance and Knowledge by Description', in *Mysticism and Logic*, New York, W. W. Norton, 1929.

15 William James, *The Principles of Psychology*, New York, Henry Holt, 1890, vol. I, pp. 221f.

16 Henri Bergson, *An Introduction to Metaphysics*, trans. T. E. Hulme, New York, Liberal Arts Press, 1949.

17 Martin Buber, *I and Thou*, trans. Ronald Gregor Smith, Edinburgh, T. & T. Clark, 1937.

18 R. S. Peters, 'Education and the Educated Man', *The Philosophy of Education Society of Great Britain, Proceedings of the Annual Conference*, vol. IV, p. 8.

19 J. S. Mill, 'On Genius', in *Mill's Essays on Literature and Society*, J. Schneewind (ed.), New York, Collier Books, 1965, p. 101.

20 See note 18.

21 R. S. Peters, *Ethics and Education*, Allen & Unwin, 1966, ch. 1.

22 Gilbert Ryle, 'Ordinary Language', *The Philosophical Review*, vol. LXII, 1953, pp. 167–86.

23 Richard Robinson, *Definition*, Clarendon Press, 1954, p. 27. The reference is to 'word-thing definition.'

24 Clark Kerr, *The Uses of the University*, New York, Harper Torchbooks, 1966.

Index

Adams, Henry, 33
Aesthetic
  appreciation, 102
  creation, 115
  education, *see* Education,
    aesthetic
  enjoyment, 97
  experience, 94–6, 99–101
  norms, 104
  performance, 102, 115
'Aesthetic literacy', 103
Agesander, 111
Aldrich, V. C., 109n.
Alienation, 111, 253
American education, 94, 96, 240–2
Anarchy, 40
Anderson, R. N., 32n.
Anomie, 11, 149, 155, 163–4
  cognitive, 166
Aristotle, 27, 36–7, 39, 70, 157–8,
  168n., 244
Arnold, Thomas, 134
Artists, 102
Arts, the, 93–5, 110
  celebrative role, 98–9, 103, 108,
    114
  distinctions among, 111–12
  expressiveness in, 100–1
  originative role, 98–9, 103,
    107–8, 114
  as sources of life-styles, 98
  technical factors in, 100
Austin, J. L., 234, 256n.
Austin, John, 168n.
Australian National University,
  141n.
Authenticity, 5, 9, 46—8, 123–5,
  133, 135, 149, 161–2

Authority, 121, 135
  educational, 106
Autonomy, personal
  and absence of constraint, 155,
    159–60
  and aesthetic education, 8, 104,
    108
  as aim of education, 4–6, 24,
    30–1, 45, 49–55, 104, 108,
    120, 123–5, 166
  and authenticity, 46–9, 104,
    123–4, 149
  as component of composite ideal
    of freedom, 167
  and concepts of the self, 40–1,
    46–9, 160–1
  development, 8–11, 127, 130–4
  educational elitism and, 54–5
  etymology of term, 40, 123
  functional, 97
  and ideals of communal life, 5, 51
  and indoctrination, 5–6, 104,
    108, 138
  influence of institutions on
    achievement of, 134–7
  Kant's conception, 50, 124, 126,
    130
  kinds of learning in achievement
    of, 138–40
  and moral goodness, 4–5, 38–45
  necessary conditions, 9–10, 125,
    161
  normative definition, 41
  political authority and, 41
  as political metaphor, 158–60
  as pre-condition of dignity, self-
    esteem, and responsibility, 160
  and rationality, 41–5, 49, 124, 166

259